# Denied

## By

### Jeffrey B. Nordella, M.D.
### with
### Kim Beyer-Johnson

## Dedication

In loving memory of:

*Carole Leigh Nordella*

Loved by all and missed every day.

She lived in Christ and died in Christ.

# Prologue

*March 16, 2013*

The day is crisp, the sky an uninterrupted blue against the scrub brush hills of Santa Rosa Valley. Nestled just over the hills from Malibu Beach, Santa Rosa is a throwback to a sleepier time in California history. Dotted with pumpkin farms, ranches, and gated custom homes, it's the kind of place you go to raise a family and escape from the artifice of Los Angeles with its aspiring movie stars, gridlock traffic, and social climbers.

Dressed in a red flannel shirt, blue jeans, and a weathered ball cap pulled down low to shade his eyes, Jeff climbs on his beat up tractor, happy to find sanctuary in the low rumble of the engine as he tills the hard clay of his twelve-acre ranch. Soon he'll plant rye grass, the perfect carpet for high heels and Sunday best boots of the 350 guests who will attend his daughter's upcoming Western themed wedding.

Dr. Jeffrey Nordella is a man with simple tastes and simple values. He loves country music, house boating, and barbequed ribs slathered with smoky hickory sauce. He believes in the principle of hard work. He treats people with courtesy and respect and hopes he will receive the same.

Jeff's mind travels to his wife, Carole. Like his daughter, he and Carole also had a Western themed wedding. But unlike Jamie's wedding, Jeff and Carole's day was a simple affair. A weekend getaway with a few family members in the nearby mountains of Tahoe, California. Like any thought of Carole, the memory cuts both ways, painful yet sweet, but today, he's grateful for the distraction. Thinking about anything except the verdict is nothing short of a blessing.

Watching the seed spill into the fertile soil, the metaphors of rebirth and new beginnings aren't lost on Jeff. He realizes for better or for worse, a new chapter of life is about to begin. He will either prevail or be crushed. There will be no middle ground. Either way, it's difficult to believe it is all coming to an end. It had been ten years, after all. Ten years since he'd spat in the eye of the giant. Ten years since he'd sunk his teeth into the hand that had fed him. Ten years since he'd embarked on what many considered a fool's errand at best, professional suicide at worst.

It had been ten years since he'd opened his lawsuit against the insurance giant, Blue Cross.

It wasn't like suing City Hall. It was like suing God. Or maybe, more accurately, the devil. The journey has nearly destroyed him, his business, and his family. But like everything else in his life, he realizes he's still standing... at least at this moment, sitting on his tractor tilling the dark, rich soil. When the phone rings, he hardly hears it above the grumble of the engine. He fumbles in his pocket, almost dropping his cell under the tractor's carnivorous blades. He cuts the engine and presses the phone to his ear, hoping he hasn't missed the call.

"Theresa?"

"Jeff!" It was Theresa Barta, his attorney who'd stood by him since the beginning. Her voice is barely above a whisper, yet rings with urgency.

"Theresa? I can't hear you!" he shouts as he leaps off the tractor and jogs toward the house, hoping to catch a better signal while his faithful yellow lab, Kinzie, lopes alongside on arthritic legs.

"I'll step outside..." he thinks he hears her say. He realizes she must be in the courtroom, and is moving out into the hallway where she can talk more freely.

"Theresa? Are you still there? Can you hear me?"

"The jury came back..."

This is it. This is what it all comes down to... He silently reminds himself that regardless of the outcome this is the end of the road. Win or lose he has to move on with his life.

"And...?"

# Chapter 1

## The Neighborhood

Everyone has a history. For better or for worse, history shapes who we are. It can dictate our choices. It sticks with us no matter how hard or how long we try to erase it from our hearts and memories. I'm no exception.

I grew up in North Hollywood, an asphalt wasteland also known as "The Valley." Don't let the word "Hollywood" fool you. My neighborhood was the opposite of glitz and glam. Long before any environmental laws were enacted, living in North Hollywood was literally bad for your health. Smog alerts were commonplace, an ever-present brown cloud trapping in not only the heat, but obliterating any shred of blue sky. Even if it was considered safe to venture outdoors, just cruising down the street on my battered orange spray painted Stingray for a couple of blocks left me with what the neighborhood kids called "burning lungs."

It was also the era of Kennedy and the Cuban Missile Crisis. Disaster, whether environmental or political, was a word on everyone's lips. Tall wooden towers were erected throughout the neighborhood. On the fourth Friday of every month sirens blared, drilling us in the event of an attack. Schools had "duck and cover drills" coaching students to scurry under their flimsy metal desks and cover their heads to ward off the feared nuclear bomb blast that many thought was sure to wipe out Los Angeles.

My neighborhood consisted of row after row of cheaply made track homes, slapped up in the '50s and left to slowly crumble in the constant heat. Ours was a 900 square-foot two bedroom, one bath home, nearly identical to every other of its kind stretched alongside the cracked asphalt streets. There were no curbs or sidewalks. Instead, we'd play in the narrow gutters that lined the street, our only playground a block-long dirt lot filled with soaring steel, potentially carcinogenic, electrical towers.

Everyone in the neighborhood ran free in the streets during the summer, left to their own devices. A favorite game was to lie on our backs in the dirt and shoot steel tip arrows up toward the humming electrical wires. We'd watch them arch up and wait for the arrows to drop, holding our ground until the last second before we rolled away, barely missing being pierced. If we weren't dodging arrows, we'd head to Brett's house—the only kid who had a pool, making him the most popular on the block considering summer temperatures soared to over a hundred degrees. There was a commercial parking lot right behind his house, and the bravest of us would scale its cinderblock wall and stare down into his kidney-shaped pool. There we'd be, two stories in the air, clinging to the edge of that parking lot wall, daring each other to jump. One by one we'd leap, our legs hitched to our chests to keep from breaking them on the bottom of the deep end. Once our rear ends slammed into the plaster bottom, we'd give ourselves one good push for the surface and pop up shouting our triumph.

As for my house, it never felt like a true home. The front yard consisted of one tree surrounded by a scrubby piece of dying grass, the place where I fractured my clavicle and learned firsthand about emergency rooms. Our driveway led to a single-car garage packed to the rafters with junk. Our clothes hung on a sagging clothesline in the backyard, a potential death trap when playing cops and robbers. The only greenery in our postage-sized backyard were thorny weeds known as goat heads that pierced my thin rubber flip flops and poked into the soles of my feet. I still remember picking them out as I sat on the back porch before entering the house. The thing was, no matter how dismal the conditions outside were, I never wanted to go home at the end of each day. I'd stay out as long as I could. If I went home, I knew I'd be facing chaos.

My parents were good Catholics, and I was the fifth of six kids, all born within ten years. The fact that we all lived in a nine hundred square foot house didn't make for the best of conditions. Mom and Dad slept in one bedroom and the kids slept in the other. Our bedroom was just big enough to hold one bunk bed, one single bed, one trundle bed, one crib, and one dresser. The four boys used the dresser for what clothes we owned, while the girls got the one small closet in which to hang their dresses. Sometimes, when I was very young, we'd use the cramped quarters to our advantage. Considering our room was essentially one big bed, we'd bounce from mattress to mattress, six crazy kids laughing, screaming, and generally tearing up the room. But more often than not, the laughter would turn to pokes, the pokes led to fights, the fights led to screaming, the screaming led to crying.

On top of the quarreling, disorganization ruled our home. Everything we owned could be found aimlessly strewn about the house: piles of papers, books, and clothes crammed into the four rooms we called home. It wasn't just space that was an issue growing up. Although we were physically close, we were emotionally distant. There were no heart-to-heart talks. No real talks at all. It was all business: "Did you do your homework?" "Where's my shoes?" "Help set the table." Or it was fighting. I think we were really just trying to survive, like most families in the neighborhood, the best way we knew how.

In the eye of our family storm was my mom. In her younger years she was a real live bathing beauty who had swam professionally with Ester Williams and balanced on the tanned shoulders of Venice Beach's famed Muscle Men. I used to puzzle over my mother's old bent photographs trying to reconcile the saucy pin up with the upbeat woman who spent her days frantically whizzing through our lives in an attempt to manage the emotional and physical clutter of our home.

Today when I think of my mother, I'm reminded of a scientific theory called Maximum Entropy. The theory goes that nature has a way of constantly moving toward disorganization. In order to stop this natural flow towards disorganization you have to put energy into the system to organize it. That was my mom. She was always positive, jovial, and the first to hand out a compliment. But, no matter how hard she worked, she could never work hard enough to organize our complaints, fights, and daily dramas. Just as the scientific theory states, everything in our home would inevitably return to a nauseating disequilibrium despite her energy and efforts.

My dad was another story. He unfortunately was part of the chaos, but not because he was filled with frenetic energy. In fact, he was like a worn out windup toy, mechanically trudging slowly through life, winding down with every passing day, ready to turn off completely at any given moment. The oldest of four, his dad walked out on the family when he was just fourteen, making him the de facto father and provider. It wore him out; made him old before his time. I don't think it helped that he married my mom and started having children right away. When he was young, he had dreams of being a comedian, and joined the USO, an entertainment division in the armed forces, where he met my mother who was a singer and dancer. Whether he'd lost his spark years ago or never really had it, I'll never know, but rather than live his dream, he ended up working retail, selling men's clothing at the Broadway department store.

Once in a blue moon Mom would pile all of us into our "three on the tree" '54 Dodge and we'd visit Dad at the Broadway's top floor restaurant where he'd treat us to grilled cheeses, fries, and sodas, the best part being the pink bubble-gum cigar he'd hand out to each of us before he'd disappear back into the bowels of the cavernous department store.

It's hard to say exactly why Dad settled for the life he ended up with, but addiction might have had something to do with it. Addiction runs in my family. Alcoholism and drug abuse were common denominators among my father, his father, my father's siblings, and my brothers. Alcohol and cigarettes were my dad's favorite vices, a standard for that era. I was his favorite runner. He'd call to me from his perch on the pull-out couch, "Hey, Jeff! How about going over to the store and getting me some cigarettes? I'll give you a note."

I'd race across the street to the local Food Bag mini-mart to get his pack of True Blues. His hands trembled so badly sometimes he couldn't even light his cigarette. When he did, the long cylinder of ashes would build like a glowing charred centipede until it dropped to the carpet. Mom used to get angry because he had a way of continually missing his ashtray, which he remedied by grinding the ashes into the worn beige shag carpet with the toe of his shoe. Seeing her disapproval, he'd get nervous and start to twist the buttons on his shirt. Now I know this twisting or "pill rolling," might have actually been a symptom of his Parkinson's disease, the reason for his shaking. People suffering from the disease for some reason rotate small objects like pills or buttons between their fingers. Unfortunately, his constant button twisting would only test my mother's good nature because the buttons would eventually fall off and Mom would have to sew them back on. Just one more thing that required her energy.

Of course, back then I didn't see my father as a man suffering from Parkinson's. All I knew was that for as long as I could remember, he was sick. One of my earliest memories involved my father and illness. I had been playing down the street when I looked up to see a hearse-like ambulance parked out in front of our house. I pedaled home and raced for the front door just as the ambulance drivers rushed inside the house. Stunned, I followed them inside and hung back, paralyzed as they lifted Dad, inert and pale onto the gurney. Peering through the living room window, I watched, confused and powerless, as the ambulance drivers rolled him out into the driveway, opened the back doors to the ambulance, and loaded him inside. I can still remember the *clunk* of the doors slamming, then the high-pitched whine of the siren and flashing lights as the ambulance sped off and disappeared around the corner. I was eight years old.

"Hurry up!" Mom ordered, as she snatched up her purse and coat. "Change into some clean clothes! We're going to the hospital!" It was mass chaos, my brothers and sisters flinging on their jackets, sliding their feet into shoes, spewing out an endless gush of questions for which Mom had no answers. "Just hurry! We're leaving now!" We spilled out the door and into the Dodge.

Mom didn't like driving LA's surface streets to begin with, but she made it a point never to venture onto the endless ribbons of Los Angeles freeways. But that day she had no choice. The car lurched and jumped down the street as she ground the gears, the older kids shouting cautions as we cowboyed down our way toward the Hollywood Freeway. I sat motionless in the back, eyeing Mom's face in the rear-view mirror. Her eyes glistened with unshed tears as she started up the onramp and merged onto the freeway.

"Look out!"

"You're going too slow!" my brothers and sisters shouted as the cars swerved around us, laying on their horns.

"Quiet!" Mom finally yelped and jerked the car onto the shoulder of the freeway. She pulled to a stop and slammed it into park. She leaned her forehead against the steering wheel, as cars whizzed past at sixty miles per hour shaking at our hulking junker. The only sound was the passing *whoosh* of car after car and my mother's heavy breathing. For once, everyone was silent.

When we finally made it to the hospital, the six of us were left to wait on the narrow polished wooden benches lining the hallway. The air was stale with the scent of antiseptic, cleaning agents, and sickness—an odor I would become all too familiar with.

Deemed too young by the hospital staff to see my father, I waited in the hall as my brothers and sisters filed into Dad's room, then back out again. Finally, a slight, precise man, looking all-knowing in his suit and tie, emerged from Dad's room and led Mom down the hall. My dad's doctor. She listened, nodding; her expression hopeful yet terrified as the doctor quietly updated her on Dad's condition. Finally, she turned away, her shoulders heavy with the weight of the news. Only then did she cover her hands over her eyes and turn away.

It was the first time I'd seen my mother cry.

My father had suffered a heart attack that would require him to stay for over two weeks at the hospital. I had wondered whether or not he would ever come home, and in a way I guess he never did. He had left for the hospital my father, but he returned a sick man. Although his body would recover, his mind would not. He saw himself as a sick person. So did we.

Whenever Dad wasn't working, he would move from bed to bed, sleeping, reading, or resting. The heart attack had far more than damaged his heart. It had destroyed his ability to view himself as anything other than someone who was marking time until death. But even before his heart attack, he seemed older than all the other dads. He shuffled, he stooped when he stood, and his eyes were sunken and circled by bruised purple rings.

And then there were those shaking hands.

Every morning he and I would sit together at our little Formica kitchen table to eat breakfast. He'd be dressed, ready to go to work in his cheap suit and thin tie, and I would watch him try to eat his cereal and drink his coffee. I'd feel the familiar wash of sympathy and shame as he'd grip the spoon with his palsied hand and try to feed himself. His hand would tremble so violently that by the time the spoon got to his lips there was nothing left. I watched helplessly as he sighed and dipped the spoon back into the cereal bowl and start the agonizing process all over again.

As a kid, I was hyperaware of my dad, yet for as much as I studied him; I have to admit I didn't know him very well. I guess there was a distance between us that I never really thought I could bridge. It was partly because of his health, which not only made me feel sorry for him, but the fact that he was sick also frightened me. This was my *father*. The man I was supposed to look up to. Someone who was supposed to be strong. But even as a small child, I would look at him and think, *I don't know how much longer you're going to live.* The thought of losing him terrified me.

It's not that my dad didn't love us-or my mother. I am sure he did. He never left us, or beat us, and the way he just showed up day after day at a job he hated told me he cared for the family. But he was never really connected with us, and there was little joy or playfulness in his love. Maybe losing his dreams and his heart attack had turned him fearful and quietly bitter, but his only real interaction with us kids was to tell us what we *couldn't* do. "When you going? Where're you going? No, you can't go to the dance. No, you're staying home tonight." His rules were strict and without explanation.

None of us knew why we couldn't do things, and my brothers and sisters chaffed at his constant restrictions. He and my mom would fight over his strict guidelines and eventually my brothers and sisters turned against him. There he was, surrounded by a houseful of people, yet he was alone. Even as a kid I sensed his isolation and would make my own childlike efforts to strike up some kind of conversation. He never said anything, but I think he was grateful for my awkward attempts.

Another thing that distanced me from Dad, and Dad from all of us was our razor edge dance with poverty. No one ever said we were poor, but it didn't take a genius to figure out it was true. Even though Dad worked, his paycheck never seemed to stretch far enough for a family of eight. The constant stress about money seemed to create an invisible wall around Dad no one could penetrate. Mom and Dad would sit bent over the linoleum table at the end of the month surrounded by stacks of bills, trying to figure out who to pay and who not to pay. They were constantly rotating their bills. Always behind.

I instinctively knew I was supposed to have a mom and dad who were happy. A nice house. Food. When we were hungry, my mom would say, "Eat an apple," because we could afford apples and little else. But I was always hungry. What little food we had was spoiled. The milk in our fridge was sour. "Just pour off the top and drink what's on the bottom," Mom would say, trying to make light of the situation. I knew even as a little kid this wasn't exactly the way it should be.

The food we did have was horrible. My poor mom wasn't exactly what you would call a good cook. I'm sure she did the best she could with her tiny food budget, but that didn't stop me from dreading dinner. Tuna casserole was the worst. Every Friday, being the good Catholic family we were, we'd have tuna casserole. I hated tuna. Every week she'd bake it in the same thick steel pan with two cracked black plastic handles. Even the sight of that pan made me feel sick to my stomach. *Clunk* it would go on the counter. Then came the tuna. *Slop.* In it would go. Then came the mayo. *Glop. Glop. Glop!* Then came the nauseating wet *squishing* sound, as she'd stir the mayo into the reeking tuna fish. Next up was the cream of Campbell's mushroom soup. Another *glop, glop, glop.* Last but not least, she'd cut the corner of a potato chip bag, press out all the air, then *crunch, crunch, crunch* she'd roll her fist across it, crushing the chips before dumping them over the top of the ungodly concoction.

It was like: just shoot me.

I remember sitting next to my brothers and sisters on the wooden patio bench we used in lieu of chairs, bellied up to our rickety Formica table dreading what was coming. She'd plop down the bubbling hot beige tuna casserole and I would literally force myself not to gag. To me it was nothing more than warm cat food--with potato chips. I forced myself to take a bite, only to spit it into my paper napkin, ditching it in the trash as soon as no one was looking. The other one of Mom's specialties was tamale pie. I have no idea what was in that aside from some olives, corn, and some form of meat. All from a can, except maybe the meat, but I'm not even sure about that. Horrible. But it was dinner and I ate it. So did everyone else. We were too hungry not to.

By the time I was in high school I was 6' 2," 135 pounds. A rail. My grandfather once told me, "Eat something for breakfast that's gonna stick to your ribs. Try this stuff..." He handed me a box of Wheatena. Every morning before school I'd put a pot on the stove with a little salted water, bring it to a boil, and then add the Wheatena. It would turn into a hard pack cereal, like oatmeal. I'd pop a couple of pieces of Wonder Bread into the toaster, and then slather them with peanut butter. Tons of peanut butter. The Wheatena would go on top of the toast. Then with the left-over Wheatena, I'd dump more peanut butter into the bowl and eat that too. A breakfast of champions. And stick to my ribs it did—for the next two hours. Then I was starving all over again.

We might have had little to nothing for food, but true to my mom's unflappable spirit, she didn't let the fact that we had no money ruin our Christmas. Determined to create a bright spot in our lives, Mom would go all out for the holiday. I'll never forget my favorite Christmas when I got not only a football helmet, but also an Army man set complete with a canteen and rubber knife that fit onto a plastic belt. I ran around with that helmet and belt almost every day for a year. I still love the holiday season. It reminds me of one of the few times our family was close and a sense of warmth prevailed. But, the closeness and the day itself would come and go and Mom would spend the rest of the year paying off the Christmas debt. By the time she did, she'd turn around and do it all over again.

After Dad's heart attack, my brothers and sisters had disconnected almost entirely from him and he turned to me. Sports were what bonded us. Dad loved sports of all kinds, spending long hours on the pull out couch watching all kinds of sports on TV. If he wasn't watching TV, he was listening on his transistor radio to Chick Hearn and Vin Scully as they called the play-by-play for our local teams. What little conversation we did have was centered on our favorite teams; players; plays; and my obsession, America's favorite past time: baseball. I loved baseball: hit the bat, over the line, three flies up, or just fast pitch up against the garage door. I was dying to go out for Little League, but when it was time to sign up, I knew my parents could never afford the $25 fee. But one day after school dad called me over to his bedside.

"You want to play ball?"

I couldn't quite understand where he was going with the question. "What do you mean?"

"You want to play Little League, don't you?"

I didn't want to hope. "Yeah, but…"

"No buts. We signed you up."

I almost couldn't take in what he was saying. You would have thought he told me I just got signed to the Dodgers. I was going to play baseball!

It didn't matter to me that I showed up on the first game with my oldest brother's beat up old glove, blue jeans, and tennis shoes. I loved every second of it. Just being one of the guys, being part of team where we were all playing together with the same goal in mind was a dream come true. I'd trot out onto the field with my teammates, the smell of freshly cut grass and grilled hot dogs in my nostrils, feeling like there was no other place in the universe I'd rather be. I loved to see the parents scattered in little knots throughout the stands, ready to cheer us on. Every catch, every hit, every "Way to go, Kid!" filled me with a sense of pride and accomplishment.

But Little League also holds some tough memories. Dad came to almost all my games. "Is that your grandpa?" my teammates asked the first time they caught a glimpse of Dad. I can still feel the sting of embarrassment. I loved my father, but at the same time, I was ashamed. The conflicting emotions were a difficult thing for an eleven-year old to bear. There he'd be, his hands trembling visibly, his ever present cigarette pinched between two tobacco-stained fingers, ashes falling like snow around his feet. As happy as I was that he cared enough to come see me play, all I wanted to do was pretend I didn't know him at all. I felt horrible.

The second blow Little League dealt me was when I was twelve years old. At that time, playing ball was my world. I put everything I had into the game and pushed myself to the best of my ability. By the time summer rolled around, everyone knew who was and wasn't going to make the All Star team. I felt confident I'd make the cut. One Saturday afternoon towards the end of the season, the phone rang. My dad picked it up. I heard him say my coach's name and I felt my heart squeeze. This was the call to tell me I'd made it. Soon I'd be wearing the All Star jersey. Dad, however, hung up the phone and turned to me.

"The coach is coming over," he said, his expression inscrutable.

"Over here? Now?"

"That's what he said."

"What for?"

My dad just shrugged and turned back to his game on the television. A half an hour later my coach, a burly man with red cheeks and a barrel chest arrived at our front door.

"Want to go for an ice cream, Jeff?" he asked.

"Sure." I still had no idea what he wanted as I climbed into his carpet cleaning truck and headed toward Baskin Robbins. Before we could even reach the end of the block, Coach blurted out the news.

"You didn't make it," he told me, his eye trained on the street ahead. The moment sat there between us. Finally, he turned to me for a response, but I was far too stunned to answer.

We rode together in silence the rest of the way. Once at Baskin Robbins, Coach tried to make small talk with me as best he could, as I slowly stirred the rocky road ice cream into a brown chunky soup. I'd been denied, and unfairly so, I thought. I had nowhere to put my disgrace and sense of outrage. As insignificant as it was in the grand scheme of things, it was a feeling I would relive to a much greater degree as a grown man. As for Little League, I never played again.

In the meantime, my father's drinking, poor diet, and lack of exercise continued to contribute to his arteriosclerosis. Eight years after his first heart attack, he was feeling worse than ever and went to the doctor who admitted him to the hospital, which then led to open-heart surgery. The procedure, although relatively commonplace today, was a risky and frightening proposition at the time.

The day of Dad's surgery, we all headed to the familiar hospital. But I wasn't prepared for what I was about to see. Stepping into the ICU was overwhelming. The rhythmic sounds of the of ventilator and cardiac monitor, the large plastic tube protruding from his slack mouth, the tangle of intravenous lines, and my father's shrunken lifeless body was too much for me to take in. The moment I laid eyes on him, I was covered in a thin sweat. I swallowed hard, struck with a wave of nausea, barely managing to fold into a chair before I passed out cold. If you would have told me years later that I would have been in the ER cracking chests, treating gunshot wounds and stabbings I would have told you were crazy.

After Dad came home from the hospital, he left the Broadway, went on disability, and took to his bed—permanently. Each morning, Mom would fold up their pull out couch in the living room. Dad would sit up long enough to eat breakfast, but as soon as the girls would go to school, he'd shuffle into their room and sleep all day. His depression was like a physical weight bearing down on all of us. In desperation, Dad turned to the Catholic Church, becoming an usher and attending mass several times a week along with my mother. While none of the kids followed suit, I think it was his way to ward off death and get right with God, or at least make some kind of peace.

While Dad slipped into a deep depression, Mom had to pick up the slack and became the sole breadwinner for our family of eight as a seamstress instructor at a local adult night school. I'd get home from school around four to find her dashing around the house prepping for her evening lesson. "Get the sewing machines and load them into the back of the car, please! I'm running late!" she'd call out as she threw together another inedible casserole to be warmed up later for dinner. I'd load the sewing machines in the back seat and *vroom!* She'd be off and en route to her six o'clock class. She'd be at school until nine, and it was ten o'clock before she dragged herself back inside and fell into bed next to my sleeping father. The next morning the same cycle would start all over again.

By the time I got to high school I felt a huge void. I was left thinking, "*Is this what life is?*" There had to be more. Where were the people I was supposed to call my family? Where were my parents? The truth was, they were trying to keep their head above the waterline. It was all about survival.

The fact of the matter is it did not leave much room for hope.

The very last thing I would have guessed was that education would be my ticket out.

# Chapter 2

## A Strange Way to Make a Doctor

My first encounter with school was, of course, confusing at the tender age of five. I remember very distinctly telling my mother, "I'm not going to school. They're going to give me a new mom." Mom, on the other hand, apparently didn't share my opinion or fears as she delivered me to my class on the first day of school. I walked into a room covered with *papier-mâché* flowers, colorful maps, and a miniature traffic signal inclusive of changing red, yellow, and green lights. It was all meant to be welcoming, but I remember I wasn't going to have anything to do with it. After taking roll call and learning the basics of what it took to be a good kindergarten student, it was game time. But unlike my classmates, I didn't want anything to do with the game of red light/green light the teacher had orchestrated.

"If you're not going to play then you have to sit up on the piano bench," my teacher scolded, not about to give in to my stubborn headedness. *Fine with me*, I thought. From my vantage point on the piano bench I observed the lay of the land, keeping a close eye on the door. The minute someone opened it–*boom, green light!* I leapt off that piano bench and darted as fast as my skinny little legs could take me toward my escape. I hit the door running and lit off across the schoolyard. I made it to the chain-link fence, scrambled up over the top, and then shot across the empty lot dotted with electrical towers, making a beeline for home. I arrived home panting, but proud of my desertion, as well as my fortitude. Mom, however, was less than pleased.

"What are you doing home?"

"They're going to give me a new mother," I tried to explain once again. She wasn't picking up what I was putting down.

"You get your butt back to school, young man."

She grabbed me by the hand, placed me in the car, and drove me back to school. It didn't matter. The second I saw my means of escape, I was off again. But the second time I was a little smarter. *I'm not going home this time,* I reasoned. It would be a little vacation. Sort of like hanging out on the street before I had to go to school.

The school called my mom. "Your son, Jeffrey. He took off again."

"Well, he's not here," my mom said, more angry than frightened.

She got in the car and the hunt was on. I remember hiding in the bushes along the street, watching her idle slowly past in our old hulking '54 Dodge. Once, twice, three times, she cruised up and down the street, knowing it was unlikely that I'd gone too far. She finally spotted me hunkered down in the bushes. She jerked the car to a stop and rolled down the window.

"Jeffrey Nordella! You get in this car right now!"

I knew that voice. I wasn't about to mess with her. I slunk out from beneath the bushes and slid in next to her, not daring to look her in the eye. My mother might have been a former bathing beauty, but she was no push over. It was the last time I tried to escape from school. But perfect attendance didn't change my attitude. I still hated it.

Education was never a real part of my family's consciousness. It wasn't a priority. Whenever my father would say, "You need to get an education," he meant that I needed to try to get a couple of community college classes under my belt so it would look good on my resume for some kind of low level service or retail job. It was assumed I wasn't going to be any different than everybody else on the block. That kind of life was reserved for a different class of people. A much more well to do crowd.

Besides, I was a C student at best. I just wasn't smart. Or at least I was convinced I wasn't smart. The only thing that helped bring my GPA to even a C level was that I got A's in auto shop and PE.

My senior year schedule consisted of PE in the morning, art, and two hours of auto shop. I'd leave school at noon where I'd report to a work-study program. I hustled up a variety of dead end jobs just to earn a buck, working as a bus boy, grocery store bagger, and selling hot dogs at a concession stand. But my favorite job was working as an auto mechanic.

Even though my father's health prevented him from being a strong role model in my young life, I did have my mom's dad, Grandpa Ovide. Although he had no real education, he did have a can-do entrepreneurial spirit and had taught himself how to paint and mix chemicals, which earned him a position as the head of the paint department on the lot of Universal Studios, a job he held for most of his life. A nuts and bolts, no nonsense kind of guy, Ovide wasn't one to sit around and chat about his feelings and he expected everyone else to deal with life head on the same way he did. If I ever came to him with a complaint, his answer would always be the same: "Look at your options, make a decision, and work hard." But there was no mistaking he wanted the best for me and became my mentor by default. I loved him, and I looked up to him.

Ovide was the one who got me into cars. He had a place out in a semi-rural, semi-industrial area on the outskirts of Los Angeles, a sprawling rundown ranch home in the hills. His ramshackle garage stored a mountain of tools of every shape and size, and he always seemed to have at least two junkers he was working on simultaneously, and I'm not talking about restoring vintage cars. I'd lie in a dirt driveway alongside my grandfather, tinkering inside the bowels of some rattletrap vehicle, relishing every moment. I loved the metallic scent of warm grease and the satisfaction of working with my hands. I was good at puzzles, dismantling, and rebuilding an engine, which served as an interesting mental challenge.

Once I knew what I was doing, I started to do tune-ups, oil changes, and replacing clutches for neighbors and friends, my front lawn serving as my garage. I even completely rebuilt two engines, one of them being for a '67 SS Camaro, a car I'd die to have today. With the cash, I installed a red phone on my bedroom wall to take calls for my growing business. My younger brother even painted a sign that I nailed above my bed: *Jeff's Automotive.*

However, my mechanical prowess did little to help the fact that I found myself on the outskirts of the high school social scene. I was fine at working on engines or working any one of my part time jobs where I felt a sense of acceptance and belonging. But school was a different story. Like a lot of adolescences I felt I was not good enough. I wasn't attractive enough. I wasn't wealthy enough. I wasn't this or that enough. I never even dated in high school. My senior year I tried to improve my looks by paying for my own orthodontic braces. But when you're a senior and smiling for your senior portrait with a mouth full of metal, it goes without saying that I wasn't the best looking or most popular kid that ever hit the halls. As far as an education went, my lack of self-esteem held me back and lead me to believe I was stupid. But not everyone agreed...specifically, my grandpa.

One day, just out of high school, our heads under the hood of yet another junker, Ovide grilled me about my future plans.

"I'm already doing what I'm going to do," I told him.

"Why don't you become something to make yourself proud."

"Like what?"

"I don't know. Get yourself a real education. Be a dentist or something."

"How? I don't have the smarts or the money to go to college for that," I answered, hoping he'd just drop it.

"Don't worry about the money. If you say you really want it, I'll figure out a way for you to get it."

"Thanks, Gramp, but I don't need any more school."

"The hell you don't. What're you gonna do? End up being some kind of ditch digger or something? I'm telling you, you need that education."

"Why? You didn't get an education."

"Exactly."

Ovide slammed the wrench back into the toolbox and stomped into the house. The conversation was over.

I had to admit, at least to myself, that the idea of becoming an auto mechanic for the rest of my life wasn't nearly as appealing as it had initially seemed. I began to notice my fingertips were always stained, and I could never quite seem to scrub the grease out from underneath my fingernails. Lying for hours on my back in the dirt was no longer a novelty, but simply uncomfortable. However, I was at a loss for what else I could really do. Most of my other friends weren't going to school. They were working in auto body shops, liquor stores, and gas stations. Although I saw nothing wrong with these jobs, I knew there was no real future in them.

Still drifting, none of my questions answered, I enrolled at Pierce College, a nearby college open to anyone who enrolled. I started taking general ed and electronics classes and soon secured a job at a stereo factory. I began to work during the day and go to school at night.

Although my new trajectory in life didn't have me exactly turning cartwheels, the factory job paid pretty good money for the time, a whopping $4.25 an hour. At least I was making enough money to save. I socked every other check into the bank, not knowing what I was saving for, but proud that I could save at all.

What happened next with Grandpa Ovide prompted me to make my first move toward a new future.

After my grandfather was widowed, he retired and moved into a small lake community three hours north of Los Angeles. Staying true to his indomitable nature and willing himself not to grow old in idleness, he slapped on a construction belt and built himself a house. But whether he liked it or not, he wasn't a young man any more. The workload proved to be too much, and he suffered a mild heart attack. I watched, slightly horrified when he returned from the hospital and washed his prescribed meds down the sink in a furry.

"If I can't live life my way, I don't want to live at all!" he defiantly declared.

Soon after, he befriended a woman, Thora, a one eyed widow cut from the cloth of a true prairie woman who lived in a little cabin about five miles from Grandpa. She was spunky and cantankerous and lived without electricity or running water except for a nearby creek. She used kerosene lamps for lighting, had an outhouse, and a dammed-up pond in the corner of the creek that she used as a bath. She and Ovide were a match made in heaven.

But just months after his heart attack, Ovide paid a visit to Thora. She had accidently dropped a wrench in the eleven-foot-deep water hole on her property and asked for Ovide's help. Unable to swim down far enough to retrieve the tool, Ovide tied a large rock to a rope and plunked it in the water. He jumped into the pond, clinging to the rope as he pulled himself down to the bottom where he grabbed the wrench. Just as he was about to come up, he was struck with a sharp pain in his chest. True to his Spartan grit, he was able to make his way to the surface, but Thora could see he was in pain. She insisted on driving him to the nearest hospital where he spent the night, while Ovide grumbled that everyone was making a big fuss over nothing. Early the next morning, he shot up in bed. His hands clutched his chest as he shouted out in pain before he went limp. He had a massive heart attack followed by an arrhythmia, and the hospital personnel were unable to resuscitate him. He died.

His loss was as unexpected as it was devastating. But at least he had died on his own terms. He had lived the life he'd wanted. He was my counselor, my mentor, and my hero. I couldn't help thinking of his words, his insistence that I get an education. If I didn't try I was disrespecting him. My mother, having always been close to her father, spiraled into a depression. I felt adrift, the tendrils of melancholy reaching out for me, too. Things at home were reaching critical mass. My father and now mother were both depressed, and my brothers fell deeper into the drug culture. And all this crammed into our 900-square-foot home where the walls seemed like they were closing in by the day.

I still wasn't sure where I was headed. I still wasn't as convinced as my grandfather was that I had the academic tools to attend college. I still didn't have a clue what I was doing. But the only thing I *did* know after losing my grandfather was this: I had to get out of the house.

I went out and found an apartment, using my savings from the factory job to put down the first and last months' rent. I had a '65 El Camino truck I'd nursed back to life a couple of years ago. I backed up to my front door, piled my belongings into the back and moved out.

My new home was a bachelor, which meant one crappy room. It cost $110 a month. It came "furnished" with two sagging couches, one of which acted as my bed, a chipped end table, a gooseneck lamp, a bathroom, and a dime-sized "economy" kitchen. The definition of bare bones in a bad neighborhood. But to me? It was a mansion.

I was finally free. *From here on out*, I decided, *the future is what I make it.*

# Chapter 3

## Endings and Beginnings

Life was starting to look up. Not only did I have a decent job, but a physical metamorphosis was taking place as well. Now with a confident braces-free smile and recently matured body, I found myself with my first official girlfriend. Even though I had a hunch it wasn't going to last forever, it certainly kept me distracted from my recent loss and was well welcomed. Life was good, at least for the moment. But my direction was still unclear and it haunted me.

Like most kids my age, I was still aimless in terms of a career. After my first year at Pierce College I transferred to Valley College where I heard they had biomedical equipment technology classes. I thought they'd be interesting. It was a certificate program, sort of like a trade school within the college that taught students how to repair and maintain medical equipment. Part of the program involved onsite training, kind of like an internship, in a hospital. The objective was to go into a hospital and experience firsthand the different machines that the doctors and techs used. A cardiologist in an affluent suburb of Los Angeles volunteered as a supervisor for the program, and I was assigned to report to his hospital.

Driving into Westlake Village was like entering into another universe. One of Southern California's first "pre-planned" communities nestled close to the Santa Monica Mountains; it was filled with majestically gnarled oaks, tasteful upper scale shopping centers, and gated communities that catered to the upwardly mobile. This haven for young executives even had its own hospital, and that's where I met Dr. Merriman.

"Hey Jeff, come on in. Can you fix any of these machines?" he asked on the first day while he pointed to the stray heart monitor.

"Well, actually, no," I said sheepishly. "I came to *learn* about the machines."

"Good, good, good!" he declared, not hearing a word I'd said. "C'mon, I'll take you on rounds."

"Wait, what...?" I muttered, images of passing out in my dad's ICU room filling my head. "I'm not sure I want to go on..." But before I could say "rounds," he disappeared around the corner expecting me to follow.

"Hurry, up Jeff!" Dr. Merriman called out. "Got to stay on schedule!"

I swallowed hard and rushed after him.

As he whisked down the halls moving from patient to patient, I closely watched the effect he had on the patients and staff alike. When he walked into a room, people stopped in the middle of whatever they were doing. They listened. In fact, they hung on his every word. It was clear to me he was a master at helping his patients feel secure, something that everyone needs when their health is in someone else's hands. People trusted him. They looked up to him. They wanted him to give them reassurance that everything was going to be okay. If he said it, they believed it.

I had my fair share of experience with doctors and hospitals because of my father and all his illnesses and had felt intimidated with the unfamiliar sights, smells, and sickness. But I also remembered another common denominator—the reassuring presence of doctors. They were the calm in the middle of whatever storm of illness my father had faced. As I continued to walk the halls with Dr. Merriman, I was reminded of another doctor who'd left a real impression on me as a sixteen-year old kid—a general surgeon who'd removed my appendix. A former football player for the Chicago Bears, his starched white coat, dark rim glasses, low voice, and masculine confidence left me feeling soothed and slightly in awe. Plus, he was easy to talk to and generally a nice guy. Sort of like the ultimate professional man's man. He even gave me a signed photo of himself when he'd played for the Bears. He was the kind of person anyone would look up to.

Dr. Merriman exuded the same intelligent confidence and kindness I'd seen years before. Not only that, but, as I was invited to observe Dr. Merriman, I watched him fix people. He did procedures with his hands, placing catheters, and suturing wounds. That meant he was good with his hands.

I felt I was good with my hands...

I would also watch Dr. Merriman pouring over charts, EKGs, X-rays, diagnosing, figuring things out, and troubleshooting.

I loved troubleshooting.

An idea began to slowly take shape inside my head...

*Maybe I could be a doctor.*

But just as soon as the thought materialized, reality set in. *What am I, nuts? How could I be a doctor?* I had no clear idea of what it took, what kind of grades, schooling, and level of sacrifice that was required before anyone had the honor of wearing that iconic white coat. But somewhere in the furthest reaches of my psyche, the seed had been planted.

By the end of my second semester at Valley College I completed and received my biomedical medical equipment technology certificate. It felt like a big accomplishment, even if it wasn't much more than a degree from a glorified trade school. I wanted to call my dad and my mom as soon as they handed me my certificate of completion. I knew they'd be proud. Mom was teaching that night, but at least I could call my dad and share my good news. I headed over to a pay phone, (yes, a pay phone), just outside the classroom and was about to dial home when a couple of my buddies waylaid me.

"Nordella, we're going out for a beer to celebrate. C'mon!" I hesitated, but ended up replacing the receiver and joined the party.

It was a decision I still regret to this day.

By the time I made it back to my apartment it was late. Too late to call my parents.

The next morning at my factory job, a voice came across the overhead speaker.

"Jeff Nordella. You've got a phone call."

A phone call? I'd never gotten a phone call at work before.

I headed to the back room and picked up the phone, silently trying to convince myself there was nothing to worry about. The moment I heard the voice on the other end of the phone, I knew something was wrong.

The man identified himself as a fireman. In the background I could make out muted voices, commotion.

"Is this Jeff?" he said. "Jeff Nordella?"

"Yes..."

"Son, do you have a way to get home?"

"I have a car. Why?" I asked, desperate for an answer, yet terrified to get one.

"You just need to get to your parents' house. Drive safely, but come as quickly as you can."

This was bad. Really bad, and I knew it. "What's going on?"

The line went silent. Then, "Just come on home, son."

I heard the panic rising in my own voice. "Just tell me. Is it my mom? My dad? Who?"

"It's your dad."

I don't even remember driving home. It all slipped by like some kind of fever dream.

As I turned down my street, the first thing I saw was the fire truck blocking our driveway. I threw my truck into park, flung open the door, and rushed toward the house. The front door and screen yawned wide open.

I stepped inside the darkness of my childhood home, no one visibly present.

There he was, on the pull-out bed, a thin sheet pulled up over his face, outlining the motionless peaks and valleys of his wasted body. All alone in the dimly-lit room, dead.

My father had died on the very same bed he'd escaped to, clung to for all those years. One of my deepest childhood fears, and my father's as well, had finally come to pass.

He would never know I had received my certificate. I would never introduce him to my future wife. He would never hug my children. He would never know that one day I would become, against all odds, a doctor. All the times he had dragged himself to my baseball games and I'd been ashamed. Why? In that moment I longed to share just one soda, have one last conversation about our favorite team. But that would never happen again.

My dad was gone.

He was sixty-four and I was nineteen.

From the back porch I could hear Mom, a fireman's low, steady voice a counterpoint to her hysterical sobs. I stepped onto the porch. She looked up, wrecked, her eyes clouded with tears, rimmed red. I didn't have words. What could I say? What could she? I stepped to her and folded my arms around her back, her body uncharacteristically frail against mine. We stood like that, clutching each other for what seemed like a small eternity.

Before long, the coroner arrived. I stood by, screwed to the living room floor as he confirmed my father's death. Numb, I stared out the same living room window I did as an eight year old boy, watching the drivers load my father into the back of the ambulance. But this ambulance didn't have the light on top. This ambulance wasn't headed for the hospital where he would recover, but to the mortuary where he would remain. This ambulance was a hearse.

In the end, my dad died never knowing much about me, just as I never knew much of him. My grandpa Ovide was gone, and now Dad. The only male role models I'd ever known had vanished within less than a year. I was truly on my own now. If I was honest with myself, the feeling was familiar. In some ways, I'd been fending for myself my entire life.

As I watched the hearse drive slowly away, I knew this would be the worst day of my life. Unfortunately it was not even close.

* * * * *

Months after my dad's death, life delivered another left-hook. Things had gotten a little rocky with my girlfriend, and we had broken up right around Christmas. My job at the factory collapsed not too long after. I can't blame them for firing me. I was showing up late; I wasn't focused. The prior enthusiasm I'd brought to the assembly line was gone.

"Your heart's really not in it," my boss told me on the day I got canned. "Sorry."

He was right. My heart wasn't in it. The fact was, my heart wasn't into much of anything.

If I were to look back at that time of my life as a movie, it would be some kind of bad student film. There's this kid, shuffling around in his shoebox apartment day after day, like some kind of warmed-over zombie. His dad is dead, his grandfather's dead, his mom is mourning, his girlfriend is gone, and he's lost his job. It was like a country western song. All I needed was a dead dog and a six-string guitar. It would've been a hit. Everyone has a different reaction to grief. Mine was anger.

Some days I'd head over to my mom's house hoping to vent, but she was getting her teeth kicked in by life too. She'd just lost her father and husband and was still struggling to keep my brothers and sisters fed.

It hardly seemed appropriate to heap any more misery on her. Without work or direction, life became a bleak, unfulfilling routine: I'd wake up, sit around the apartment, go get a burger, come home, hang around the apartment, listen to music, watch a little TV and crash. Next morning: repeat. I let my hair grow long and tangled past my shoulders and I had a mountain man beard to match. I found myself staying in more and more, as if hunkering down against an invisible siege. I'd never been depressed before, but now I was.

With my savings from the factory job depleted to just a few dollars, I took a day job tarring roofs. The blasting summer sun, amplified by the black tar, beat down on my bare back as I spread the thick, toxic mixture across the papered roofs, day after day. I breathed in the acrid fumes, my shoulders aching, working alongside the other day laborers that seemed to be carrying silent burdens of their own. Once again, here I am thinking, "*This can't be what life's about.*" It was like I was doing everything I could to swim up to the waterline to catch a deep breath, but the world just kept dragging me back under.

My depression clearly took me to a crossroads. I could choose my dad's road: give up and accept the status quo. I could just pack it in, and drag myself from one metaphoric bed to the next. Or I could listen to the voice in my head bred by years of my Grandfather's no non-sense approach to life: *get your ass up and move forward.*

When I look back, it took the tragedies and heartbreak for me to finally step back and take a long hard look at where I was going, or in my case, *not going.* Some would say it was bad luck. Some would say it was God's hand. Who knows? I remember sitting in my apartment listening to music thinking, "*Enough of this shit.*" I needed to take charge, control my destiny, and not be a victim. I just needed the proper tools to do the job, something my grandfather taught me. What did I really want to do with my future?

When I was working with Dr. Merriman, I'd had an idea, but had just as quickly discarded it. This time I really bit into the concept, and once I did, I wasn't about to let go. It was my way out toward a new life and I was never going back.

* * * * *

"You want to do what?"

"I want to be a doctor."

Mom stared at me from across the kitchen. "Really?" was all she could say. It wasn't the kind of "really" I'd hoped for. It wasn't an excited "really" or even a proud "really." It was more of an "*Are-you-joking*"? "*Really.*"

"But you have to go to college to do that. Like a real college."

"I know. I'm going to figure that out." I was not very convincing.

"But you have that certificate in electronics. Why don't you do something with that?"

"It's not what I want to do, Mom."

"But you'll have to go back to school, how are you going to support yourself?"

"I know. I'm working on it." I certainly wasn't earning any points.

"And get really good grades, right?"

"Yes, I am aware." Ouch, that one hurt.

She just looked at me, almost as if she was waiting for me to yell, "Got ya!" But I wasn't going to give an inch. It didn't matter what she said, or didn't say. I'd made my decision and nobody was going to talk me out of it, and I meant nobody.

Even still, I could see her doing the mental math and it wasn't adding up. She was my mom and I loved her and she loved me. She didn't want to tell me straight out something like, "Who are you kidding! *You*, a doctor?" I believe she related to those well-educated, well-dressed, well-spoken, intelligent doctors she remembered from her husband's long-term illness. I was just the kid she remembered lying in the dirt, grease under my nails, replacing a fuel pump on a '62 Plymouth Valiant. I knew what her hesitation was all about—she didn't want me to get my hopes up, only to have them crushed by some impossible, pie in the sky goal. On the other hand, she didn't want to discourage me. She knew, like her father, that I was stubborn, driven, and a hard worker and would not be denied once my mind was made up. Maybe, just maybe…

"Well, if that's what you want to do, then you should do it," Mom said, making an effort to sound sincere. "But don't you think you should cut your hair first and shave?"

"Why?" I joked. "Jesus was the ultimate healer."

It wasn't exactly the kind of *atta boy* I was hoping for, but if I were going to make my new dream of becoming a doctor a reality, I would have to be my own biggest fan. I secretly had my own doubts—big doubts—but I couldn't let that stop me before I even got started. I'd set my goal, and now I just had to figure out what I had to do to achieve it.

# Chapter 4

## Starting Over

It was time to rejoin life. The first thing I did was take Mom's advice. I cut my hair and shaved. I kind of liked it. It was as if I was announcing to the world and to myself that I was a new man with a new beginning. But the reality was, I had no idea what it took to be a doctor. It didn't really occur to me all the courses I'd have to take, all the flaming hoops I'd be jumping through for the next eleven years of my life.

Back then, the average number of applications for most medical schools was somewhere around 4,500 applicants for an average of 130 slots. And the applicants weren't just your run of the mill academic slouches. These were kids who, for the most part, had been groomed. Prep schools, academic camps, and private tutoring were commonplace for most aspiring medical students. For most, money was also no object. Many were sons and daughters of doctors with grandparents who were doctors, lawyers or other professionals before them. They knew how to work the system, how to guard and maximize their grades. They spent summers shadowing doctors and setting up their own research projects. Many had connections that greased the wheels of the medical school machine. All so they could one day walk the polished linoleum halls of a revered hospital with a stethoscope around their neck and a nametag on their white coat that read, "medical student."

I didn't have a clue about any of this. Nada.

But most importantly I was also carrying a big fat nothing in my academic backpack. By this point I'd had two years of college, but I had no real education because it was all about electronics. I hadn't even taken the basic general education college requirements. My high school resume was even worse. I had a killer 2.4 GPA, graduating maybe 500th out of 600 kids. I had cut class and rarely studied, and even if I did hit the books I'd be happy to wind up with a C or D. I didn't know how to write, my spelling was horrible, and my reading and comprehension skills were poor at best. Math was the same. It wasn't that I had left-brain skills or right-brain skills. It was that I had no skills at all.

What I did have was an idea and a long, difficult path to obtain a title.

Medical Doctor.

As naïve as I was about the requirements for getting into medical school, I knew I had to start over and that starting line would involve getting my academic act together. I reached out for the first opportunity that came my way. A buddy of mine, a fun-loving guy who was into sports and baseball, had just graduated from a prep school in Los Angeles and had a scholarship to play baseball at College of the Canyons. He knew I'd just finished up my certificate program at Valley College and proposed, "If you can get to my house," which was in Panorama City about five miles from my house, "I'll drive us both over to COC," he told me.

College of the Canyons had just broken ground on a one hundred-fifty acre new campus with the help of a $11.2 million grant from of the statewide Community College Construction Act and another $8 million matching bond supported by the local community of Santa Clarita. Valencia, another growing preplanned community within the Santa Clarita Valley, was situated just over the hill from the Los Angeles basin. It catered to young executives and their families who couldn't quite afford the more exclusive areas in LA like Beverly Hills, Brentwood, or Malibu Beach. Everything about it was new, ordered, and wreaked of optimism. It felt like the perfect place to get a fresh start.

"Okay, sounds good," I told him. "Let's do it."

And that's when my life started over.

I'd pour water into the leaky radiator of my '62 Ford Falcon just to make the five-mile drive from my apartment. We'd hop into his new truck and sail up the 5 freeway toward the brand spanking new junior college, COC. The first thing I needed to do was sign up for classes. The kind of classes that would put me on track for medical school. I headed to the academic counseling department for a scheduled appointment, cruising past the newly sprouted grass and into the modern cement and glass building to find my place on one of the slick plastic chairs inside the waiting room. I took in the smell of freshly-laid carpet, blinking back at the harsh overhead florescent lighting, feeling equally nervous and excited. I was finally going to embark on a road that actually led to a worthwhile destination.

A trim, pleasant looking middle-aged woman in a lime green polyester pantsuit, mascara lining her eyes like two fat caterpillars, stepped into the waiting room. "Jeff Nordella?" she asked, glancing around the room.

"That's me!" I answered, jumping to my feet.

"Come on back."

She ushered me through the little swinging door leading to the counselor's bullpen, pulled my file off from the top of a large stack of other student transcripts, and glanced through it.

"So, I see we have an electronics certificate, but no real courses in general education. What were you thinking of majoring in?"

Well, here it goes, I thought. "I want to be a doctor, so whatever I need to get into med school would be great," I said with the kind of confidence only ignorance could muster.

The friendly smile drained from her face. Thank God she hadn't been drinking coffee. If she had been, she would have done a spit take all over me.

She quickly glanced down at my transcripts again and flipped through my miserable history as if trying to unearth some buried nugget of hope. I could see she wasn't coming up with anything. Instead, she looked back up and attempted to plaster back on her best professional counselor's smile. "Isn't medical school a little... ambitious? I mean..." she waved a hand at my file, waiting for me to fill in the blank.

It was the professional version of my mother's response, but much worse. Clearly, this would be everyone's knee-jerk reaction to my new ambition. It just kind of pissed me off, to be honest. Not that I was angry with her, per se. If I were in her position I would have thought the exact same thing. I knew I didn't have much proof to indicate otherwise, but then again, nobody was going to deny me before I even got started. *Please don't tell me I **can't**. Just tell me **how**.*

I wasn't about to be defined by a couple of sheets of paper. I was willing to travel the road, to shoulder that boulder up the steepest slope. I just needed someone to point me to the right mountain.

I looked her straight in the eye. "I'll do whatever I have to. If you say I have to start over, so be it."

"But Jeff... "

"Just put me down as pre-med," I interrupted, as politely as possible. "That's my major. Please. Just tell me what classes I need."

She stared at me for another long moment before she sighed and signed me up.

My first weeks of class were terrifying.

I knew I had to complete my general education requirements and premed courses, and like I told the counselor, I was willing to start over. On one hand I'm a very impatient guy and I wanted to get through all of it quickly, but on the other hand I thought, "*Oh, boy, you better slow down because you've got a lot of catching up to do. A lot.*"

I took a couple of classes to test out the waters: psychology, math, and an EMT class, which I figured would get my feet wet in the medical field. However, I very quickly realized I didn't have the tools to get me through. Something my grandfather had taught me a long time ago. The issue wasn't how slowly or quickly I wanted to complete my coursework; the issue was that I had no academic foundation on which to stand. I sat there in class listening to the instructors talk, and I didn't know half of what they were saying. I literally didn't have the vocabulary to understand what the hell they were even trying to get across.

How was I supposed to become a doctor if I couldn't even get through a basic psychology class?

However, a small glimmer of light soon pierced its way through the darkness of my growing panic. That glimmer had a name: Don McGinty. It turned out that COC was attracting a cadre of young, talented instructors. McGinty was one of them. I signed up for his class, intermediate algebra, which wasn't much more than a high school level algebra class. I couldn't help noticing when I stepped into the lecture hall on the first day that I was a little older than most of the students, which was simultaneously intimidating and humiliating. My humiliation only compounded when the concepts Don taught sailed right over the top of my head.

My first test didn't help my anxiety. When Don passed back the results, my eyes landed on the large "C" scrawled in the right corner of the test. *Oh God, I'm in trouble. That counselor was right.* Next test. I studied my butt off. Another "C." *What the hell...*

I stayed after class and talked to Professor McGinty.

"I just don't get it. None of it makes sense to me," I admitted.

He nodded, with compassion. "Sometimes it just takes time."

"But I have to get a good grade in this class," I almost pleaded. "It might sound stupid, but I'd really like to go to medical school." I think he could see how much I wanted it, even if I had nothing to back up my dream except grit and pure desire.

"Stop pursuing grades and start pursuing knowledge," he said. "Pay attention to the concepts and put in the time. If you don't get it, do it again. It'll click eventually."

I went to class. I took notes. And most importantly, I studied. And then I studied some more, then more. And of course it didn't hurt that I refused to quit. This time I focused on understanding not only what I was doing, but also why I was doing it. It wasn't about proving to myself that I could get the "A." It was about proving to myself that I wasn't the person I had convinced myself of being.

Just like McGinty suggested, I'd go to the math lab. I'd work the problems, over and over-and over again. I put in the hours, lots of hours. My whole life disappeared. I didn't socialize. I didn't go out. I jettisoned "free-time" altogether. Night after night, there I'd be, inside my crappy bachelor apartment, bent over my cheap desk working problems. Reading. Then working the problems again.

The hard work began to pay off. My next algebra test came back... an "A." My first A in anything other than auto shop. Just like McGinty advised, I went to class, I listened, I took copious notes, I studied, then I studied some more, again focusing on concepts. The grades followed, C's turned to B's, then B's to A's. Before I was like a V8 engine operating on two cylinders. Now I was operating on all eight. I finished my classes for the semester and got my grades... EMT: A. Psychology: B. And as for McGinty's algebra class... A. It was just one quarter of good grades. But it was much more than that to me. It represented that months of hard work and sacrifice could pay off. It convinced me I had the potential to reach out and grab a whole new life.

Every day, as my buddy and I drove over the hill from the Valley into the expansive landscape of Santa Clarita, I'd crank the Fleetwood Mac song: "Don't stop thinking about tomorrow. Yesterday's gone... yesterday's gone." The song spoke to me.

I looked around as we topped the hill and sailed through the rolling hills of the Santa Clarita Valley. "I would love to have my own clinic here one day," I blurted out.

I knew he thought I was half-joking, but I couldn't have been more serious. The idea of having my own practice there in the Valley I passed through every day, motivated me. Even though the clinic only existed in my mind's eye, it gave me something concrete to work towards. All I had to do was continue to work. I knew it was going to be a long road, but now it was just one step at a time.

When I signed up for my next quarter's classes I decided to jump into the deep end to fulfill the pre-med requirements. And when I say "jump in" I really mean headfirst. I filled my schedule with the maximum number of classes. No electives. I decided that with my newly full schedule, I didn't want to take the time driving over the hill every day with my pal. An acquaintance of mine from my first quarter EMT class mentioned he needed a roommate and I was it. I sold everything I owned to make the transition to a dreary but cheap, two-bedroom condo up a rural canyon in Santa Clarita, just ten minutes from school. I didn't have a stick of furniture, but who cared? I was closer to school and that's all that mattered. I took a foam pad that someone had given me, tossed it on the floor, and put sheets over it for a bed. I supplemented my blankets with a bunch of old coats that I'd collected throughout the years. Oh, and did I mention that the heater didn't work? So what? I could always just throw on another jacket.

My EMT (Emergency Medical Technician) instructor, a lanky, wannabe mustached firefighter, seemed to like me. He chose me to volunteer in front of class when he was doing his demonstrations, and he could see I was working hard in his class.

"What are your plans?" he asked me one day as the students filed off from class.

"I'd like to be a doctor," I proudly announced.

"You want a job as an EMT after you finish the course? It might give you a little background."

"Are you kidding? I'd love it."

"You have a phone?"

"Yeah."

"Good. You'll be the second unit backup. If the first unit is out and we get another call, you can run the call out of your condo."

My first day as an EMT in training was a ride along and much more of a shock than I expected. I was hoping it would be something simple, like a broken leg, or an elderly transport from a nursing home. Something routine. Instead, it was a DOA, Dead on Arrival. And who? A young man in his early twenties. Just a year or two older than me. He'd crashed his car into a tree and had gone through the windshield. Now his life was over.

The two seats in the front were taken by the two more experienced EMT's. "You're gonna have to ride in the back, kid," the driver said as he exchanged looks with the guy riding shotgun. I could see they knew how tough it would be, especially for someone as inexperienced as I was to this new world. But if I were going to be in this business it was something I'd have to get used to.

I crawled into the back of the ambulance and settled in next to the body. A white sheet had been pulled up over his face, just as it had been when I'd last seen my dad. An immediate déjà vu. I was struck with an involuntarily wave of emotion. Loss, fear, and a familiar emptiness I had so recently buried after my grandfather and father's death, came swimming to the surface. There was no escape. He was lying right in front of me. Nothing but my thoughts and feelings for the twenty-five minute ride. A flurry of questions flew around inside my head. *Who was this kid? What was he doing before he got into the car? Why did he crash his car? Was he speeding? Was he drunk? Who's going to get the phone call? How many people would be affected by his death? God, if you're there, why did you allow this to happen?*

My racing mind sent me deeper, making me question my newly minted commitment to medicine. *Is this what it's was going to be like? Do I really want to see death? Am I going to go through this every time I see somebody die?* This wasn't a TV show. Riding in the back of the ambulance next to death itself, I felt as vulnerable as I ever had in my life. But before long, the work became routine. Instead of allowing myself to become overwhelmed by the life and death nature of the work, I focused on what needed to be done in the moment.

I had to make this work.

The EMT job ended up paying some unexpected dividends. During the runs to the hospital, I started talking with an ER doctor by the name of Ruth Degas. She was everything I wanted to be as a doctor— smart, energetic, decisive, yet kind and personable. The patients loved her. One day, after bringing in a young girl with a broken arm, we both found ourselves in the break room sharing a couple of cups of black oil that barely passed for coffee.

"So what are you going to do with your life, Jeff?"

"I'd like to go to medical school."

"Really?"

Oh no, I thought, not this again. "Why? You think I'm not cut out for it or something?" I joked.

"No, it's not that. It's just that my husband is a pulmonologist and he's on the admissions board at USC. Would you like to meet him?"

Does the Pope wear a funny hat, I thought. "Absolutely! When?"

"Any time you want. Just let me know and I'll make sure he sees you."

I made an appointment. Fast. This was a very big deal. USC Medical School? Hoping to make the best impression possible, I put on a second hand tie and drove down to USC County Hospital. I strode through the endless maze of hallways, getting lost three times, before I tracked down the nurse's station closest to his office. I was nervous as hell, but hoped if he saw how utterly determined I was to become a doctor, he would give me a step-by-step formula of how to negotiate the gauntlet of admissions.

That wasn't exactly what I got...

A middle-aged, round-faced man, Dr. Andrew Degas, with thinning red hair and a firm handshake, soon ushered me into his cramped office.

I gave him a brief rundown of my background, hoping he'd be impressed. He was anything but.

"I'll be honest with you, Jeff," he said, not unkindly. "It's gonna be tough. You're going to have to get into a good four-year college. I'd recommend the UC system, but those schools are hard. *Very hard.* You'll be competing with the top minds in all of California and, for that matter, in the country."

I read his expression. Although he seemed to be more compassionate, he gave me the same look the counselor had given me at COC. He wasn't saying I had no chance in hell, just that I had *almost* no chance in hell.

Not what I wanted to hear but, as they say, it was from the horse's mouth. For the next forty-eight hours all I could think was, *What am I doing? Am I delusional or what? So what if I've gotten good grades for a year or two? So have tons of other people, and not just for one or two years, but their whole lives.* I have to admit it was totally deflating. All around, my friends were out there having fun, partying, getting married, working their jobs. I momentarily considered chucking it all. Would it really be so bad working in a factory, getting married, saving up for a vacation to Hawaii before I retired? No. Who was I to think I could have anything different?

But when it came right down to it my gut told me, do not quit! The seed had been planted, and I was not going to be satisfied with anything except the goal I had set. It didn't matter how high the odds were stacked against me. If I didn't have an academic foundation, I simply would build one.

Unable to go out to the movies or bars until two in the morning, all the relationships I had built evaporated as I hunkered down and attacked my classes, biology, zoology, botany, anatomy and physiology, calculus based physics, and calculus. All of these while I continued to expand an academic foundation. I hit the reading lab and drilled myself on basic comprehension, cramming my brain with years of lost educational skills.

In the meantime, with the $2 an hour I got from my EMT job along with Dad's social security death benefits, I had just enough to cover rent on our rural condo. But my grocery budget was thin at best. So I'd grab two cartons of whole milk and a chocolate pie at a near-by 7-11 on my way to campus, filling myself up with cheap calories. On the way home, I'd stop at the same 7-Eleven and load up on chicken pot-pies for dinner at thirty-eight cents each. I'd throw one of those in the oven, serve it up alongside my books waiting for EMT calls, and I'd then study until two or three in the morning. I'd then get up at seven, get to class by eight and start all over.

That was life.

If I came up short, that's where my mom came in. She was struggling on her own, but she'd give me $25 whenever she could. And that made all the difference.

Towards the end of my first year a friend told me about a summer course in Utah, a program that squeezed thirty weeks of organic chemistry into eight weeks. I barely arrived in Utah two days late after an overheated engine, fried valves, and a nearly-missed flight. Hardly taking time to say hello to my new roommates, I hit the books. The pace was relentless and before long two of our roommates dropped out, taking with them the only cars we had, leaving the remaining three amigos to hike three miles to school as we quizzed each other for our daily tests.

It was a grueling summer, but I hit it off with my two remaining roommates who both attended UC San Diego. The more I heard about their school, the more I liked it, especially because the pre-med students had an exceptionally high acceptance rate into medical school. I plotted a new course. UC San Diego would be my four-year college, and I would stop at nothing to get there.

Returning to COC for my last year, I found that my brain had, somewhere along the line, finally "clicked" into gear just as the professor had stated. It wasn't an overnight transformation, and it certainly wasn't magic. It had been a gradual two- year process that had started the day I'd stepped foot onto the COC campus. But once I'd built up a knowledge reservoir, once my brain finally turned on, the subjects became easier. I was finally *integrating* all the disciplines.

I had finally built that cornerstone I needed to stand on if I was going to make it at a four-year university and later medical school. I'd walked into COC unable to understand nearly a word of lectures and ended up as a tutor for chemistry, math, and biology. And the counselor who thought I was too ambitious with my academic calendar? She ended up nominating me for an academic scholarship, and I got it.

It was now time to transfer to that four-year college. I was accepted to the University of California San Diego, La Jolla California, affiliated with the institution where Jonas Salk earned the Nobel Prize for creating the polio vaccine.

It was unbelievable.

When it became a reality, all I could do was reflect: "*Me, the kid who'd flunked his high school biology class, the kid who'd barely learned to read and write in high school, the kid who was going to be an auto mechanic, was going to a prestigious university noted for hard-core sciences.*"

# Chapter 5

## Acceptance

When I got to UC San Diego, I felt like I was standing on a new stair platform getting ready to start a long climb all over again. The students were brilliant. The first class I took was physical chemistry of biological systems. The dreaded P-Chem was a complex course, combining a mixture of calculus and chemistry. Knowing I was entering a whole other stratosphere of competition and difficulty, I went down a month early and got the textbook. I dove right in, reading the book and working the problems to get a head start.

Once I finished all the problems, I did them again. And again. Nothing new, just hard work. Nevertheless, when I got to the class I was still unsure if I was going to perform. Sure I'd done every problem, but did I understand the concepts? I'd never gone head to head with this caliber of student before. They were brainiacs. By the time the end of the semester rolled around, despite the fact I was going toe-to-toe with the other students, I was still fearful I would fail. I can still vividly remember the final...

"You can have one piece of paper," our instructor told us a week before that last test, which was fifty percent of our final grade. "And only one side of that paper can be written on. But you can write anything you want on that one side of paper."

That's all I needed to know. If I ever decide to give up medicine I might consider becoming the world's smallest handwriting scribe. If you've ever seen those guys who write microscopic print on a grain of rice—the ones who set up at county fairs—they couldn't hold a candle to me when it came to that one stinking piece of paper. Everything that had ever been written on the subject of P-Chem was crammed, jammed, and squashed into that paper. Well, not *everything*, but *almost* everything. After I'd finished, I read that cheat sheet over and over and over. On the day of the final I folded it up and stuck it into my jean's pocket.

And that's where it stayed.

I got an "A."

It was another turning point. A big one. I could do this! As long as I kept firing and putting in the hours...

But everyone I went to class with had the same goal: medical school. The pre-med kids had become my friends, but they were also my competition. I needed to make sure that every class I took was right on target, exactly what was required to get accepted. But I wanted to go beyond that. Take physical chemistry for example. It was pretty clear this was yet another tool for weeding out students. If it was recommended, I was taking it. UC San Diego also had a pre-med club that taught us how to interview and reminded us of important deadlines. I went to every meeting.

I continued to stick to the ascetic lifestyle of no partying and no real socializing. I might have gone to three parties in two years. I was either in class or in the library. Finally, after all the work, and all the sacrifice, it was time to apply and show the schools who I was. I pored over all my choices. I talked to other students. I studied the best schools, the mediocre schools, and all the other in between schools. I weighed my options. I thought, then rethought my strategies for optimizing my chances of getting in. In the end, I applied to fifteen separate medical programs.

I applied in July. Within weeks I had a request for an interview.

*Holy Crap! How did I get an interview that quickly?* Not only that, but getting the interview meant I had passed the first rung of acceptance. My chances had gone from 1 in 4,000 to approximately 1 in 800, still mind-numbing odds against getting in, but I was heading in the right direction. Before I knew it, I had a fistful of letters requesting interviews. One of them was to USC, one of my top picks.

*This is a good thing*, I thought. *A potentially **very** good thing.*

I ironed my one dress shirt, slipped on a suit, and headed to USC. It was a round of three interviews in one day, one at ten o'clock with a physician, then with a medical student at noon. My third interview was scheduled for two hours later and gave me some time to burn. I decided to browse the medical library. Waiting nervously in the beautiful Gothic library, the light streaming through the stained glass windows, my eyes caught the familiar rounded red face and red thinning hair of Dr. Degas walking through the library. The same Dr. Degas who had put a hitch in my confidence back when I was an EMT. I loped across the library, tapping him on the back.

"Dr. Degas?"

He spun around to face me, confused.

"Jeff Nordella. I was the EMT that worked with your wife? I came to see you a couple of years ago."

Recognition finally spread across his face, "Oh right. Of course. How are you?"

"Good. How's your wife?"

"Very well, thanks. So what brings you to SC?"

"I'm interviewing."

He tried to piece that together and came up short.

"For medical school," I added.

"Here?"

"I know. I can't really believe it either."

He smiled, clearly shocked, but also impressed. "That's great! Congratulations."

"Well, I haven't gotten in yet."

"That's okay. It's quite an accomplishment to get this far."

"Thank you, sir."

"Good luck."

"Thanks. Would you tell your wife I said hello?"

"I will. She'll be glad to hear you're doing so well."

We shook hands and he disappeared into the library.

It felt good to have his approval. Even though I hadn't been accepted anywhere yet, it felt as if I had made it just to be standing there in the USC library, lucky enough to even be interviewing.

I later found out he wrote a letter on my behalf to the admissions board. Something along the lines of "... his background is a bit unconventional, but this young man has overcome incredible odds and shows remarkable tenacity." I guess he really was impressed after all.

I was happy, and more than a little surprised, to see that more invitations for interviews started to roll in. Soon I was whisking off to San Francisco, Boston, Chicago, and then back to Los Angeles for my number one choice, UCLA, along with several more. My interview strategy wasn't much of a strategy at all. It was simply to tell the truth. When the fateful question arose: "So why do you want to be a doctor?"

Rather than pulling out some kind of beauty pageant answer about humanity, saving starving orphans, and world peace, my response was simple and forthright. "I've always liked to work with my hands, solve problems, and I like to work with people," I'd tell them. "Medicine allows me to do those things. Also," and this was the dead honest piece, "being a doctor allows you to make a good living." That was the one that seemed to shock everyone. But it was the truth. I did want to make a good living and I wasn't going to apologize for that, or pretend it wasn't part of the equation. Money certainly wasn't the sole reason, or even close to the biggest reason I wanted to become a doctor, but I had struggled my entire life. The idea of working hard and living a comfortable lifestyle was something I aspired to. A couple of the interviewers looked at me and said, "Wow, nobody has ever said that to us." I think they appreciated my honesty.

But it was too early to get my hopes up. On one level I knew I could do it. I knew I was qualified to go to medical school. I felt my resume, despite my slow start, was pretty decent since I'd gotten excellent grades ever since starting at COC and even my biomedical technology and EMT training set me apart from the other applicants. It didn't make me better, just different. And I was absolutely certain I'd worked my ass off and it showed. I believed I really had what it took to be a doctor. However, on another level I was still that kid who was lying on his back fixing cars alongside Grandpa Ovide. *Is this really going to happen?* It was almost too good to be true.

I had just finished up one of my last interviews at University California San Francisco. The interview had gone well, but I was bone-tired. Having flown into Burbank airport, which was about a three-hour trip back to my apartment in San Diego, I decided to spend the night back at the house I grew up in and take an early train in the morning. The next day, after everyone had left for work, I showered and got ready to catch the 9:45 A.M. train. Eating my cereal alone at the same rickety linoleum table from boyhood, my mind canvased the sum total of the interviews. I'd been honest, I'd been myself, and I'd given it my best shot.

Mikey, my mom's shaggy white-haired mutt stared up at me and wagged his tail, as if reading my thoughts. "You're right. Now comes the waiting," I told him before he jumped up on his hindquarters and scratched my leg, making the most of my attention. "No, you can't have any Captain Crunch," I reminded him.

It was then I heard the familiar *creak* of the early morning mail slot.

I looked toward the front door just as the little brass door on the mail slot clanged shut. A small pile of letters and fliers littered the floor. I scooped up the mail, casually leafing through it, until my heart clenched. Everything stopped.

It was a letter addressed to Jeffrey Nordella. The envelope was stamped with the USC School of Medicine emblem.

*Oh God. It's thin.*

I thought a thick packet would be a welcoming acceptance letter with all the forms, brochures, and glossy advertising that comes with admittance. This was anything but. *Don't worry,* I thought, trying out a little positive self-talk to try to calm my galloping pulse. *You've got a bunch of other schools to go. Everybody gets rejected.*

I steeled myself and tore open the envelope. It contained a single letter. Not good. I barely needed to read it to know what it had to say.

I slowly removed the letter, braced myself for the worst, and let my eyes fall onto the page...

*"It is a pleasure to notify you that the Committee of Admissions has recommended that you be accepted into the School of Medicine."*

*Wait. What?*

My eyes flicked back over the sentence. *I must've read that wrong.*

*"Pleasure... Admissions... accepted...* ACCEPTED?

*I JUST GOT ACCEPTED INTO MEDICAL SCHOOL?*

"I did it!!" I shouted into the empty room. "I got in!" Mikey started yapping hysterically, running circles around my legs. It's true that dogs are man's best friend. I scooped him up and cheered. "I'm going be a doctor, Mikey!"

All of it had been worth it! All the chicken pot-pies, all the missed parties, all those hours in the library shivering from coffee overdoses bent over endless piles of books, everything.... It was all worth it for this single letter, this single sentence, this single word: acceptance. I had made it into the tribe. I had successfully negotiated the gauntlet. It was like the veil had been lifted. I could see the sky above me, reaching out into a never-ending galaxy of possibilities.

I glanced around the room at the place I had come from. I stopped, my gaze traveling out the living room window where my father had been taken away in a hearse. So much heartache in that house. It had all been such a struggle. But now...

The path of my life would change dramatically forever.

My younger brother got home a few hours after I opened the letter. He just shook his head and smiled. "I can't believe it. My dumbass brother is going to be a doctor. How're you gonna tell Mom?"

"I've got an idea."

\* \* \* \* \*

Mom looked tired as she dragged in after teaching a morning class. I was slouched on the couch with my brother when she stepped inside.

"Oh, I didn't think you'd still be here," she said as she wearily shelved a small bag of groceries. "Weren't you supposed to take the train?"

"Yeah..." I said, putting on my best long face.

"Is something wrong?" she asked. It was the question every parent dreads asking, especially when they can already see something's not right.

I took a deep breath, playing it up the best I could, nudging my brother who had to walk into the hall in order to keep from bursting out laughing. "I've got something to tell you..." I muttered.

She stopped shelving and focused on what I was saying.

"What happened...?"

I held up the measly looking letter from SC. "I heard from SC," I said, handing her the paper. She reluctantly took the letter, reading the faux disappointment on my face.

"I'm so sorry, honey. But you know how hard it is to get in..."

"Yeah. Almost impossible. Obviously."

"You've still got other schools, don't you?"

"Yeah, but there's no way. I'm just going to quit. It was a dumb idea anyway."

"Quit school? But you're almost finished. Don't you want to at least get a college degree?"

I just shrugged. Now I was feeling bad. I was torturing her, but I knew she liked a good prank even more than I did. Even still, I couldn't draw this out too much longer. "Go ahead," I prompted. "Open it. See what it says."

She sighed and unfolded the letter. Her eyes traced over the words before she looked up at me totally and utterly confused…. "But…"

I shrugged again….

She looked down, rereading the sentence over and over. It was just too much for her to compute. "But… this says you got in?" I just smiled. "*I know.*"

Her hand flew over her mouth, tears instantly clouding her eyes. "Oh, Jeff…"

My brother loped into the room and crowed, "Guess we'll have to take down the Jeff's Automotive sign, right, Mom?"

Mom reached over and pulled me into a hug. I could barely make out her words, her voice was so husky with tears. "I'm so proud, son. So proud."

Some days are meant to be remembered. That was certainly one of them.

* * * * *

Before I knew it, I received one, two, four acceptance letters, and I still had yet to hear from several remaining schools. But my number one school remained UCLA. Who knows, maybe it dated back to that very first day when Grandpa Ovide had mentioned he'd pay for my education and pointed to the August UCLA campus, but for me UCLA stood head and shoulders over the other schools. First of all, although I loved Tufts and Northwestern, two schools which had offered me acceptance, being a California boy, the Boston and Chicago winters were something I could live without. My priority was to stay close to Mom in Los Angeles to help ease her through her widowed years. That made USC a contender as well, until I found out about the tuition.

"How much does it cost to go to school here?" I asked their very polite admissions counselor.

"Per year, semester, or in total?"

"Why don't you give me the entire price tag?"

"About one hundred thousand dollars," she said, smiling. She didn't even blink. And remember, this was 1978. That was *big* money.

"How many zeros is that after the one?" I joked.

As I was waiting to hear from other schools I got a phone call. On the other end of the line was a UCLA interviewer, an infectious disease specialist. The interview went very well and we certainly had a connection. I was totally shocked!

"So where are you going to school next year?"

"Well, I really don't know."

"Where are you looking?"

"It's between UCLA and SC."

"Well, that's an easy choice, then. So when can you come back up for a tour?"

I was so stunned I could hardly answer. Was I actually being *courted* by UCLA?

After we toured through the entire medical school and hospital, a complex he described as the second largest structure in America second only to the US Pentagon, he offered to take me to dinner.

We headed to a swanky little white table clothed creperie in Westwood Village as I kept repeating to myself over and over, "*Is this really happening? Does everybody get this kind of treatment from admissions?*" But there I was, sitting across from an established physician as he waxed poetic about UCLA and what a good fit it would be for me. The more he talked about UCLA, the more I could imagine myself inside the brick labyrinth of a hospital, hurrying past rooms that held the latest research, cutting edge technology, and housed everyone from the indigent to the most famous movie star. How did I, a guy who never thought he'd get the grease out from underneath his fingernails, end up sitting across the table from a doctor who not only was paying the bill, but was selling me to become a physician at a top ten medical school?

At the end of our meal, over chocolate crepes with crushed hazelnuts, he put down his fork, wiped his mouth, and looked me square in the eye. "So, what do you think? Can you see yourself at UCLA Medical School?"

"Cut me open and I'll bleed blue… and gold."

"Now *that's* what I wanted to hear."

The deal was sealed. I was going to become a doctor. And I would be a Bruin. I would study medicine with the best of the best. I was blown away. And as for the doctor who took me to dinner? I never heard from him again. I never laid eyes on him in the hospital, on campus, *anywhere.* Just like a real angel. His appearance had rolled out an unending ribbon of highway I would travel for my entire life.

On top of everything, I received a full scholarship. Another much needed miracle. I was headed for UCLA.

*My dreams were about to become a reality.*

# Chapter 6

## Becoming a Member of the Tribe

You have to be driven if you want to survive medical school. First of all, there's the sheer amount of material you have to consume day in and day out. Secondly, all the material is purely foundational, each piece laying the stepping-stone for the next. It's painstaking, it's thorough, and it's obsessively detailed. And it never lets up until you finally get your medical degree and then, of course, continues on for perpetuity.

If I had looked at the big picture, all the areas of medicine I was going to be required to study and digest, I would have said it was an impossible task. But rather than focusing on the mountain of material I had to plow through, I compartmentalized my life and my studies into each day, each class, each hour.

I was no stranger to sacrifice, but medical school required more than I'd ever imagined. It was the same kind of sacrifice I made back at COC and UC San Diego, but tenfold. There were no parties or going out drinking or dancing like most young adults in their mid-20s. It was a sacrifice, but I was ready for it.

The way I looked at medical school was that it was just another hurdle in an endless series of hurdles that had brought me to that place. I was prepared to go over, under, or right through any obstacle they put in my way.

I viewed medical school much like a primitive tribal initiation I had read about years before. If a young boy wanted entrance into the tribe, he had to run the gauntlet of tribe members who held clubs of all shapes and sizes. The initiate would take off down the long line of tribesmen as each one took a whack at his ankles, swung at his head, and slugged him in the gut. He must survive the punishment and make it to the end in order to belong. Like that initiate, I knew the process of becoming a doctor was going to hurt, and I also knew it wouldn't be a short line, but a very, very long line of abuse that I'd have to endure. I'd question myself many times along my seven year medical school and training journey, but at the end of the day I'd always come to the same conclusion: Put your head down, one day at a time, and keep working.

In a way, there was no alternative for me. Becoming a doctor provided so many avenues I could pursue that were just not open to me with any other profession. That feeling of having options and freedom resonated with me. The years of being restricted, confined, and limited, both literally and metaphorically in my younger years is something my spirit could never settle with. In fact, I still have one reoccurring nightmare. In the dream I realize I never got accepted to medical school. I never made the cut. Even today, after practicing medicine for thirty years, the dream continues to haunt me.

But more than any of that, the fact was I loved the idea of becoming a doctor. It utterly excited me. It wasn't just a profession or a way to make a living. It was a passion.

* * * * *

In the first year of medical school there was an obscene amount of material to commit to memory in a short amount of time. They say you really only retain about fifteen percent of what you learn. I believe it. We used to call it choke and puke. You'd get it all in and then you'd throw it all up for the tests. Then it would naturally slip away over time. But it's what you did. It's what everyone did to make it through that first year.

The UCLA biomedical library, open every day from eight until midnight, was my main squeeze, along with all my medical student pals. It's a squat 60's cement and brick building located on the south end of campus next to the sprawling brick hospital. The library itself wasn't much, just a bare boned, barely maintained space stuffed with stacks of books, periodicals, and students. Students hunched bleary-eyed over their books, students surrounded by empty paper coffee cups, strings of drool escaping from their loose lips asleep on their books, students furiously wired on caffeine reading their books. It was our wheelhouse for learning. Our sanctuary of study. Our home away from home. Or more accurately now that I think of it, our home.

After pushing through the heavy glass doors, I'd see the same faces in the same places day after day, each of us quietly territorial as we carved out our own nooks and crannies to pour over notes and textbooks. My favorite spot was on the second floor where a series of long battered wood tables spanned across the quiet room. Breathing in that warm reassuring scent of old dusty tomes, I'd nod to the other medical students seated at their usual spots, pull the heavy books from my Army surplus backpack and spread out across the polished table to claim my space for the long day and night to come.

Within weeks I found myself making fast friends with the other medical students. In this way, medical school was far different that my earlier college experience where everyone was fighting for the same seat. Now that we had all been accepted into "the club," competition turned to camaraderie. We helped each other, formed study groups together, lived and died over our tests together, carved up our first cadavers together, and shared cold cups of coffee together. Dinner was always a treat. My friends and I would happily take a much needed hour break and wander into Westwood Village, a buzzing, eclectic community that bordered the four hundred acre campus. Westwood was the prime location for movies and star studded premieres, boasting the famous Fox Village Theater as well as several other trendy boutiques, restaurants, and movie theaters.

We had a favorite Mexican restaurant we'd always seem to wind up at and dessert was a must, usually at the same yogurt shop, a fad that was taking the country by rage at the time. We'd amble back to campus with tall spirals of exotic frozen yogurt topped with nuts and candies, only to suffer from the blood sugar crash not soon after. But we could always rely on our trusty coffee machine to get us through the night. The tinny *plunk* of quarters falling into the bowels of the machine, the soft *clunk* of the cup as it dropped down onto the metallic plate, and the trickling stream of weakly brewed coffee spilling into the thin paper cup will always remind me of my first years of medical school.

The second year was all pathophysiology or more commonly, diseases. If the volume of material that was covered in first year med school seemed unreasonable, the second year was preposterous. There was always a test, always more material to cover. Whenever I felt like I was going to fall asleep from too many hours bent over my books, I'd force myself to run the library stairs, come back, get more of that famously horrible machine coffee, sit down, and start again. Each class, thankfully, had a person who was paid to take notes on the lecture. I'd take the lecture notes and go through them, point for point, matching them up with the material in the books so I was sure I wasn't missing anything.

At the end of my second year, I took part one of the national boards exam. It was a grueling two-day test, six to eight hours a day. Thankfully, I passed. It was time to hit the hospital as a third year student and start doing medical rotations known as clinical years. Finally, after all the years of studying, all those tests and sleepless nights, it was time to *practice* becoming a doctor.

Those library seats my friends and I had so faithfully occupied for the first two years were now given over to the underclassman below us. Sure we might go back to our beloved biomed library to look up a research article, or review a disease process, but the same old gang was gone. The names and the faces had changed, the circle of medical school life continued to spin forward, just as it should. If I did happen to see a fellow classmate it would be in passing as they trotted after the rest of their rotation team. We'd exchange a wave, a quick "How's it going?" and then disappear into a patient's room or around a corner. Unfortunately, we just didn't have the time to maintain the once close friendships forged at the bottom of our academic foxhole.

With the transition from the second to third year came a transformation that wasn't just academic, but was physical as well. Now, as third year students, we were going from classroom bookwork to being in the hospital and interfacing with patients. This was our first opportunity not only to learn how to be a doctor, but *look* the role as well.

Each of us was presented with the quintessential emblem of doctor hood: the black bag. Yes. A real live black bag complete with stethoscope, otoscope, opthamaoscope, and a reflex hammer with a tuning fork that traveled with us. Additionally, all guys wore ties, and men and women alike donned the archetypal white coat with our nametags. I still have my nametag stashed away in a shoebox somewhere in the attic. It reads: "Jeffrey Nordella UCLA Medical School." I couldn't have been more proud.

Before we headed off to our various assignments, we all appeared early to hang out at the student affairs center, everybody feeling a bit awkward yet complementing one another on how professional we looked. We'd all come a long way, and as much as we felt like kids playing dress up, it was a proud moment.

For my first clinical rotation, I received Cedars Sinai Hospital for internal medicine. The rotation, like all the others throughout the rest of my medical training, would be a six to twelve week stint depending on the rotation. The moment I walked into a hospital with my coat and nametag was surreal. I would be working with the same team of doctors, residents, and interns throughout my rotation. I felt as if I had finally become an official member of the Tribe of Medicine.

Nine years after graduating high school I was at last learning the nuts and bolts of caring for patients. I was doing the job of a doctor. As a third year medical student, I would get an admission, and then be responsible to perform a history and physical along with every member of our team. After Cedars it was off to another rotation at another hospital. By year's end, I'd successfully rotated through all of my mandatory rotations, internal medicine, surgery, OB/GYN, pediatrics, psychiatry. After all that came the second part of national boards, basic sciences mixed with some clinical medicine presentations. Another two days, eight hours a day, another pass, and I was moving on to my last year.

By the fourth year of medical school students are asking themselves, "What specialty do I want to spend the rest of my life doing? I could have gone off and specialized as a surgeon or a gastroenterologist, or better yet an obstetrician. This is where the money was, but money wasn't a decision factor. I was going to be fine financially. I'd never have to struggle. I'd never have spoiled milk in the refrigerator or a bed made of foam and old jackets. To me, I thought of a doctor as someone who treated the whole person and knew about everything that ailed a patient.

The decision was easy: primary care. As a primary care physician I would need to know a little bit of everything, including pediatrics, internal medicine, obstetrics and gynecology, psychology, and I could assist in surgeries. That was exciting to me because I knew I'd always be learning. I also had a tremendous amount of energy. Considering that, ER was alluring. If I focused on ER and Family Medicine I could get the best of both worlds. My decision had been made. I decided to apply in Family

Medicine, see where that went, and then I'd specialize in ER as a secondary choice.

At this point in medical school I had the opportunity, like all my fellow students, to leave the area and check out different hospitals across the country. I could get on a plane and head to wherever I thought I'd like to live and potentially practice medicine for a series of four to six week stints. It gave both the students and the hospitals an opportunity to check each other out for future internships.

Most med students have an idea of where they might like to practice, and I was no exception. First of all, I knew I wanted to be on the West Coast. Eager as always, I scheduled all my rotations back to back with no breaks in between and I finished all my elective rotations six months before I was to receive my official MD diploma.

A few days after I finished my rotations, student affairs called me back into one of the offices.

"Hey, Jeff," one of the staffers said, "There's a position over at Cedars. Would you like to go over and apply?"

"What's it for?"

"A student fellowship in the emergency room. There's a stipend that goes with it. You want an application?"

"Absolutely."

It turned out there were actually quite a few kids applying throughout the country for this spot. I knew the competition would be stiff, but I really wanted the position. I decided to give it a shot. I ended up interviewing with the medical director, a huge man, 6' 8", three hundred-plus, with an easy smile that loved baseball almost as much as I did. We talked about our favorite teams and players, which I guess gave me an edge over the other students. In a couple of days I got a call.

"How would you like to start in January?"

"The sooner the better!"

I was psyched. Being in the mix at a popping ER was an adrenaline junkie's dream come true. I loved the fast paced drama of the emergency room and the docs were all great. Not only did they joke around and have fun as a team, but they also didn't waste a second before tossing me into ER's meat grinder.

"Go work up the abdominal pain in bed three and present the case to me."

"There's a laceration waiting in bed ten!"

"Can you work up the eye infection in the ENT room, Jeff!" the attending would call out as the ER buzzed with standing room only crowds.

I was just this little fourth year medical student, but I was part of the team. I'd do my work up, do my notes, work all of these shifts, and still I got my stipend. I was stoked.

I couldn't believe just a couple of weeks ago I was itching to get my feet wet, and there I was thrown into the deep end. All of the ER docs were incredibly kind and very knowledgeable and they loved to teach. So I took advantage of it. I worked dayshift as well as night shifts. I saw anything from sick children to observing full cardiac arrest.

I was becoming a doctor. And not a half-bad one at that.

It was time for match day. And when I say match, I'm not talking about dating...

\* \* \* \* \*

Right before graduation, all medical students go through the same medical mating ritual: Match Day. It's like a huge computer dating game, setting up the doctor with the hospital for a grueling three-year relationship at minimum. It works like this: You fill out a Scantron sheet prioritizing your hospital and specialty, but you're not the only one choosing—the hospitals also list their favorite candidates as well. Those two factors get sucked into the computer, the computer does its computer magic, matching doctors and hospitals, and out pops where you'll be spending the next three years of your life. You might get your third choice because your number one choice may not want you. You might not get a match at all. If that happened, the dean would have to go in and personally call the medical programs to see if they could get you placed.

Match Day comes with a lot of stress. We were all ushered into a drab room with chairs, several boards, and nothing else. On the board, under the letter of our last name, there were numerous envelopes, one for each member of our class.

The Medical School dean gave a short speech, warning us that some of us didn't have a match.

"If you don't," he said, "see me in my office. Okay, everyone. Have at it!"

We all crowded around the boards and grabbed our envelope. I was as excited, as I was nervous as I ripped into the envelope.

"Yes," I said, breathing a sigh of relief. "UCLA." *My first choice.*

I'd be an intern at my beloved Alma Mater. I'd be a Bruin for life.

# Chapter 7

## Internship and Residency: A Handbook on Survival and Love

I can sum up internship in two words—physical survival.

It's not nearly as grueling now because they've implemented laws against working interns too many hours in a row, but back then, getting worked to death was a rite of passage, and intellect wasn't the secret to surviving as an intern. It was more like, how am I going to stay up for thirty-six straight hours every third night?

I'd come in on Monday morning at six o'clock and then wouldn't go home until Tuesday evening at six o'clock. That meant I'd be in the same clothes I came in with, many times not having laid my head down for thirty-six straight hours. My skin was oily, my hair felt matted and dirty, my body smelled, and a vague ever-present sense of nausea dogged me from lack of sleep. When I'd finish my shift, I'd stumble home, fall into bed, and set my alarm for five o'clock so I could get back to the hospital by six and start work again. The one day off a month I had was reserved for laundry and running errands. When people drove home from their shifts, it wasn't unusual to find them slumped over their steering wheel at a red light, fast asleep. Although that never happened to me, there were many times when I'd have to get out of the car and do a quick Chinese fire drill before I got back inside to head home, praying I wouldn't be overcome with exhaustion before I pulled into my apartment's garage.

I was *so* tired.

*All* the time.

I slept on gurneys that were splattered with blood and I couldn't care less. I fell asleep leaning against the wall, at the nurse's station desk, once even in the bathroom. And as soon as I did that and got into a twenty-minute sleep, then,- *beep!* My pager would go off.

I'd be up and running again.

I quickly learned that an intern was not the most prestigious title to hold within the medical community. I remember an attending doctor I did a rotation with. Every time he'd find me, he'd clap me on the back with a smile.

"You know what's lower than dog shit on the sole of your shoe?"

"What?" I mumbled, already knowing the answer.

"An intern!" he crowed and sailed off, laughing, freshly showered, and with a good eight hours of sleep under his belt.

It was true. I was a lowly intern.

It was misery for everyone. The doctors were annoyed by us because they were often times too busy to teach us what to do. The nurses also hated us because we didn't know what we were doing, but were nevertheless obliged to follow orders. In fact, the nurses knew more than any intern did, and many of them didn't let us forget it. Not like I would've forgotten to begin with.

I was sweaty. I was hot. I was miserable. Plus, I had to be there for what seemed like *forever.* Nobody liked me. I was tired. Life sucked. I'd been up a day and a half.

And did I mention that I was *TIRED?*

As an intern I did the same basic rotations I had as a medical student, rotating through general surgery, internal medicine, psychiatry, coronary care unit, pediatrics, and OB/GYN, but now with an increased level of responsibility. I had been thoroughly sleep deprived by the time I was doing my OB/GYN rotation. It was Christmas time, but not like any Christmas I had ever known before. This year I was catching babies. And since I was catching babies that meant that I wasn't having any Christmas at all. Or New Year's. Both of the holidays were something I'd really looked forward to in the past, but this year the days would be just like any other. I did spot a little Christmas tree sitting on a nurse's station, but that was it.

Honestly, whether it was because I missed seeing my family for the holidays, or just that all those sleepless hours had started to pile up on me, it was a depressing time of my life. But, ironically, one of the most depressing times of my life led to the best thing that had ever happened to me.

It was December 27, 1983. The first day I saw my future wife, the one true love of my life.

I was still on my OB/GYN rotation when one of the unborn babies started to crash. The resident prepared for an emergency C-section, and NICU, the neonatal intensive care unit, was called in to attend the birth. I was my usual grimy, smelly bleary-eyed self as I got into my surgical greens preparing to observe the C-section. Stepping out into the hall, I spotted her walking through the large door connecting NICU to labor and delivery. I recognized the pediatric resident at her side, but it was the first time I laid eyes on Carole. Her eyes flicked over toward mine. It was the kind of awkward moment when two people both are checking the other out, but neither wants the other one to know. She smiled and looked away as she breezed past and disappeared into the dressing room.

I watched on the periphery as the resident performed the C-section, Carole and the other pediatricians all the model of professionalism, caring for the baby. My glance slipped over to Carole maybe a little more than was clinically necessary. With her high cheekbones, along with her brown hair and eyes, she was a combo of pretty and cute.

My reaction to her was purely physical, a function of biology—stimulus in through the eyes, zapped to the limbic system, and she was a green light. What can I say? I was a doctor in training; I knew how these things worked. Before I could even introduce myself, the C-section was over, the baby secured in the isolette, and Carole hurried out of the room, down the hall, to be lost behind the locked door separating our two domains. But one measly locked door wasn't about to stop me.

That day, I cornered a friend of mine who was a pediatric intern.

"What's the 411 on the brunette in the Neo Natal unit?"

"What brunette?"

"The cute one."

"Oh right. Yeah, she is cute, isn't she?"

"So who is she?"

"I've seen her, but I really don't know much about her."

"Okay, thanks anyway," I said, and started down the hall.

So it looked like if I wanted to pursue her, I'd have to do my own recon.

I started to wander into NICU in between deliveries. Mind you, I had no business being there. It wasn't part of my training, and Carole knew it. I'd just stroll in and casually look around like I was interested in everything except her. "How's that baby doing that we delivered?" I'd lamely try in an effort to strike up a conversation.

"Pretty good," she'd say smiling, and then go back to her work. I guess she enjoyed playing me.

"Good, good," I'd say, then walk out and accuse myself of being a bonehead.

This went on for a couple of weeks. I tried to come across as the confident, take-charge doctor, but the reality was I was nervous. How did I know if I would make the cut?

Finally I got busted one day when I found out she was in the break room and I "just happened" to swing inside for a cup of coffee.

"Funny running into you again," she smiled. It was a smile that said, *You're fun to torture.* I liked that about her. She was sassy.

"Yeah, funny."

"So why *are* you over in NICU all the time?"

"Ahh...." I mumbled. What could I say? I could make up some stupid excuse or I could really surprise her and tell the truth. "I come over to see you."

"Oh..." She smiled that smile again. She really *did* like to torture me. "Well, have a seat."

I was in.

One thing I'm good at is listening. And that's exactly what I did during that first conversation. Carole talked about almost everything in her life during our first talk. I found out about her family, that she spoke French fluently, and how she wanted to hike across Europe. I discovered where she went to nursing school. Her ambitions of becoming a nursing supervisor at UCLA. I found out she'd just come out of a relationship. A messy one. I'd learn later that she was married for a short time to someone she'd met in the church she attended. But at the time, all she said was she was just coming out of a relationship and that it was over. The fallout left her questioning her faith. On this matter we could relate. I didn't have much of a spiritual compass. I was familiar with questioning a God who so many others accepted on blind faith. My father had clung to the Catholic Church more and more the sicker he'd become. He had tried to convert me, but I'd never saw the logic or appeal in religion. I was more about the facts.

Spirituality aside, the more Carole talked, the more interested I became. That first conversation with her was a real indicator to me. Even though I wasn't ready to dive headfirst into a relationship, Carole was different from all the other nurses, doctors, and interns I'd met so far. She could go deep. It was something I craved.

"Oh, my gosh," she said once she glanced up at the break room clock. "I've been talking like crazy. Tell me about you." At that exact moment, my beeper went off.

"Saved by the bell," I teased with a quick smile. I wasn't above torturing either.

I got up and hurried away hoping I had made an impression upon her, because she'd certainly made an impression on me. Something told me this wouldn't be the last conversation we'd have.

The first months our relationship consisted almost exclusively of late night phone calls. That is if I could get to a phone. Or there was always the ever-romantic hospital cafeteria.

"Hey, you want to go down and have a cup of coffee?"

"Have you had lunch?" I'd ask one or the other in my typically romantic fashion. Okay, I guess I wasn't much of a sweet talker.

After a few months I knew I really liked this girl. I had just gotten my first credit card and decided the first purchase I would make would be flowers for Carole. I had the florist write on the card *"From a secret admirer."* At that point, I wasn't really sure if she was dating anyone else. And if she was dating, how serious was it. I'll admit, besides doing my best to make some kind of romantic gesture, I was sort of curious to see if I was her number one admirer after all.

I decided to have the bouquet delivered to NICU. One of the attending doctors there had the reputation for being the biggest busybody on the ward, the queen bee of the hive. If something was buzzing, she wanted to be in the center of it. At this time I was doing a rotation up on the sixth floor in the coronary care unit, a world away from the NICU. Suddenly, my beeper went off from her unit. I had a hunch this was about the flowers.

I got on the phone and said, "Doctor Nordella."

"Thanks for the flowers," Carole said, sounding confident.

"I'm sorry? Flowers?"

Silence. Then...

"Didn't you send me flowers?"

"No, was I supposed to?" I could hear the gears inside her head grinding away. I leaned into her hesitation. "Now I feel bad."

"No, don't feel bad," she said, momentarily off her game.

"So, who sent them to you?"

"Uh... I'm not sure..."

"I guess I have some competition?"

"Uh... this is really awkward," she said. I started to feel like I was taking it a step too far.

"Yeah. Maybe we should meet for coffee and talk," I told her, trying to sound equal parts hurt and miffed.

"Jeff, it's fine. I'm sorry I called."

"No, I wanted to see you anyway. Can you get away?"

When we settled down with our usual bad coffee and stale muffins, I finally came clean.

"So did you like them?"

"What?" she asked, obviously not relishing the idea of bringing up the subject of secret admirers again.

"The flowers I sent?"

She looked at me for one shocked moment before rearing back and landing a solid slug into my shoulder.

"Hey, don't try to hurt me, I sent you flowers, remember?"

"You still deserve it."

"Sorry. So what happened up there? I thought I could hear the buzzing from the sixth floor."

"Oh my god, the staff attending physician was following me everywhere wanting to know where the flowers came from and who had sent them."

"What did you tell her?"

"Don't worry. Your secret is safe with me." Then she leaned in and gave me a kiss before she smiled. "Thanks, Jeff. I love them."

It was the best forty bucks I'd ever spent.

I think one of the reasons Carole was attracted to me was because she'd been through some really tough times with her marriage. It left her feeling pretty insecure. I had my insecurities, too. We'd both walked through our own separate fires and not only had they left us with some scars, but also with some strengths along with a real understanding about what we wanted and didn't want in life and in a relationship. Besides that, Carole was as wise as she was smart. She knew I had experienced a chaotic childhood, and because of that my *modus operandi* was to do everything within my power to create security for the people I loved. The one thing Carole didn't want in a relationship was insecurity and drama. She'd had enough of that already. Now she wanted a rock. And I wanted to be her rock. We had all the potential for the kind of match that could go the distance.

As exhausting and grueling as my internship was, at least I had Carole to lighten the load. Before I realized it, I'd served my sentence. I was officially a licensed doctor. If I wanted to, I could forego the rest of residency and go out to hang my shingle as Dr. Jeffrey Nordella. But, of course, I wasn't about to give up the training and experience I could get with two more years of residency. Not only did I have my license to practice medicine, but I also got something almost as good, a one-week vacation.

"One whole week," Carole said. "What are you going to do?"

"I don't know. What are you doing?"

"Working. But I'll get it off. Come to the river. It'll be fun."

Carole's parents had a little place in Blythe, a small desert town that lies along the lower Colorado River Valley.

"We could waterski, hang out, and swim. And you could even play golf if you want to."

She'd said the magic words. Golf. I loved the game. Everything about it. Still do.

"You're on."

A week on the river, Carole, golf and no more internship? I felt like a pig in mud.

Carole had a friend, a receptionist at the NICU, and we set her up with one of my best childhood buddies. They came along with an orthopedic surgeon friend of mine who was an expert water skier and golf nut like both of us, and he also just happened to have a little plane. The girls headed down together, and us guys threw our golf bags into the back of the prop plane and headed down like the three amigos, completely white, out of shape, wearing cowboy hats and sandals, ready to live in shorts and go crazy for a week. A scene right out of the show M*A*S*H.

We landed at the Blythe airport and met up with the girls. But I couldn't really relax, because not only were we going to her parents' house, her parents were also going to be there. An entire week with my girlfriend's parents and I'd never even met them before.

We pulled up in front of their little wooden shack on the water.

I was nervous. Who wouldn't be? This could work out all right or it could be a very, very long week. We knocked on the door and it swung open. There stood Carole's parents, blinking at three guys they've never met, all looking like stand-ins for dumb, dumber, and dumbest. Before they could as much as say hello, my orthopedic pal, being the lovable, crazy whack job that he was, threw open his arms and screamed, "Mom! Dad! How are you!!" He grabbed Carole's mom, lifted her in the air and plunked her down to face him. She took a beat, then smiled.

"Wait, you don't look anything like my daughter described."

The ice was broken and the dye cast. It was going to be one of the best vacations ever.

I slept on the carpet with the spiders. The surgeon crashed on the lumpy couch. My other friend made a bed outside on the broken lounge chair. Let me tell you, it was just everything we expected it to be.

It was crazy.

We were out of jail and we acted accordingly.

The guys got up at 4:30 because we were all used to only sleeping for two hours at a time and that was a luxury. As soon as our feet hit the floor we were heading for the golf course. We'd jam over to the little rundown 24-hour grocery store in the dark and stack up on six packs of Gatorade, Coke, and jugs of water and toss all of it onto the back of the golf cart before we'd hit the course. We knew the thermometer would be edging toward 118 degrees by ten o'clock, and I didn't want to die from dehydration on my first vacation.

The three of us would tee up our first ball just when there was just enough light so we could see our drives fly down the fairway. It was beautiful to see the sun peeking out from behind the low ridge of purple mountains edging the course. We were living again. We'd play eighteen holes, and then we'd come around and play eighteen more. We'd return to the house crowing about our best drives and almost-holes-in-ones before we'd dive into a breakfast of waffles, pancakes, eggs, bacon, and sausage. Carole's mom was a wonder.

By noon it was time to hit the water. We'd work the river up and down, up and down all day, water skiing, drinking, laying around in the sun. As the sunset, we'd swing back to the shack were Carole's dad would throw some thick steaks on the grill and then we'd eat like pigs again. We did that for a week. And through it all Carole was there. We laughed, we skied, we joked, and we bonded. I'd known her for less than a year, but something told me this girl was a real keeper.

# Chapter 8

## The Work Of Doctoring: Junior and Senior Residency

By the time I was ready to enter my second year of residency, Carole and I had cemented an exclusive relationship and now I had to firm up how I wanted to spend my career as a doctor. It was now time to report to the emergency room for further training. Everything I had learned in Family Medicine laid an invaluable medical foundation, but my experience at Cedars' ER room had ruined me to any other type of medicine. I had such a blast mixing it up with the docs, zipping from one curtained room to the next, that once I stepped back into my Family Medicine internship it seemed like I was doing doctoring in slow motion. Throughout my internship it didn't matter if I was dealing with heart attacks in the ICU, delivering babies in OB/GYN, or taking care of a child with meningitis in pediatrics, they all had a sense of routine and order that I found mundane after experiencing the heart-thumping pace of the emergency room. ER was like supersizing those ailments and throwing them into a blender. Not only did the shifts fly past because of the continual stream of patients, but the illnesses themselves where always much more acute. Now I had to put together the pieces of the puzzle to discover the right diagnosis with the clock ticking.

Part of my ER training was rotating though other hospitals. My first was Wadsworth Hospital, a Veteran's facility a couple of miles from the UCLA campus. Going from being an intern to a resident was a huge leap. Remember, I'd only just finished my internship. I'm not far from being just a stupid intern who mostly just watched the real doctors do their thing. Now as a resident, I'm supposed to be the all-knowing doctor. It's sort of a joke, but a not-really-very-funny one.

Regardless, I pushed back my shoulders and walked inside the dilapidated grey building and wound my way into the coronary care unit or the CCU. For most people, CCUs are scary places and for me it was no exception. The CCU is the floor of the hospital where very, very sick people go. Basically it's where any and all serious heart problems were admitted. I knew the CCU was a serious place to be, but there was something else I didn't expect. The patients place the physicians on pedestals, which made me more uncomfortable. It was understandable. They were sick, and they needed to believe in someone who had almost God-like abilities, but still didn't make me feel any less squeamish thinking they'd look at me in that light.

I walked into the CCU at 6 A.M. Monday morning without even a toothbrush or a change of clothes. I found the cardiac fellow, the boss, marched up and extended my hand.

"Good morning, I'm Dr. Nordella. I'm your visiting resident."

"Oh, great. Here's your intern. Mitch Chung. And by the way, you're on call tonight."

"Oh, great."

I looked over the fellow's shoulder to see Mitch, fresh out of medical school, small, shy, bespeckled, and looking as bewildered as I felt. He offered me a nervous grin and a half-raised hand.

"Hi…" was all he could manage.

"So good," the fellow said, obviously anxious to get out of there. "Here's a list of your patients, and here's my number if you really get in over your head." He handed me a beeper attached with a little scrap of paper containing his phone number. "Good luck, guys," he added and dashed off, leaving Mitch and me to spend the rest of the day hustling from bed to bed doing our rounds on existing patients. On top of that, we continued to take patient after new patient from the ER.

But it wasn't until 5 P.M. when the two other resident teams left that it got really interesting. First one, then the other resident team approached, giving us a run down on their patients and then handing us their beepers.

"Don't sweat it Nordella, you can handle it," the last resident said to me, before he escaped out the door.

I looked down at the three beepers lying in my hand. Each of them equaled about eight to twelve patients.

And Mitch. And me.

How did that happen?

I'm in charge?

Holy shit.

And I'm going to have to do this for a month and a half.

"Okay, Mitch. Here we go."

Turns out Mitch and I were a match made in heaven. We shared a telepathic communication that said *Let's get this done.* It was a seat-of-your-pants, can-do attitude that's born out of being left to your own devices and loving what you do for a living.

We just went at it.

First of all, Mitch was a super nice guy. Like me, he was willing to wing it and he knew a thing or two about busting his ass. Neither of us were exactly prepared I had a stethoscope and so did he, but that was it.

That first night I wasn't completely through meeting all the patients when- *beep!* I looked down at my pager and saw 001, which was the ER. I picked up the phone in the nurse's station, employing my best form of delusional thinking, trying to convince myself I wasn't about to buy another patient.

"We have an admission for you, Dr. Nordella. Chest pain."

"Okay, I'll be down."

I got eleven admissions from the ER on my first night—three times more than the norm.

The difficult part wasn't just the sheer amount of patients, it was also the mountain of paperwork. Back then there were no computers to lighten the load. All the histories, physicals, and patient orders were handwritten. But it was what it was. Mitch and I were doing our best not to run from room to room we were so slammed.

By 4:30 A.M. we got the last critical patient in. We had to shock him and then stabilize him. I'd had it. I was officially in over my head. Time to finally take the fellow up on his offer. I get to the phone and dial is number. *Ring, ring, ring...* then...

"I'm sorry the number you have dialed has been disconnected."

*What? Did I dial it in wrong?* I look down at the little scrap of paper, and dialed again...

"I'm sorry, the number..."

I didn't wait to hear the rest before slamming down the phone and turning to a grey-faced Mitch.

"We're on our own, dude."

We were completely on our own. I just tried to hold on to make it in until the sun came up because I knew the other two teams would be coming in. I realized, like with pretty much everything else in my life up until then, and even beyond, I'd be the one steering the ship whether I had the navigation skills or not.

And guess what?

I had the most awesome six weeks of my life. I freaking loved it. Once I got comfortable, Mitch and I had a blast. We ran codes, we assessed all manner of critical cardiac care, congestive heart failure, pulmonary edema, myocardial infarction, and pericarditis. Oh, and did I mention doing invasive procedures?

One of my favorite and most involved was to float a Swan Ganz catheter, a procedure that ultimately allowed us to read waveforms within the heart, which was necessary to prescribe the appropriate treatment. It was usually reserved for only the most experienced cardiac fellows. I'd start with a central line, driving a large needle that went into the patient's neck under their clavicle, then thread the needle into the large bore subclavian vein, nick it just right, and then feed a catheter in, snaking it all the way into the right atrium, then the right ventricle, then the pulmonary artery where a tiny sensor picked up waveforms which we'd see on the monitor. I relished the experience.

Every night, Mitch and I would gather around the big white boards getting our patients' lay of the land.

"Hey, Mitch?" I'd say as I settled into my chair. "What do you feel like?"

"I could go for Mexican."

"We had that last call night. What about Chinese?"

We had three favorites: Mexican, Chinese and Indian—all of which delivered. We'd never rotate the same cuisine two call nights in a row, but never deviating from our favorite places. There we'd be, sitting in front of that patient white board with our cartons of chow mein and General Tso's chicken and plot our war plan for the night. Then we'd hit the floor working through the night and taking care of business, until we went home 24 hours later, exhausted but satisfied.

I immediately noticed something different about the patients and the hospital. Mind you, at UCLA and the other hospitals I had rotated through, it was all about research, high level academics, and state of the art procedures and equipment. As for the patients, at UCLA, they were often wealthy, sometimes even famous celebrities, and if they weren't wealthy, at least they were middle or upper middle class. Don't get me wrong, UCLA certainly had their share of the poor, who also needed health care.

But here at the VA, these men and women were different. Many of these vets were poor and often homeless. Some of them would get their VA benefits and chart their course across the country using the VA hospitals as their homes just so they'd have a place to sleep at night. Just as a way to keep off the streets. It was a horrible way to live. Many of them were very sick and had no family or friends to support them. But almost across the board, these patients were thankful for the care they received and were very trusting of us young doctors. And I was equally thankful for their trust in allowing me to take care of them.

"You're *my* doctor, aren't you?" they'd say with pride as I walked into the room.

When it came time for me to perform a procedure, I'd always take my time, explaining all the risks the procedure itself, what they could expect, and why the procedure was necessary. This was often very invasive, frightening stuff. But these patients would just nod and say, "Whatever you think. You're the doc." I was in my mid-twenties, caring for men who had served in Vietnam and even World War II, and they gave me their respect. In turn, I gave it back. I listened to them, not only about their health but also about their service, their long and often fascinating lives. In some ways it was heartwarming, in others sad. It was an honor to give that to them. It also inspired me. These patients, in my mind, deserved the best medical care possible, and I'd be damned if Mitch and I weren't going to give it to them.

When Mitch and I finished our six-week rotation, I thanked him like a brother in arms with a hearty handshake.

"Hey, man. Really appreciate all your hard work. It was great working with you."

"Thank you, Jeff. Good working with you, too."

"Good luck, man. You're awesome."

I never saw him again.

I handed my beeper off to the newbie, my classmate, another wide-eyed junior resident, and a hulking young doc with a halo of wild black hair.

"Any advice?" he asked, sounding rattled as I handed him my beeper, just as the fellow had done before me.

"At first you're gonna hate it, but then you're gonna love it."

When I saw him six weeks later back at UCLA he had the same shine in his eye I had when I'd left. It was an experience both of us would take to the grave.

* * * * *

All junior residents are required to take radio calls in the hospital emergency room from the paramedics in the field. My moment arrived as my first call came in. I tried to convince myself that it would be a breeze, but I was jittery with nerves. I hoped for an easy turn, maybe a senior citizen with a relatively minor complaint, or a minor car accident with minimal damage. But I didn't get off that easy.

The call came in and it was from a paramedic group not more than a mile away. In fact, the call was coming from UCLA's upper campus. When the paramedic's voice came in over the radio, he was almost screaming. Not a good sign for a veteran emergency caregiver.

"UCLA, this is unit 37! UCLA THIS IS UNIT 37!"

This was going to be bad. I heard the anxiety in his voice. Despite telling myself to remain calm and professional, I internalized his anxiety and multiplied that by a factor of ten. "This is UCLA. Go ahead unit 37."

"37 is at the scene of a 16-year old female on the upper campus of UCLA in full cardiopulmonary arrest! We are doing ventilations and compressions at this time."

*Oh shit. What do you mean you've got a 16 year old who's not breathing and has no pulse?*

"Orders!" he repeated, his desperation growing. As a seasoned paramedic he would have had far more experience than I did and he was *panicking.* But he was looking for my guidance because I'm the doctor at his base station.

I had to focus. Clear my mind. Focus on the patient not the craziness.

"What cardiac rhythm is the patient in?"

"Ventricular fibrillation."

"Has the patient been defibrillated?"

"Affirmative!"

"Repeat defibulation at 360 watts per second. If possible establish an IV and transport."

"Roger that. ETA in 7 minutes!"

The adrenaline had hit my system full force. When I pressed the button to announce the patient's arrival, my whole body began to tremble. "Full arrest coming in in 7 minutes!"

When the paramedics slammed through the swinging ER doors, continuing to ventilate the young cheerleader as they ran inside, a team of doctors and nurses were waiting. She was still in full cardiopulmonary arrest. I couldn't help thinking just how wrong it seemed, seeing this young, beautiful girl lying inert, while I intubated her and the rest of the team moved around me, a frenzied melee of confusion, an entire team of professionals caught up in the unlikely drama of a sixteen year old on the brink of death. All of us could relate to this young girl in some way. We remembered our own youth and when we believed we were invincible. I am sure others thought about their own teenager that they had at home. Either way, this wasn't a situation of a dying elderly patient who had lived a long and full life. This just shouldn't be happening. We worked on her for forty-five minutes. In the end, it was to no avail. The attending called the code. Time of death: 3:47 P.M. *How did this happen? How was it possible?*

It turns out she was a high school cheerleader. She and her girlfriends were training out on the intramural field where Poly Pavilion now stands. Seven girls had formed a human pyramid with this girl on the bottom. When the formation collapsed, at first the girls recovered, laughing and ragging on each other for messing up. It wasn't until they noticed their friend was lying motionless on the grass that they called 911. Most likely she probably had some cardiac anomaly she never knew about, until the stress of the others on her back pushed her heart into a malignant arrhythmia. But whatever happened, I never found out.

Her parents were quietly ushered to a private room. The attending took a moment to gather himself before padding inside and closing the door behind him. There he broke the news that their daughter, a vibrant, seemingly happy, healthy young girl, was now dead. Their cries broke through the closed doors and suddenly, the door burst open. I had to take a quick step back as the devastated parents rushed past me to collapse over the body of their little girl.

I'd seen death before. I would see it thousands of times again. Yes, it became routine, but never easy. This was not something from a soap opera or a TV series. This was real life, or rather *death*. The reality is, if you're going to be a doctor it's impossible to save every patient. If you buy into the lifestyle of a doctor, you also have to understand you are buying a front row seat with death. No matter how talented, no matter how skilled, no matter how compassionate the doctors and nurses are, death is always present. Death is always waiting.

I was learning to become a doctor and I loved it, but it was changing me. Yes, I had more control, something I'd yearned for since I was a kid. But I also knew just how capricious life could be. I wished I could change that. At least for the people I loved most.

* * * * *

As the senior resident working in the emergency room you get to receive the golden beeper. Actually it never beeped, it screamed at you with one loud constant tone. It was a rite of passage you earned, the honor of being the flight physician on a trauma helicopter. Some of the residents were not thrilled, but I absolutely loved it! Not only did we receive the beeper but a card key to the elevator system throughout the hospital so that no matter where we were we could just inserted it and it would automatically take us to the third floor roof. That's where she sat, an Italian made Augusta twin-engine helicopter, UCLA MedSTAR. Custom-made and equipped with all the state of the art medical equipment.

It was about 1 A.M. in the emergency room and patient flow was average. I was discussing a case with the junior resident when the helicopter beeper suddenly let out with that obnoxious tone. Sprinting to the elevator, I inserted the card key and bingo! In moments, I was climbing aboard. After a quick scanning of the panel and instrument gauges and a few flips of some toggle switches, the pilot fired up the engines. First the one and then the next, it was a very distinctive sound. The nurse was already present with her headset on.

"Where are we heading and what do we have?"

The nurse responded.

"To a small downtown ER all I know is it is a gunshot wound to the abdomen." The blades were now at full RPM and the pilot interrupted and asked,

"Already back there?"

He got clearance from the Santa Monica flight tower.

"UCLA MedSTAR to Santa Monica tower."

"Go ahead, MedSTAR."

"UCLA MedSTAR requesting approval to lift off UCLA to transition LA."

"Santa Monica tower, UCLA MedSTAR, clear for transition across LA."

He pulled up on the collective, we ascended straight up about thirty feet, the helicopter rotated 90° left and transitioned forward, dipping slightly as we crossed the entrance to UCLA hospital. The city lights created an almost mesmerizing effect of beauty and calm as we transitioned across LA. But soon this would be lost like a snap of the fingers from a hypnotist removing someone from a trance. A quick twenty minutes and we were now hovering over the small ER parking lot. The pilot ordered,

"Okay both of you beware of the power lines."

At that command we both opened our side doors and gently hung our heads out looking for wires.

We reporting, "All clear."

We then completed our decent into the parking lot. Once we were safely down we grabbed our equipment bags and headed for the back of the emergency room. There, we were meet by the ER physician and he quickly gave us a run-down.

"The patient is a Spanish-speaking male in his mid-twenties that was working a small ice cream cart and was ordered at gunpoint to turn over his money and when he did not, he was shot twice at close range in the abdomen. The patient was brought in by paramedics in a MAST suit." This is a pneumatic suit that is inflated to very high pressures around the legs and abdomen so blood will be shunted to the vital organs as a priority.

"His blood pressure is 90/60 and he is tachycardic. The patient is on a Venti mask with high flow O2. He has one peripheral IV in his arm running in lactated ringer's solution. His airway is patent and he is ventilating well but clearly needs more fluids." I decided to quickly put a large bore IV line into his upper chest so we could pump more fluids into him. He needed the operating room like yesterday. Bing, Bang, done, IV hung, MAST suit inflated. It was time to scoop and run or rather, fly.

While we packed and loaded the patient into the helicopter, the pilot fired it up and got ready to lift off quickly questioning again, "Good to go?" Up we rapidly ascended again hanging out scanning for power lines, to approximately fifty feet above the telephone poles. Suddenly the alarms in the helicopter started screaming deafeningly loud.

"What the hell!" the pilot shouted.

The pilot seemed confused and clearly concerned and, of course, the first thing that went through my mind is that we're going to go down. The pilot managed to quickly set the helicopter back down gently in the parking lot.

Reassessing the patient, his blood pressure was now lower. We pushed fluids as fast as possible but what the patient needed most were blood and/or blood products. Or more importantly, an operating room to stop the bleeding. After a quick assessment attempting to trouble-shoot the problem, the pilot lifted off again. And again, at about the same height as before, the obnoxious alarms sounded off.

By this point we were all concerned and mentally entertaining the thought that we might not make it back to the main hospital. A decision had to be made in mid- hoover. If we landed and transported by ground ambulance across town, that would certainly be a death sentence for the patient. The pilot could not find anything perilous to our flight and said, "Fuck it, let's go!"

We began our forward transition and were en route back to home. About halfway there the alarms spontaneously stopped.

Again, the pilot's yelled, "What the hell!"

We made contact with UCLA and I requested that they take the patient directly to the operating room. The trauma surgical team agreed to rush him off from the helipad. The MAST suit was deflated and the patient shortly thereafter arrested. Just too much damage and too much blood loss; the patient sadly died.

It was now time, I was ready to take on a little moonlighting. I reported to my first shift at a large community hospital emergency room outside Los Angeles. I arrived at 9 P.M. ready to go into my surgical greens, carrying my white lab coat and briefcase. Not really knowing what to expect, I strolled in through the emergency room entrance and into the waiting room.

It was a friggin' zoo.

Every chair was taken with patients and loved ones. Some leaned against the wall, nursing bandaged hands, looking pale and sick. Others milled around frustrated and bored from the long wait times. They all silently turned to me, as though help had arrived!

I quietly headed to the hardened receptionist and said.

"Dr. Nordella. I'm working the evening shift."

She offered me nothing more than a cursory nod and buzzed me inside.

The E.R. was *packed*. Every bed was taken. Gurneys with moaning patients lined the halls. Paramedic units were parked just outside the door waiting for beds to open up so they could unload their patients. The dayshift ER physician, grey with exhaustion, signed out a handful of patients and headed out the door. I looked around.

No other doctors except me for the next twelve hours.

"You might need this," the supervising nurse suggested by way of introduction, handing me a stale cup of coffee.

*Okay, I think I can handle this*, I thought as she walked me through a quick in-service on the department. Suddenly, we both stepped aside to make way for the paramedics who rushed in with a woman screaming, screaming the unmistakable scream of impending delivery. They whisked past us and headed for Labor and Delivery. One thing was sure—I wasn't going to be bored. I gulped my coffee, shrugged on my lab coat and got to work, quickly digesting the patient charts when I heard the tinny blare over the hospital speaker system:

"Code pink! Code pink!"

I continued to read, but could feel the supervising nurse's stare burning two holes through the back of my head. I turned to face her with a questioning look.

"Well..." she flatly stated.

"What?"

"Aren't you going?"

"Going where?"

"Didn't they tell you?"

"Tell me what?"

"You have to cover labor and delivery, too."

"There's no OB?"

"No. That's why they're calling for a code pink. It's upstairs. Follow the signs," she said, waving me in the general direction before turning her back.

I jogged toward the stairs, reading the signs as instructed. *So now I have to go deliver babies on top of handling a full ER? Crap. I haven't delivered a baby since I was an intern. Where's the delivery room, anyway?* But her primal scream was all the direction I needed. This mother was about to deliver. There was no wasting time.

After scrubbing up, I flew through the door into the delivery room where I found three nurses attending to the screaming woman. Obviously, this mother-to-be hadn't had any anesthesia. There was no anesthesiologist. Nothing to help this poor woman with the pain.

One nurse gave me a towel to dry my hands and avoid any contamination while another quickly helped me into my gown as I was filled in on the woman's history: 30-year-old woman, thirty-seven weeks, no prenatal complications. *Just stay calm, I told myself. You've got this. Control the head. Make sure she doesn't get any tears that need to be repaired. When the rest of the body follows, clamp and cut the cord, and deliver the placenta. I'll be out of here in about 30 minutes.*

I slipped on my first glove and I turned to see the amniotic sac bulging out from between the mother's legs. I fit my hand into the last glove and took a step toward the mother when the sac spontaneously ruptured. I looked, then froze…

Two small feet poked out between the mother's legs. A dual footling breech.

A heavy curtain of disbelief cloaked the room. We all stood frozen in panic for one sickening second, then…

Chaos.

Two of the nurses snapped into action and started rushing around, shouting out instructions and observations. I instantly felt a cold sweat envelop my entire body as my mind started to whirl like an overheated computer, scanning for every scrap of knowledge that could get this young mother and her child out of this situation alive.

I looked to my nurses and said, "Okay. Here we go."

One nurse moved to the woman's head, trying to calm her as the mother continued to wail. The other nurse hung close to my side as I went to the two protruding feet. With my right hand, I grabbed onto the baby's feet and applied gentle traction, simultaneously delivering the child's arms with the other hand. But once the torso had been delivered, the cervix began to constrict around the neck and umbilical cord restricting the flow of blood and much-needed oxygen to the baby.

I quickly checked the cord for pulses. They were dropping with every second. *Oh, shit. We need to get this baby out. Now!*

"Hey, we need an extra set of hands," I called out to the third nurse. I turned to look, spotting her propped in the corner, looking deathly pale. Her knees gave out before she slid down the wall and vomited on the floor.

Biting back my growing panic, the mother howled like a wounded animal as I slid my left hand up the back of the infant's neck desperately attempting to move the cervix off of the umbilical cord to reestablish the cord's pulses, but the cervix only continued to squeeze down on the baby's small neck, continuing to cut off blood flow. Any thought of finesse was out the window.

"Get on top of her!" I ordered the nurse at my side. "Straddle her!"

The nurse responded, leaping up onto the bed and doing exactly as I instructed.

"Push down on her fundus while I pull! And give it everything you've got! We've got to deliver this baby!" To the terrified mother I yelled, "*Push!!*"

I grabbed both feet and pulled on the baby as the nurse pushed, all the while yelling for the woman to *push* as she shrieked from the effort and the pain. As I pulled, I was terrified about what I was doing to the infant. *I'm going to break this baby's neck.* But I knew there was no other option but to continue. "Again! *Push!*" I ordered the mother.

It wasn't working.

Suddenly, I had a flash of what I hoped was an option. I remembered reading that in extreme breech cases such as this you could cut the cervix. But as quickly as I remembered this, I discarded the notion in the next instant. The cervix is filled with arteries. If I damaged any one of them by cutting into the cervix the mother could bleed to death.

I felt the cord, again checking for the baby's heart rate. It had dropped to life- threatening levels. We had to deliver this baby or face the worst. This was our last chance. *Where the hell is the OB or that anesthesiologist!*

"This is it," I coached. "You need to push with everything you've got!" I looked to the nurse, still straddling the woman as sweat poured down my face and into my eyes.

"On three we're going as hard as we can, okay?" The nurse nodded at me, her determination steely as the mother continued to scream hysterically. "Okay, here we go. One, two, *THREE!*"

I *PULLED!* So hard I was convinced I had injured the infant. Then...

*POP!*

The baby exploded into the world!

A baby boy.

I've never known a baby's cry to be that sweet, before or after.

I cut the cord and gave the child to the nurse who happily pinked the little boy up in the nearby isolate, while the other nurse cooed to the mother who quietly wept in relief.

Just then the mother's OB came waltzing through the door.

"How's everybody doing!"

I have to admit, I wanted to bust his jaw.

"You can deliver the placenta," I told him. Not my most polite moment. "I'm going back to the ER."

I backed away from the room, snapped the paper gown off with my bloody gloves, and looked down at my greens...

If you would have taken me out back and sprayed me with a garden hose full bore, I couldn't have been as wet as I was than after that delivery. My pants, my chest, and my face were literally drenched with sweat, and I felt an immediate chill. It was then, my body buzzing with left over adrenaline and cooling sweat that I started to shake.

I barely made it back down to the ER, pale, freezing, looking like something the cat just dragged in from a hunt. The supervising nurse gave me the once over. "What happened to you?"

"Dual footling breech. First time ever."

"Oh, shit. Go inside the call room. Get yourself a new set off greens. I'm going to get you a fresh cup of coffee."

"That's okay, I think I'll pass."

"I wouldn't. We have a full arrest hitting doors in less than 10 minutes."

Like I said, boring was the last thing you'd call this E.R.

Around midnight I asked the supervising nurse to call up to Labor and Delivery to check on the status of mother and baby. She returned with yet another cup of coffee and the news.

"Mama and baby are both doing just fine."

Wow. Life was incredibly fragile. But other times nothing could extinguish its tenacious flame. I didn't know whether to call it luck or divine intervention.

* * * * *

Not only was my career moving forward, but so was my relationship with Carole. We'd been dating for a year and a half when my yearly vacation came up and there was nobody I wanted to spend it with more than her. One of the perks of dating Carole was her family. We both really enjoyed spending time with them, and ever since our first vacation, waterskiing had become a family tradition. We all decided to spend a week together on a houseboat at Lake Orville. We spent the week at the lake zipping around with a little ski boat, waterskiing and fishing. At the end of the week, we all hugged goodbye and Carole and I hopped into my car, a Bronco, my first new car ever and headed for home.

We cruised down from Northern California on the I-5, an endless stretch of straight highway through California's central valley. I popped another Advil, still aching from living a week on water skis.

"You looked like a pebble skipping across the lake," Carole laughed, recalling my most dramatic fall.

"Most girlfriends wouldn't laugh if they saw their boyfriends make an idiot of themselves."

"The only thing I feel badly about is missing it on video tape."

"Did anyone ever tell you nurses are supposed to be compassionate?"

"Let's face it, you're getting too old for spending eight hours on the water," she laughed.

"I'm thirty-one!"

"Exactly," she joked, popping the top of the Advil bottle. "Here. You better take another. Nurse's orders."

Just then... *whoosh,* we got sucked into the airstream of one, then two extended passenger vans, sculls secured to the rooftops.

"Geez," Carole said, "They must be going 90."

"Or more."

I didn't think much of it and Carole and I continued on, gabbing and relaxing. But about 15 minutes later, as the sun began to dip out of sight behind a distant mountain range, I noticed what looked to be a huge cloud of dust hanging just above the road. I squinted ahead trying to make it out.

"What is that?" I asked Carole.

"I don't know. It looks almost like a dust storm or something."

It was that time in the evening when the sky hangs suspended between day and night adding a surreal, ominous quality to the mysterious cloud. We moved closer and as we did the looming brown haze came more and more into focus.

"It's dust. But not from a storm," I said, squinting as we approached the brown haze. As we continued, I spotted dozens of brake lights bleeding through the cloud. *Whoa, what happened here?*

"Jeff, look out!" Carole said, bracing herself. I slammed on the brakes. In front of us, dozens of cars locked up and swerved to a stop, some on the road, others pulled out onto the side of the highway, kicking up even more dust. Within moments the Bronco cut into the curtain of dust. It was like driving onto the set of a disaster movie.

In front of us lay a crippled van, the same one that had passed us minutes before, one of the wheels missing a tire, bits of shredded tire and beer cans strewn across the road. Tangerine flames licked out the smashed windows. I quietly scanned for passengers, but it thankfully appeared to be empty. I found out later that the van had blown a tire. Fifteen college students, all members of University of San Diego's crew team, had been thrown from the van as it tumbled end for end across the highway.

"Stay here," I told Carole, leaping out of the Bronco. I whirled around to run to the accident scene, the smell of the burning gas and toxic metals and, the cries of the students rising up into the unsettling swirl of dust.

"I'm coming with you," Carole insisted, materializing suddenly at my side. It wasn't the time or place to argue.

Together we raced towards the accident. Kids were screaming, some lay inert on the ground, others stumbling across the road, confused and bleeding. As I jogged closer and closer, two hulking guys came striding toward me, arms extended. I stepped around them, anxious to get to the kids, when one of them grabbed my arm.

"Hey, where're you going?"

"I'm a doctor."

"What kind?"

"Emergency medicine," I said, then Carole nodded, "And she's a nurse."

"Great. C'mon, first victim." It turned out they were both off duty firemen, and they had done some triaging themselves. As we hurried toward the injured kids my mind raced, threaded with insecurities. Even though I was a licensed doctor, I was still a doctor-in-training. Nevertheless, despite whatever fears I had, I knew I was the best thing these kids had at the moment. As for Carole, she was used to a controlled environment only, a far cry from anything like this. We had to work together, check our emotions, and stay focused. And that's exactly what we did.

The first kid I went to was lying motionless on his belly, unresponsive, and arms splayed out.

"Okay," I said to the fireman. "Stay with me. You too," I said to Carole.

I had no stethoscope, nothing. I slid my hands under the boy's head to do a log roll along with the fireman, knowing I had to stabilize his head in case he had a C-spine injury. I inwardly cringed as I felt the disconnection between the boy's skull and spine. *I believe his neck is broken.* I checked his vitals. No pulse. No spontaneous respirations.

"He's dead," I pronounced him.

"Next?" I said to the fireman, willing myself to compartmentalize. I couldn't think of this poor young boy, so full of life in one moment, gone the next. I could do nothing for him. I had to do whatever I could for the next victim. And I had to act fast.

The fireman hurried us over to the next victim, a young blond-haired girl crumpled on the asphalt, her legs and arms at impossibly unnatural angles. I checked her vitals. Nothing.

"Dead."

"Oh Jeff..." Carole breathed, choking down her own emotion as we moved on, trotting after the fireman who led us to the third victim.

A young boy. Unconscious. Unresponsive. No vital signs.

Another dead.

All around us kids were crying, some screaming, delirious in their pain and shock. We split up, trying to take on as many kids as possible.

"Jeff!" Carole called out.

I finished securing a kid who had been lucky enough to come away with nothing more than a broken arm and road rash and I ran to Carole.

"My eye! My eye!" A young, muscular boy cried. He sat crouched on the side of the road, rocking back and forth, one hand clutched to his injured eye.

"I got you, let me see," I said trying to reassure the boy, pulling his hands away from his face. A quick examination told me he had possibly perforated his eye, the oozing fluid and blood flowing from the orbit.

"He's going to be okay," I said to Carole.

In the distance I heard the thin wail of several oncoming ambulances, growing louder by the moment, quickly followed by the *whoop, whoop, whoop* of approaching chopper blades.

"Stay with him," I told Carole. She did.

"You're going to be okay," she reassured the boy, her voice steady, professional yet caring.

"It hurts!" he wailed.

"I know. Help's coming. Don't worry."

"Doc! Over here!" The fireman called out from across the road. I jogged over to another boy who was doubled over, clutching his abdomen, screaming in pain.

"Where am I? What's happening? What is this?"

*This isn't good. He's disoriented. If he's disoriented, that means he's got a head injury.*

I dropped down beside him. "Hey man, you've been in an accident. I'm a doctor. I'm here."

"Who are you? Where am I?" the boy continued to babble, his eyes wild. Upon closer examination I saw that he was cut over every inch of his face, bite-sized pieces of glass clinging to his cheeks, chin, and forehead.

"Lay him down," I instructed the fireman. "Carole!" I called out. She was there in an instant. "Help me get him down." Carole and the fireman helped me carefully ease the boy into the dirt, just as I heard the diesel rattle of the fire truck pull onto the scene.

"Is he the last of the critical patients?" I asked the fireman.

"Yeah, we think so."

As the paramedics rushed toward me, I scanned around to make sure. The roadway was filled with dozens of rescue units, their ghostly white headlights piercing the newly fallen night, EMT's and paramedics hunkered over the students as the sounds of young girls crying out in pain and anguish for themselves and this unspeakable tragedy rang through the darkness.

I turned back to the task at hand, securing the boy with the head injury. "Let's get him on a C-spine board and get vitals and blood pressure," I ordered, as one of the paramedics handed me a stethoscope. The other paramedic got him on the board and sand bagged him so he couldn't move, standard procedure to avoid further injury. But as soon as the boy was immobilized he started to scream, something very common for head injuries.

"Stop it! Stop! Who are you!" he shouted.

I quickly wrapped a cuff around him. His blood pressure was dangerously low and his heart rate fast. *This is not a good sign.* I gently palpated his abdomen, hoping to distract him. His belly was as hard as a board. That meant there was the possibility of blood pouring out of his circulatory system and into his belly, accounting for his low blood pressure, rigid abdomen, and racing heart rate. *He's either lacerated his spleen, liver, bowel, or some other major vessel,* I thought. We put two saline IV lines in him to raise his blood pressure and started pouring the fluid in him.

"He needs to get to a hospital. Now! And in an ambulance." Just then another blanket of dust and grit swirled around our heads as the chopper landed nearby.

"What're you doing? Who are you? Stop it!" the boy pleaded.

"We're all here to help you," Carole murmured close to the boy's ear, doing everything she could to calm him. "My name is Carole, I'm a nurse. The doctor's here too. Everything's going to be okay." They loaded the boy into a helicopter and they were off. All of the patients had been loaded onto the ambulances and were whisked to the ER.

As I watched the last ambulance peel out, sirens blaring, I turned to Carole. We held each other's gaze. Our work was done, while it was only beginning for those who would care for them at the ER and beyond. It all ended as abruptly as it had begun.

We finished up the report with the CHP and police on scene.

"Listen, thanks a lot, Doc," the officer said as he shook my hand and then Carole's.

We shuffled back to the Bronco and started down the lonely stretch of road, in silence. I spotted a Denny's up ahead and pulled off the road for a much needed break. We walked into the brightly lit diner, catching sideways glances as we dragged ourselves to the bathroom. We were filthy. Covered in blood. Bits of gravel and dirt clung to our faces and clothes. I waited outside the bathroom as Carole slipped inside. Behind the door I heard her muffled cries. When she stepped out, her mascara smeared, her face still smudged with dirt and bits of dried blood, I pulled her into my chest and gently hugged her.

"Are you okay?"

"Remember what day it is?" she asked. I took a beat, thinking before she answered her own question. "It's Mother's Day."

With that, she broke into unrestrained sobs, grieving for the unseen mothers and fathers as well as the students who had suffered such a sudden and catastrophic day.

We'd dated for a year and a half, but we'd never been through an ordeal like that before. I hoped we never would again. But that day taught me something. Carole had fought through her own fears, her own feelings, to unselfishly help people she never knew and would never see again. And she had never left my side. We had done it all together.

"You did great, out there," I whispered.

Carole looked up at me, smiling through her tears.

The ordeal had bonded us. We really were a team. That day and every day after. We were in this life together.

# Chapter 9

## Giving Back

Having done my rotations at Children's Hospital for Pediatric ER, Olive View and UCLA for ER, I was near the end of my training. It had been hard work, but a blast. Flying on the helicopter during my senior year of residency was probably the highlight. It was everything from gunshots, to fractured spines, to pediatric drownings. Soon it was time for me to get my board certification in Emergency Medicine. After a day of written tests, followed by another day of orals, I was done. Six weeks later a letter came in the mail. My results. I passed.

Finally, after 14 years through college, medical school, and training I was a licensed, board-certified physician. I was accepted to a large inner city ER that had a reputation as a knife and gun club. It was time to get on with the work of being a doctor and move forward with the kind of life I would have never dreamed possible. Jeffrey Nordella, M.D. I couldn't believe it. I was a lucky man.

I felt grateful. I felt like the first thing I wanted to do was give back in some way. I had an idea what I would do to celebrate, and as soon as I secured a steady income from my profession. I couldn't wait to make it happen.

* * * * *

It was a particularly warm summer day when Mom and I wound our way up the 118 freeway past the prehistoric rock formations dotted with tidy ranch homes.

"It's a brand new development." It has community pools, a nice little clubhouse. It even has a golf course a couple blocks away.

"Don't you want to show Carole before you buy a house?" Mom asked.

"I'm not thinking of buying anything right now. I just thought you'd want to see it. You know, if Carole and I decide to get married."

"If?" Mom was one in a long line of Carole's number one biggest fans. And she didn't let me forget it.

"Can we please not talk about Carole and me right now, Mom?"

"You're the one who brought it up," she teased.

"*Anyway. If* we moved out here, we wouldn't be too far away from you, you could visit all the time."

"That would be nice."

"You think you'd want to move out here someday too? It's not that far from your friends."

"Oh, I don't know. Maybe. It is beautiful out this way," she answered, her voice soft. I knew what she was thinking. She could never afford to move out of the old neighborhood. The house she'd lived in for the last 35 years. The house that had grown increasingly run down, just like the neighborhood. Thinking about how the neighborhood was deteriorating kept me up at night, worrying about Mom's safety.

"Oh, this is lovely, Jeff," she said as we pulled up past the development entrance, all smoothly manicured lawns, adobe and wood fences, and newly-constructed Spanish style homes. The place exuded friendliness, serenity, and above all, safety.

"You like it?" I asked her.

"Who wouldn't? It's beautiful."

"Good. I like it too. C'mon, let's check it out."

I took Mom on a tour through the four different models, each one nicer than the last. There was one model, however, that I had my eye on, and when mom saw it, I saw her light up. She moved from feature to feature in the home, showing me pantries, vanities, closet space, appliances, flooring, explaining just how great everything was. I could see she loved it.

Afterward, inside the model home office, we bent over the 3-D plot map of the development, complete with lot sizes, tiny pieces of artificial green shrubbery, translucent blue plastic indicating pools, and house after tiny house lined up along the artificial golf course.

"I like this one the best," I said pointing to a teeny home on a cul-de-sac, a small red dot stuck to the roof. "I really like this model. And it has got the biggest lot. What do you think?" I asked Mom.

"It would be nice to live on a cul-de-sac. I like that one too. But what's the red dot for?"

"Unfortunately, that one is in escrow," the realtor, a well-coiffed young woman poured into a powder blue business suit, told us.

"Oh, that's too bad, Jeff," Mom said, disappointed for me. "Well, you said you're not quite ready to buy yet. Maybe something else will come up later that you'll like better."

"Maybe..." I said, looking glum.

"Do you have a restroom?" Mom asked the realtor, almost as if she wanted to change the subject.

The moment Mom turned the corner for the ladies room, the realtor smiled. "I just got the message ten minutes before you got here. That home has fallen out of escrow."

I made a quick check down the hall to make sure Mom couldn't hear. "Where do I have to sign? We've got to do this before she gets back."

Mom padded back into the office the moment I pocketed my checkbook and stood to my feet.

"Guess what? That house just opened up. I bought it. Just wrote the check for the deposit," I announced, beaming.

"You're kidding!"

"Nope. Do you really like it? I mean, you think I should buy it?"

"It's a beautiful home. I think you'd be very happy there."

"You mean you're gonna be very happy there."

Everything stopped. The smile fell from her face, replaced with utter confusion.

"It's yours, Mom."

"No it's not," she sputtered, still trying to make sense of what I was saying.

"I just wrote the check. It *is* yours."

"Jeff, no. No... I can't... you can't."

"Yes I can. I want to."

"But you don't even own your own house yet... you can't..."

"Don't worry about that, Mom. That will come..."

"Congratulations, Mrs. Nordella," the realtor said.

Mom remained glued to the carpet, helplessly glancing between the realtor and me before her eyes glassed over with unshed tears. "Jeff... I don't know what to say..."

"You don't have to say anything, Mom. Except that you want it."

She stepped to me, wrapping me in the kind of hug only moms can give, unable to hold back the tears any longer. I looked over the top of her head to see the realtor, dabbing at her eyes as well.

It was a pretty incredible feeling. Mom had had such a tough life. Enduring my dad's drinking, ill health, and early death. Lugging those heavy sewing machines around every night, doing whatever she could think of to keep the family afloat. And through it all she'd unselfishly been there for me. Everything from those horrific tuna casseroles, to the $25 whenever she could spare it just to keep me afloat, to biting her tongue when her auto mechanic son announced he'd someday be a doctor. Giving her this one little piece of happiness, getting her out of the old neighborhood to help brighten her last years after all the years she'd sacrificed, wasn't only a pleasure, it was an honor.

She stepped back, wiping the tears from her eyes. "I love you, Jeff."

"Love you too, Mom." I might have held back a tear or two myself. It was a great day.

# Chapter 10

## A Change of Heart

Ever since I had sprinted across that kindergarten playground to make my escape I felt as if I'd been headed as fast as I could in one direction. But during one of my rare down moments, when I was kicking back with a beer, Carole's dad focused a long look at me.

"What?" I said.

"Just thinking that's all."

"About what?"

He took a moment before answering, "You know, you've got a lot of tenacity."

"Thanks, I think," I said, not sure what he was mulling over. "But I'm not sure what that really means."

"It just means you strike me as a young man in an awful hurry."

He was right. For some reason I was in a hurry. I couldn't pinpoint exactly why that was the case. Maybe it was habit. I had focused so intently on getting my M.D. for so long, it was almost like I didn't know how to be anything but single-minded, directed, and intense. But now I was a doctor. I had a good job at a busy emergency room. I was also the medical director of our pre-hospital care program and taught not only EMTs, paramedics, and nurses, but also family practice resident doctors as well. Considering that I had started as an EMT, I felt as if I had come full circle. I loved my job, and I had a good income. I secured my mom in a nice little home where she was thriving, after which I bought a nice small house for Carole and me in Valencia where we lived happily together.

The one thing I was certain about was that I wasn't going to rush into getting married and potentially relive my childhood. "Look," I'd said to Carole more times than once, "I just want to make sure I have enough to take care of us." But it was hard to argue that I'd hit that mark and passed it. For so many years I'd had my head down, taking step after step, always moving forward, focus on becoming a doctor. Then all of a sudden I looked up and said, "Wow, where am I?" I was 34. Carole was 32. It was like I stopped and said, "What am I doing?" What good was being a doctor if I was alone? I loved Carole. It was time to seal the deal. But how would I go about the proposal? Well, that's another story...

I proposed over the telephone.

It was horrible. It's not something I'm proud of. For quite some time I actually felt really bad about being such an unwitting butthead, but eventually it became a joke between Carole and me. Among all Carole's positive attributes, forgiveness and being able to go with the flow were right up there.

As for the proposal itself, it was something that wasn't really planned. It just sort of happened. I got her on the phone, and we were talking and then, it just spontaneously popped out of my mouth. To be honest, I couldn't even tell you what the conversation was about, and then all of a sudden it kind of evolved into our relationship. The topic of children came up.

"I don't know, Jeff. You say you want to have a family, but do you *really* mean it?"

"Yes." I did. Completely.

"I want a family, too. With you."

A long silence ensued. She let the unspoken then-what-are-you-waiting-for lay there between us. This was it. I might as well go for it.

"You know you're an awesome woman," I sputtered. Another silence. "And you know I love you."

"Right..."

"I think it's time we got married. Will you marry me?" Another silence.

"Did you just ask me to marry you?" Now it was my turn to skip a beat. But it was what I wanted. Of course it was what I wanted.

"Yes. I mean it. Will you be my wife?"

"Jeff!" she squealed. "Of course! Oh my gosh!"

That was it. Not the most romantic proposal ever.

Actually, on the list of top ten most unromantic proposals in the greater U.S. or maybe the world, I'd rank right at the top. I recognized I was clearly a bonehead. But what can I say? All I'd done for the last 14+ years was study and rumble around hospitals and libraries. I didn't know anything. I didn't know you were supposed to run over and grab a ring and take the girl to dinner and have people in the bushes and write love songs and hire photographers and skywriters like all my kids are doing now. I was just an unromantic doofus who had a girlfriend I probably didn't even deserve. I had no preconceived idea of how to ask her, so I muddled through the only way I knew how: badly.

Days later, I went on to the second bonehead move. I knew nothing about rings. Nothing. I couldn't tell you what a karat was unless it was orange and you ate it dipped in ranch dressing.

"Look, Carole, I said, I want to get you a diamond, but I don't know anything about this stuff."

"Okay..." she said, not sure where I was going with this.

"So I can get it and surprise you. *Or* I can give you a blank check and you take your friend and buy your own engagement ring. That way you can be sure you'll like it."

What's not logical about that?

Now some people would call me a total idiot. Guilty as charged. Put me in jail. I

In the end I handed her the check.

"You're gonna regret this," she said with an evil grin, as she quickly snatched it from my hand.

I stood at the door watching as Carole and her girlfriend drove off in the Bronco for a "day of ring shopping" and lunch in LA's downtown jewelry district.

"Don't forget!" I called out, "Budget!"

She found exactly the ring she wanted. I think she punished me just a little, too. It was quite expensive. But she absolutely loved it. That's all that mattered.

We were getting married.

* * * * *

We started planning the wedding. And when I say "we," I mean Carole... and then both the mothers started getting into it. What started out as fun quickly devolved into one giant ball of stress for Carole. I could see the walls closing in on her more and more each day.

"It's not even fun anymore," Carole confessed. "I wanted to keep it simple, but everybody seems to want something different, and it's getting bigger and bigger every day."

"Why don't we just make it simple, then?"

"How? It's not as easy as you make it sound."

"It can be."

"What are you thinking?"

"What about if we go to Tahoe? We'll invite just family."

"I would love that, but don't you want a big wedding?"

"No. I just want to marry you. Why stress?"

A smile crept onto her face and she said, "Perfect."

We set the date for June 1. Carole made all of the arrangements. We all flew up a couple of days before the wedding and had a blast waterskiing, hiking, and doing a little night clubbing and gambling.

On the day of the wedding we headed to a working ranch where we said our vows in a little church, up in the mountains surrounded by ancient pines and slabs of towering granite. After a brief ceremony we hopped into an antique car complete with cans tied to the back fender and a sign: "Just Married." We took a spin around the property and ended with a beautiful dinner overlooking Lake Tahoe.

Carole wore a simple but beautiful wedding dress. I still have it to this day. I wore a suit and tie. When we came home, we had a reception at our house, and about 100 people joined us for a big pool party. We played basketball and everybody jumped into the deep end celebrating together. No pressure. Just family, friends, and fellowship. Perfect for Carole and me. We'd finally done it. We were married. We were happy.

Carole was very excited to start having kids right away. As she put it, "I'm not getting any younger." Although we certainly weren't old, we knew we wanted several children. Just like clockwork, six months after we were married, Carole got pregnant. We did the test together. When the plus sign showed up on the stick, I blurted out, "Oh my gosh, I'm gonna be a dad!" I was totally excited, and then I just went, "Oh my gosh, I'm gonna be a dad?" It really hit me. Dozens of thoughts tumbled through my head. Did I really have enough money in the bank? Was Carole going to be okay? Were we ready to take on this lifelong responsibility? Would I be a good father? Did I really know *how* to be a father? The one thing I did know: I would do anything to keep my future children and Carole happy, safe, and well provided for.

I was still working at the ER outside of L.A. and it was going well. Almost immediately after getting pregnant, the hormones really hit

Carole. She'd always had a bit of a problem with migraines, but they got considerably worse as the pregnancy progressed. One day, driving to work, she was literally blinded by an oncoming migraine and had to pull over to the side of the freeway. We both felt it was too dangerous for her to continue to work when her symptoms were so severe, but she still wasn't sure if she wanted stop working when the baby was born. She had worked her way to her own goal of administrator at the UCLA NICU, a position that would be hard to give up.

"Come sit next to me, Jeff," she asked as she lay on the bed one day, a wet towel over her eyes as she rested in a dark room.

"What do you think I should do?"

She didn't need to ask "once the baby is born." It was on both of our minds.

"I think you need to do what you think you should do."

"But I want your opinion."

"That is my opinion. It's your life that's going to change if you decide to stay home. Or go to work for that matter."

We both sat and thought about that for a while.

"Okay," I said, trying to think through this with her. "Let's think about what you'll be giving up if you decide to stay home."

"Well," she said, "I do get a lot of positive feedback from work."

"Right," I agreed.

"And it took me forever to get where I am now."

"Exactly."

"And if you stay home you'll be sacrificing all of that," I reminded her.

"But if I stay home I'd be with our baby. I wouldn't miss any of it."

"Right."

"But could we handle it financially?"

"If that's what you want to do, we'll figure it out," I said.

She removed the cloth from her eyes and took my hand. "It's really not a decision, is it?"

It wasn't. At least for us.

"So you want to stay home?"

"Yeah, I really do."

"Then that's what you'll do."

She smiled and slipped the cloth back over her eyes. The decision had been made.

It was a good thing Carole quit work when she did, because she was sick– morning sickness, what is referred to as *hyperemesis gravidarum*. But Carole's case was no ordinary morning sickness where the best prescription was a handful of saltine crackers or B6 vitamins. The poor woman was sick, really sick. No matter what it was, she couldn't seem to keep *anything* down. It actually concerned me more than a little. I ended up driving a three-inch penny nail straight into the wall and kept it there. I'd come home from work with two liters of normal saline and a third liter of injectable multi vitamins and hang it onto the nail. Then I'd slide an IV into her arm and open up the fluids. We tried everything for the nausea that wouldn't affect the baby. But none of the meds helped too much. After taking in three liters of fluids, more times than not she'd get up and throw up. It was bad.

But when Carole hit sixteen weeks it was like magic. Gone.

"Oh my gosh, I'm so hungry," she said.

Music to my ears. I took her to Scottsdale Arizona to celebrate. We got a nice room and while I played golf during the day, she sat in the bathtub and relaxed. I'd come back and we would watch movies. Sitting there on that big, plush bed was the first time we saw *Die Hard*. That movie and food. That's what I remember. We both ate like pigs. She ate everything: shrimp, steak, and desserts. I just looked at her and smiled. "Good, have fun."

We were starting a family. Life was just the way I'd always pictured it.

My daughter was born. All of Carole's morning sickness and, all of my panic over being a father all evaporated the moment we laid eyes on our beautiful, healthy new little girl, Jamie Ellen. What a day. We were officially a family of three.

The first time I held Jamie, I was instantly in love and grateful that she was healthy. It didn't matter that I'd delivered hundreds of babies before. None of them were our daughter. But the euphoria of being a new father, changed when I went home that day. I don't know why, but I had nightmares on the first night. Horrible nightmares. Jamie was involved in a car wreck. An accident. She was hurt. I couldn't get to her. I'd seen so many bad things at the ER. Now I had a *daughter*. A precious girl. She was so little and delicate. The feeling that I had to be not only a provider, but also a protector overwhelmed me. It's hard to describe, but she was so innocent and she needed us 24/7, and it was my responsibility to make sure nothing happened to her.

I tried to do everything: feed her, change diapers, play with her. I loved being involved. But then I'd have to go away for three nights at the ER. I was constantly afraid I was missing something. Whenever I was at work, I'd call and talk to Carole before and after every shift. I wanted to know everything that was going on, everything that was happening without me. I missed them. Especially when I'd come home and see Jamie had passed through yet another developmental landmark and I wasn't there to witness it.

The distance started to wear on me. The emergency room was about an hour and half away from home. I ended up getting an apartment close to work that I shared with two other docs. Not exactly the most ideal set up for a new dad and his family. My routine was to get to work for a 7 am - 7 pm shift, grab something to eat, then go to the apartment and go to bed. Get up and do the same thing for two more days in a row. Then I would come home to Santa Clarita to be with Carole and Jamie. The hour and a half drive to work seemed like a world away.

But something else happened too. Something more profound.

My work at the ER was still my life's blood, but I began to see things through a different lens. The lens of a father. As an ER doctor you see a huge swath of humanity. From rich to poor, young to old, homeless, raving insanity, gang bangers, alcoholics, drug addicts, abusers, rapists, nuns and priests. The good, the bad, the wholesome, and the corrupt. What had previously excited me, now as a young father began to wear me down. But the worst cases were the ones that involved children.

Like the time I saw a dad screaming at the top of his lungs, running into the ER holding his unconscious four year old who was in full arrest, the pregnant girlfriend tailing him. The dad threw his little boy on the gurney and when we tried to establish and IV, he had been beaten so badly his arm just dangled at a ninety-degree angle over the side of the gurney, broken completely through. Almost every inch of his body was bruised. Apparently, the girlfriend was giving the boy a bath, got pissed and simply beat him. He died. She was taken away in cuffs right in front of us.

Then, when Jamie was still an infant, a nine-month old child came in seizing like crazy. I worked to access a vein, finally getting some Valium into him to stop the seizures. I managed to stop the seizing, but the source of the problem was still a complete mystery. The child had no temperature. No sign of trauma. His white count was normal and the spinal tap was unremarkable. *What the hell is wrong with this child?* I wondered. Finally, on a grim hunch, I decided to bag the baby for a urine toxicology screen. I mean, why would anyone in his right mind need to run a drug screen on a nine-month old baby, right? Tragically, my hunch was right. The baby tested positive for PCP. It turns out the baby's father was a drug dealer who manufactured PCP in their apartment. He was storing it in baby bottles. Apparently he didn't bother to wash the bottles very well before making one for his own child.

But the turning point came when a mom came in, lugging a crying baby. She was so drunk she could barely stand, her equally sloppy drunk boyfriend trailing in minutes afterward. We quickly wrestled the baby from her as she kept raving, "It was an accident! I was just an accident!"

We examined the child and noted a large hematoma on the head. The CAT scan confirmed a severe skull fracture and in intra-cerebral bleed. The mother and boyfriend were arrested. The intoxicated mother had dropped the child on her head because she was too drunk to hold onto her. It was a baby girl. Eight months old. She was the exact same age as Jamie.

I couldn't get that baby off my mind as I slowly drove in a haze back to Santa Clarita. When I got home, I stood over Jamie's crib as she slept, pure, innocent, trusting, her small tummy rising and falling with the rhythm of contented breaths. Carole found me standing there in the dark.

"You okay?" she whispered, coming up to circle an arm around my waist as I continued to look down at our baby girl.

"I don't think I can do it anymore."

"Do what?"

"The ER. My job."

"What's going on?"

"I'm just tired of all the pain and suffering and the people who cause it. I'm tired of being sweaty and sleep deprived. I'm tired of catching ten minutes of sleep on a gurney, then running off to another stabbing, another gunshot wound. I think the medical staff cares more about the patients than the patients care about themselves."

"What happened today?" Carole asked, knowing me too well.

"There was a baby. Same age as Jamie. It was bad." I didn't need to say anything more. Carole knew and she really did not want to hear about it. She understood what I faced every day. She knew what it cost me to come home day after day with a smile on my face pretending to be like any other dad coming home from a humdrum day at the office.

"So quit," Carole told me.

"I have been thinking about private practice."

"Do it, then. It's time. I don't want you to keep doing something that doesn't make you happy. We'll get by. I know we will."

Within a month, I got a call out of the blue.

A local Santa Clarita doctor I had worked with during one of my rotations in my fourth year of medical school contacted me.

"Hey," he asked, "how would you feel about joining my practice?"

Not only did he want me to join him, but he really wanted to leave, although he didn't tell me that at the time. So I started working part time at his practice and part time at the ER, hoping to make the transition to private practice. Not long after, he made his true intentions known and asked me if I wanted to buy the practice.

"What do you think?" I asked Carole.

"Would it be enough to support us?"

"He has a good practice and he has a good reputation in the community. But it's not salaried like the ER. Whether I make it or not is all on me."

"It's what you want, isn't it?"

It was. I just couldn't face the ER any more. "I just have to see if I can make it work."

"Let's do it," Carole agreed.

I was going to start an urgent care. I thought it would be a good idea, given my training, to combine ER with family practice. It would be a perfect marriage. You could make appointments to see the doctor or you could walk in. The third prong would be occupational medicine: work related issues. I thought it would be a great combination, but it was risky. At the time, urgent cares were around but none were structured that way. It went against the prevailing wisdom of that time. But I really believed in the idea. And I was willing to throw the dice.

I drained every dollar in our savings account. Took all of it and used it as a down payment to buy the practice. The existing practice was upstairs, which made it unworkable for a medical walk-in. Injured people don't want to climb a flight of stairs. So I opened up a little 2,000 square foot facility on the first floor. It was really pretty dinky for an urgent care, but it was what I could afford.

My timing wasn't exactly the best, at least on a personal level. Jamie was ten months old and Carole had just gotten pregnant with our second child, Kristen. She was throwing up constantly as she tried to chase around a toddler and needed me more than ever. As for me, I'd just left a lucrative job, didn't have a penny in the bank, and now had not only a mortgage on our house, but a mortgage on my mom's house, and a mortgage on a business too. But what I did have were tools, the same tools that got me through school and into medical school, the same tools that got me through training, and the same tools that allowed me to become a practicing physician. As my grandfather taught me, you need the proper tools to get the job done. And one tool I knew I possessed was tenacity.

And with that, I opened my doors. I went into opening day with high hopes and even higher expectations. After decorating my new waiting area with balloons and a popcorn machine per the recommendation of a marketing guru I had hired, I unlocked the doors to my clinic for the first time. This was it! My ultimate dream had come true. Fourteen years of schooling and seven years of working in the ER had led to this moment. I recalled all of those days commuting to COC dreaming about owning my own practice in Santa Clarita Valley, and here I was, just as I had dreamed. Expecting a generous turnout for my grand opening, I cleaned the rooms and the equipment one last time, popped some popcorn, and waited.

And waited. And then waited some more.

I could almost hear crickets chirping. Suddenly, the balloons and popcorn maker seemed childish. Even my startup auto mechanic service had been met with more enthusiasm than my licensed medical clinic. My fears grew with each passing hour as the rooms with fully equipped, state of the art equipment sat unused.

At the grand opening I saw just four patients in thirteen hours.

I may have been able to keep my cool in the face of any traumatic life-threatening event, but if there was ever a cause to panic, now was the time.

It was like that for far too long for my taste, about two to three months. I sat there in that empty space and felt the despair. *What did I do? Am I completely nuts? What a horrible provider I am.*

There were quite a few sleepless nights. But after all the soul-searching and all the conversations I had with friends and family, I knew I had to make this new business work. I kept asking myself what I had done wrong and what could I do differently to reboot my failing practice. I committed myself to a simple philosophy: I made sure that every patient that came in was happy. I would attempt to give my patients the best care they'd ever had. I'd treat them like I would want to be treated if I were the patient. I would take care of them in my office; I would take care of them in the emergency room; I would take care of them in the hospital. I would assist in their surgeries if need be, and I would take their calls after hours. Just like an old-fashioned doctor. If I did that, I trusted that they would come back, and not only that, they'd tell their friends.

People started walking in the door. Once they did, I retained about 95% to 98% of the patients. I think people also loved the convenience of being able to walk in without an appointment. Those patients started telling their friends and they in turn told their friends. Word began to spread. It was a word-of-mouth community, thank heavens. Within six months I was so busy I didn't know what to do with all of the new patients. We couldn't make appointments fast enough. Suddenly I constantly had a full waiting room. I was slammed! I took the proceeds and used a lump sum to pay off the practice completely. It was now mine, free and clear.

I think part of my appeal to patients was that I didn't put on any airs. That's just not me, whether I was a physician or not. I wasn't about to come off as the stereotypical all-powerful, all-knowing doctor. In fact, I felt as if comfort was a key ingredient in the patient's care. If they were comfortable, they would be able to open up to me. It was a relaxed environment and I believe people appreciated it. In fact, one of my trademarks was I threw out the white coat for a polo shirt and shorts. It didn't take long for me to be known as "the doctor who wears shorts in Santa Clarita."

The other thing was I could relate to most everyone, whether they were an auto mechanic or a high-powered business owner. Why was this important?

Because, in my opinion, communication is the most important quality needed for being a good doctor.

Sure you have to have knowledge, but if you cannot communicate that knowledge, what good is it? You've got to be able to hear people to be able to properly treat them. Some doctors don't want to relate to their patients as human beings, but just as symptoms. I disagree with that. Relationships are very important. When you have a relationship, if you treat people as if you actually care, your patients open up and tell you things they wouldn't if they felt rushed or marginalized. The more information I have, the easier it is for me to make a diagnosis and a decision about how to handle their care.

I've also always respected people to be smart enough to choose their doctor and make decisions in their own medical treatment. I would tell them, "Look, I'm just here to recommend and to give you whatever I know. You can throw it in the trashcan or you can use it. It's up to you." And I truly meant that. Finally, and maybe this was the most important thing, I had a motto: "Everybody is family."

To me it's simple, give your patients the same respect and attention you would a family member. This was very important in regards to referring patients to specialists. Referrals should not be made on a financial or political basis. They are made because the specialist will take good care of them and address their issues. After all, they are a direct reflection of the referring doctor.

It's something taught in the first days of medical school, treating your patients as human beings is not only morally correct, but medically correct as well.

# Chapter 11

## The Golden Years... and then...

Life was great. I had a thriving practice, a great wife, and after Kristen was born, Jeffrey, our third, followed. I'd come home every night, change my clothes, and get down on the floor with the kids to wrestle, tickle, and play. At night, Carole always made the rounds with the kids talking and praying with them. Since we'd been married, Carole had found her way back to her Christian faith, becoming more and more devout.

At first, it drove an awkward wedge between us. After all, one of the things that had drawn us together initially was that both of us questioned our religious upbringing. However, as Carole turned more and more to her faith, my love for her, along with the birth of the kids, began to soften my attitude towards God. I decided to put my questions aside for the harmony of the family and became a believer myself. Carole was thrilled at my conversion and we began to raise our children with like minds and hearts. All in all, we were an average, normal, happy family. I had everything I had ever wanted and I loved it.

Jamie: *We did everything as a family. I think I was sixteen years old before I saw a movie that my brother and sister hadn't seen. No matter what, we went to church on Sunday morning. Every single night in Valencia, those hot nights, we'd swim in the pool until nine or ten. We lived on a cul-de-sac. We had a yellow lab. We got along with all the neighbors. All the kids would play together and all the adults would sit in their lawn chairs and watch us kids. Dad would come home from work and always wanted dinner right away, so we'd have an early dinner so he could go out and play catch with us every night before it got dark. All of the neighborhood kids loved him because he'd play with us. Sometimes he'd set up games—cops and robbers or something. He'd be like, "Okay, everybody come around, grab your bike." Then he'd assign who each of us were—cop, robber, cop, robber. When he was into something, he was in it. One hundred and fifty percent, just like everything else in his life. So if he was going to put on a neighborhood game, it was going to be the best game EVER and everyone was going to play and everyone was going to have a great time.*

Jeffrey: *I remember the summertime. It felt like almost every day was a barbeque. All of our relatives would come over. Colorful bowls of fruit salad and ribs slathered in barbeque sauce, swimming with 50's and 60's oldies music blasting in the backyard.*

When Jamie was halfway through the first grade, we decided we wanted to take a trip in our motor home. A road trip. But it didn't fall into summer or spring break. We just took a week in the middle of the year. When Jamie got back to school she was inundated with work. I couldn't believe we couldn't even take a week off as a family. I just felt it was wrong that a six year old had to be that stressed already. I could only see it getting worse. Also, we wanted to teach our children Christian values and if Carole homeschooled there were some great programs that had a solid academic program along with the religious teaching we both wanted.

Jamie: *It's not like my mom knew anything about homeschooling, but she just dove into it. There wasn't even the Internet back then. I don't even know how she found out about homeschooling, but she got the entire Christian curriculum and that's when we started.*

Once Carole started to homeschool, our actual home became even more important to Carole and me. We both had always had a dream of spreading out and having our own ranch where the kids could run around and play in the safety of a large open area. We researched the area, and I found the Santa Rosa Valley in Camarillo. It was a quiet, safe area that seemed to be far away from the rougher elements I had been exposed to as a kid. We found a twelve-acre plot of land that was perfect for our needs. Situated behind the gates of a privately planned community, our piece of land was our own slice of paradise. Our parcel was at the end of a cul-de-sac nestled against seventeen miles of a park, which could never be built on according to open space initiatives. I got to play amateur architect as Carole and I drew up the plans and started construction on our ideal home... complete with a regulation baseball field. I bought a tractor and started working the land, which was terrific therapy in contrast with my busy work schedule. It was my sanctuary.

Kristen: *My dad was in the process of building our house for a year and a half. We were living in a motorhome on the property, which was so much fun for us kids. Mom really used the torn up space to her advantage, integrating it into our homeschooling lessons. I remember how she'd take army men out into the dirt and create the battle scene of whatever history lesson we were learning about at the time.*

Jamie: *During that time, when we were building the house and later, after we moved in, Mom continued to homeschool us. She poured her heart and soul into it. Even though she wanted us to excel in academics, she focused so much more on our character. There would be days when she'd say, "We're not doing any schoolwork today, but I'm meeting with each of you privately to talk to you about who you are and what's going on. So, we'd go in her room and she'd list off everything she loved about each of us and our great qualities and also the things she thought we needed to work on. We'd look at Bible verses and we'd have our memory verse that week that we needed to work on, and that's how we'd spend our day.*

Jeffrey: *I had a green electric scooter and I'd follow behind my mom as she jogged around our property with our three labs. It sounds like we got no work done, but we did. One day she was on the phone all day with the Internet company trying to get our Internet working while we swam in the pool. Finally, she was so brain-dead that she walked out and just jumped in the pool in her shirt and out-of-style overalls. I still remember all of us swimming around, mom fully clothed. She was just like that. She loved to laugh, especially at herself. She was just so goofy. She was the kind of person everybody wanted to be around.*

I could see that Carole was not only the perfect mom, but was turning into the perfect teacher for our children as well. She just had a way with them. Every mother has a bond with their child, but the depth of connection Carole felt with the kids as well as their connection to her was extraordinary. It was a beautiful thing to see.

As my children's faith grew with Carole's help, so did my own. But even though my faith was growing and my practice was thriving, and I had a happy marriage and a loving family, I couldn't quite shake an almost indescribable need to protect them. I started to get the reputation with friends and family for being the overprotective dad, being too "strict." Just like my dad. It was the one point of contention between Carole and me.

Jamie: *My parents definitely had a great relationship. They communicated a lot. They'd drink coffee in the kitchen together every single morning while they'd sit and talk. And then when he'd commute to Valencia, they'd talk on the phone the entire time. But we could tell that if they closed the doors to their room, it was arguing instead of talking. A lot of times it was about our mom fighting for our freedom. We weren't allowed to ride in other people's cars. I had my first sleepover when I was fourteen. I remember in first grade one of my classmates invited me to sleep over. I didn't know how to tell her that I wasn't allowed to sleep over. I was so embarrassed. I just cried to my mom that I didn't know what to do. I hated being different. To put it into perspective, there was one time when my mom had us training for this physical challenge we were doing throughout homeschooling group. So I was running in circles around our cul-de-sac and it was pitch black. Our black lab, Buck, got out and ran in front of me and I didn't see him. I tripped and I hit my head really, really hard. I remember blacking out and the next thing I remember is my dad holding me. I was holding my head and I was in so much pain, but I kept saying over and over, "Don't kill Buck, it's not Buck's fault." He would get angry if we got hurt, not at us, but it was like he was mad that we had to be going through any pain. It was definitely very frustrating at times. I remember making a list of all the reasons I wished I was a boy. I think I still have it somewhere. I remember thinking,* if I was just a boy it wouldn't be this bad.

For me, having control was always about providing safety and security. Maybe this need stemmed from my childhood. Perhaps because my home had been so unstable, I was now doing everything I could so my own children wouldn't experience the level of chaos I had found to be so damaging. Or maybe my obsession with creating a perfectly safe, perfectly controlled environment for my children came from all those years I'd spent in the ER. Maybe I just couldn't seem to shake the bizarre, the strange, and the evil of those experiences.

Like the woman who followed a sheriff into the parking lot of the emergency room. The Sheriff pulled in and parked. She parked right behind him. She motioned for the sheriff to come over. He didn't think much of it and headed over toward her car. It wasn't until he stood at her open window that she pulled a gun out from between her legs and pointed it right at his chest. The cop dropped to the ground, screaming at her to relinquish her weapon, but she didn't flinch, continuing to aim the barrel straight at the officer. Finally, with no other recourse, the officer opened fire. He hit her three times in the chest. Hearing the gunfire, the staff quickly responded to the parking lot. We grabbed her, placed her on a gurney and got her into the emergency room. With no vital signs, we split her chest open, attempting to do everything we could to save her, but it was no use. As we were packaging her for the morgue, we found a little note tucked into the pocket of her shirt. It read: "Sorry. I couldn't do this myself." She succeeded in her wish: suicide by cop.

Then there was the guy who drove to the mortuary at two in the morning and tried to get inside. A security guard jokingly told the guy, "Sorry, we're closed. You can't get in there unless you're dead." The guy, not finding the joke funny at all, just looked at the security guard before responding, "I'll take care of that." He got in his car, drove up onto the 605 freeway, and quickly pulled off to the shoulder. Soon after, thinking he had a disabled vehicle on his hands, a CHP officer rolled up behind him. The officer headed to the vehicles driver's side and tapped on the window.

The driver slowly looked over at the officer. When their eyes met, the driver took out a ten-inch kitchen knife, held it over his heart and rammed it into his chest. The CHP officer immediately called for paramedics. The patient, a young male in his mid-twenties, was in full cardiopulmonary arrest from penetrating chest trauma. I performed a thoracotomy but unfortunately was not able to repair the huge laceration in his left ventricle of his heart. He died.

How could I reconcile that kind of world with the world I wanted for my family? I wanted what was best for the people I loved. I wanted to make my family immune to pain. I wanted to do everything I could to control their situation and make them safe, but there was something else I couldn't quite shake, and it wasn't about my childhood or about my years in the emergency room. It was a feeling that was impossible to describe, a low-grade foreboding I learned to discount, but could never quite shake. If I believed in premonitions I would have called it just that, a premonition that something was coming to destroy the family I had worked so hard for so long to secure.

* * * * *

I would soon learn that there are some things no one can control.

The first blow came in my professional life.

It was a day like any other. The clinic was slammed. People stacked up in all the rooms. My practice was firing on all pistons. I'd taken a shot, believing that family practice and emergency room medicine could find a perfect harmony within the walls of my urgent care, and that shot had hit the bull's-eye. As they say, be careful for what you wish for because it might come true,. I had built the practice of my dreams.

But one day, in the midst of what I thought was my chrome-plated, bullet-proof existence, my billing person, Lindsey, walked into my office.

"What's up?" I asked.

"We've got a family that's having their claims denied."

"Okay, what's going on and who is the carrier?"

"Blue Cross. They say they're being denied because we didn't file on time."

The way it works is the physician's staff needs to provide the insurance company with a standardized form called the HCFA form—Health Claim Financial Admission. The form basically lets the insurance company know who the patient is and what medical services were performed. Blue Cross will pay the doctor for his services, only if this form is sent to the insurance company within the contractual allotted time, and in this particular case, twelve months after the doctor has performed services. If this doesn't happen, the company has a contractual right not to pay the claim.

"Did we send it out in time?"

"Yep. In fact, we sent them four times and never got a response. The claims department is on the phone right now. Can you talk to them?"

"Sure. No problem." I really didn't think it would be an issue. How could it be if we sent in the forms? "I'll talk to them and clear it up. What's her name?"

"Jennifer C."

"C? She doesn't have a last name?"

"Nobody has a last name at the insurance company. I don't think they want anybody to know who they are."

"Afraid somebody's gonna go postal on them?"

Lindsey shrugged. "Stranger things have happened."

I picked up the phone and said, "Hello Jennifer, I hear we've got a little bit of a problem with these claims."

"Yes, I'm sorry," she pleasantly replied. "We don't seem to have proof that the claims were sent out before the one-year deadline."

"Well, we've got the forms stamped with the date."

"Alright, fine. Just send us any proof you have and we will evaluate it."

"Okay, Jennifer, no problem. Thanks for your help."

"Thank you, Dr. Nordella."

I looked at the paperwork we had for the claims. It didn't seem to be a problem. It was stamped and mailed well before the one-year date that Blue Cross required. I had the office send out another copy and also wrote a cover letter explaining the circumstances, the conclusion of which read, "*SCV Quality Care has had an excellent relationship with Blue Cross of California for the last ten years as we see thousands of your subscribers. I therefore ask for your consideration in resolving this issue for the Warner family. If you have any questions please feel free to contact me at my office.*"

*Well that's easy,* I thought. Little did I know...

A few weeks later, Jennifer called back. This time her previously pleasant demeanor had just the slightest bit of an edge. As if she wanted to cut off any objection I might have, or else she was worried I would kill the messenger, or maybe a bit of both.

"Sorry, Dr. Nordella. We've received your proof of timely filing for the Warner family, but it is inadequate."

"Inadequate, how?"

"I'm sorry, but we will not be paying the claims."

I immediately knew I wasn't going to waste my time with Jennifer C.; I had patients to see. My clinic was backed up. The last thing I wanted to do was get into a petty argument over a few claims that amounted to less than nine hundred dollars.

"Please let me speak with your supervisor," I requested.

"Absolutely, please hold," Jennifer mildly replied.

Another person got on the line. "Provider relations, this is Juanita W," the voice announced, her tone clipped and steely. *Provider relations? I wondered. What the hell does provider relations have to do with an unpaid claim? Jennifer C. was from claims. I should have had a billing supervisor. How did I suddenly get over to provider relations?*

"Hello, Juanita. We seem to have a problem. My office sent in proof—"

"I am familiar with the case," she said, cutting me off. "These claims are too old. You are going to have to drop this matter."

"Why would I drop this?"

"Because your proof of timely filing is not acceptable."

"It's the only proof I have."

"That's why you should stop pursuing these claims immediately."

"That's not fair. It's not fair to us and it's not fair to the patient. They pay your premiums. I've done the work. We sent in the claims on time."

"Well, you can't prove it."

"I've given you proof."

"Your proof is not acceptable."

"Not acceptable, how?"

"It's just stamped."

"Are you saying I falsified the stamps?"

"I'm saying it's not acceptable."

"What would be acceptable?"

"You could send electronic copies."

"I don't have that kind of computer system. And even if I got one today, what are we going to do about these claims?"

"Nothing. They're not acceptable."

It was like talking to a robot rather than a person, a robot with only one computer chip that repeated, "Not acceptable" over and over and over.

"I don't understand. This proof has always been acceptable before. Why isn't it acceptable in this case?"

"The only way it would be acceptable would be if you had sent your claims by certified mail." Was she actually serious?

"What doctor sends you claims by certified mail?"

"I don't know. But that's what you'd have to do. But the claims are all now past due anyway. We will not be paying these claims."

It was like trying to knock down a steel door with a toothpick. And it made no sense. I averaged over a hundred claims a day. Did she actually think I would go to the post office and say, "Excuse me. Here's a hundred HCFA forms. Can you make them all certified?" Nobody does that. Nobody. Clearly they were establishing a standard that would be impossible to comply with, a standard that no other physician would ever do or does. This was just a way for them to not pay the claim. This was nothing more than a profit-saving strategy. If they did this occasionally with every doctor in their network, they could maybe save millions a year.

Besides, I was on the phone with provider relations. I'm the provider, the doctor. I had always assumed the Provider Relations department was supposed to be the ambassador of goodwill. Shouldn't the attitude be, "How can we help you, Dr. Nordella? We know you're out there busting your butt seeing all of our subscribers. Thanks to you we're making tons of money on your work. What can we do to make your life easier?" Instead, it was clear they were the tail, I was the dog, and they were going to wag me.

Finally understanding that this conversation was going nowhere, I knew I had to take a different tact. "What's your name?"

"Juanita W."

*Juanita W?* "What does the W stand for?"

"We do not give out our last names, Dr. Nordella."

"Okay, then, where do you sit in the company?"

"Why?"

"Because I need to know how to contact you. You leave me no alternative but to file a small claims court action."

There was a bitter silence on the other end of the phone, then, "You have no right to do that."

"Well, we'll have to wait and see about that." I hung up and looked at the phone. "Wow. Are you kidding me, provider relations? You really know how to cater to your doctors, don't you?" I said to the empty office.

What in the hell had just happened? I marched back to Lindsey's office, the claims clutched in my fist. "They're not going to pay for these."

"What do you want me to do?"

"Just hold onto them. I've got patients to see."

Three weeks passed. It seemed that whatever I was doing, seeing patients, playing with the kids, or talking with Carole, I kept running different scenarios about what I should do with the unpaid claims. *Should I drop it?* I wondered. It was, after all only a few hundred dollars. But the injustice of it kept hitting me in the gut. It just wasn't right. It wore on me. But was it really worth the effort to take Blue Cross to small claims court? Was I nuts for even considering it? One evening after seeing patients all day, I was working in my office when Audrey stepped inside.

"Dr. Nordella, a Dr. Garfinkle is on the phone for you."

I searched my mental computer. Garfinkle? Who was that? Audrey read my expression.

"He's a medical director at Blue Cross."

*Medical Director. What the hell is this about?* I'd never spoken to a medical director from any insurance company in my life. I picked up the phone.

"This is Dr. Nordella."

"Hello, Dr. Nordella, how are you today?"

"Fine," I said cautiously. "What can I help you with?"

"Dr. Nordella, we here at Blue Cross are concerned about providing quality healthcare to our patients."

"Okay..." I didn't like the sound of that. Like I *wasn't* concerned with quality healthcare?

"Yes, we care about the quality of healthcare for our subscribers and therefore, we wanted to just tell you we have some problems with you."

"Ah, huh... And what are those?"

"Well, you are billing for particular CPT codes." CPT codes are simply a code assigned to different types of treatments and medical services. I couldn't imagine why he was talking about CPT codes.

"You're a family practitioner, correct?" Garfinkle asked.

"I'm not a typical family practitioner. We are an urgent care center."

"Yes, well, I see here you seem to have an excessive amount of CPT codes for splints, which doesn't comply with the standard for family practitioners."

"That's because we see a lot of patients, several urgent care patients require splints. About 100 to 120 patients a day." I knew this was far above the average for a family practitioner whom treats about 20 to 25 patients a day.

"Yes, but as I said, the CPT codes were for splints. That's far above the average."

"Well," I said, gritting my teeth, "like I said, we have an urgent care, a medical walk-in center. More people than average come in with orthopedic problems." I remained very calm, but inwardly I was screaming questions at him. We had patients with broken legs, arms, and ankles. What did he want me to do? Not give a splint to someone with a fractured leg?

"It's not just the splints, but there are an excessive amount of X-rays."

My head was swimming. I just told him I was an urgent care. That meant not just splints, but X-rays, too. *Hello!*

"I'll repeat what I just told you. I am an urgent care. Urgent cares give X-rays. Typically, family practitioners do not bill CPT codes for X-rays because they don't have the equipment on site. They might send their patients to an imaging center or to the hospital."

He moved on as if he hadn't heard one syllable. "I see also that you have CPT codes for lab work."

"That's because I have a licensed lab in my office. If you'd read the HCFA form, you'd see that." Most family practitioners will send their patient across the hall or to another office for lab work, but I had invested thousands of dollars to have a lab and a full-time lab technician on the premises, licensed by the Department of Health, for the patient's convenience.

"We also see you're screening for cancer. That is also outside the norm."

"I just told you I have a lab. If I can pre-screen a patient for an early cancer diagnosis, that is good not only for the patient and their long term health, but also potentially in the best financial interest for the insurance company, wouldn't you agree?"

Silence.

"Well, the other doctors don't send us these codes."

"Of course they don't send them. That's because they send the order to the lab. Not to you. The lab would bill you, not the doctor."

"Well, our computers compared you to two hundred and twenty-five other family practitioners and we are concerned about false billing for those codes."

"False billing? I just told you I have a lab, and you know I have a lab. If you don't believe me, call the state and look up my CLIA license."

Again, another long silence, then, "We don't have to do that, Dr. Nordella. Our computers run very accurate comparisons. Again, we're just concerned about quality healthcare for our patients. We're afraid you're an over-utilizer."

Over-utilizer. There it was. The insurance industry term for: you provide *too much care* for the patients. And the inference was, I was providing services that weren't necessary. He was insinuating I was a crook. Or at worst, a quack that was giving medical care that wasn't necessary. I had suddenly had it.

"C'mon, you're not concerned about quality healthcare."

"Excuse me?"

"What you're concerned about is money."

"Oh no, that's not it. We're concerned about quality healthcare."

"Let's call this what it is. You're concerned I'm spending your profits."

"That is absolutely not true," he said, his previous business calm quickly evaporating. "Like I said, this is about quality healthcare."

"Ordering splints, pre-screening for cancer, ordering X-rays. All that costs you money and you don't like it," I said, going for the jugular.

"It has nothing to do with money! Like I said, this is about *quality healthcare*."

"You can call it anything you want, but we both know it's not about quality healthcare. It's cost containment healthcare."

"It is not!" he shouted and abruptly hung up.

I slowly laid the receiver back on the cradle, reeling. That phone call was nothing more than one thing: attempted intimidation. I thought to myself, *I wonder if provider relations told him about the first phone call when I had threatened to take Blue Cross to small claims court.* The message was clear to me: Back off. If you go to small claims court, we have the power to hurt you. We can brand you an "outlier," an "over-utilizer." So don't screw with us.

The conversation with Garfinkle infuriated me. On the one hand, it was a small amount of money, but on the other, it wasn't right.

I had a decision to make.

If I fought them I could be in for a bloody battle. But if I walked away with my tail between my legs, I'd be like all of those other physicians, the ones who bitched and moaned about the insurance industry strong-arming physicians. The same physicians who constantly complained and did nothing about it. Besides, it wasn't in my upbringing and it certainly was not in my DNA just to lie down and take the abuse. And for what, all to protect their profits over their subscriber's healthcare? I didn't think so.

I just needed the boss's approval.

I talked to Carole about it that night over dinner.

"A medical director?" Carole asked.

"Yep."

"Why would he call you? You've never heard from a medical director before, have you?"

"Nope."

"So why is Blue Cross doing this now?"

"Because I threatened to take them to small claims court. And miraculously they just happened to identify me as an over-utilizer, isn't that convenient?"

"*What?*" she said, starting to sound just as exasperated as I had felt.

"Thank you."

"What do they expect you to do? Just drop it?"

"I think that's exactly what they expect me to do."

"And if you don't?"

"Well, he didn't come right out and threaten me, but he also left a lot of room for reading in between the lines."

"What could they do if you don't drop it?"

"I'm not exactly sure."

"You sound like you pissed them off."

"I'm sure I did, but I wasn't going to take any of their bullshit."

"I can't believe an insurance company would be so unethical. It's not right, Jeff."

"Agreed."

I could see Carole had her back up.

"So how do you feel if I take them to small claims court?" I asked her.

"I'm right behind you."

It was a go! That was all I needed. The bully in the schoolyard was about to have his nose bloodied.

\* \* \* \* \*

I alerted my staff to get together all the paperwork I needed to go to small claims court. I also contacted my private attorney, Tris Cannon.

"So do I have a right to take them to court?"

"Of course you do. They'd prefer you to go to arbitration, but you're not compelled to do that."

"What do we need to do, Tris?"

"We file and then we serve Blue Cross."

Tris put the legal wheels in motion. Not long after Blue Cross was served I got a call from Blue Cross' legal department. Idiot that I am, I actually thought, *Finally. Someone from the legal department is looking at this. They'll realize how stupid this is, process the claims and get this thing done with.* I guess I'm very naïve.

"I'm hoping Blue Cross will see how unnecessary all this is," I tried to reason with the Blue Cross paralegal. "Why don't you just pay these claims and everyone can move on."

"I don't have the authority to authorize anything," the Blue Cross paralegal claimed.

"You're the *legal department.*"

"That is true, but I still can't authorize payment. That's up to Blue Cross."

"But you *are* Blue Cross."

"I'm the legal department."

It was the runaround all over again. "Why are you doing this?" I flatly asked.

"Doing what?"

"Pissing off one of your primary care doctors. I service thousands of your subscribers. You're creating all this bad will on one stupid set of claims."

Of course, she wasn't about to answer anything directly. Instead she went back to square one. "I just want to inform you that you don't have a right to take Blue Cross to small claims court."

I took a deep breath. "I disagree and so does my attorney. We'll see you in court."

Now I was angry. This was unjust to me and more importantly, to the patient. Blue Cross wasn't welching on just one visit, but numerous visits. And then they had the nerve to tell me I didn't have a right to take them to court. It was nothing more than bald-faced intimidation. I didn't want any of this, but it was placed on my plate. If they were going to serve it up, then I was going to make a meal of it. Next stop, small claims court.

* * * * *

*Dec 27, 1999. Valencia Courtroom.*

It was a mild 65 degrees, overcast and grey, as Tris and I walked into the large city courtroom. I was glad Tris had made the trip. Even though he wasn't there to represent me, knowing he was there for moral support helped calmed my nerves somewhat, if not completely. We walked inside to find the place packed with clusters of defendants and plaintiffs whispering amongst themselves as they waited their turn to be called before the judge. I noticed that I recognized quite a few faces. I nodded to one husband and wife as Tris and I found our seats and settled in.

"You know those people?" Tris whispered.

"Not just them. I've treated a lot of people in this room." I never expected to go to court on such a contentious and personal matter, especially in front of people who trusted me with their wellbeing. I wasn't a fan of airing dirty laundry, and this felt like staging a major washday with other patients in attendance. I could read their curious stares—*what is my doctor doing here?* However, there was no way I was backing out now. If I had to face Blue Cross in front of patients then so be it. After waiting for nearly an hour, the bailiff finally announced, "Jeffrey Nordella M.D. vs. Anthem Blue Cross."

All the whispering immediately stopped. Heads turned.

"Looks like you're the main event," Tris whispered, as I gathered my paperwork. "Good luck."

I approached the judge, my rarely worn dress shoes echoing on the hard floor, all eyes in the audience tracking my every step. I stood before the judge, the Blue Cross legal rep finding her place at my side. The judge, a harried looking middle aged man with a ruddy complexion and a bad shave job, continued to shuffle through the piles of paperwork on his desk, not bothering to look up as he addressed me.

"Okay, Dr. Nordella, tell me what this is all about."

"I'm here to request payment on medical services rendered from Blue Cross of California. All claims were billed in the contractual timeframe required by Blue Cross, Your Honor."

"Do you have any paperwork for me?"

"I do," I said. I extended a fistful of paperwork to the bailiff. The judge pursued the papers as I continued, "Those are the stamped and dated claims. As you can see, they were submitted well within Blue Cross' one-year timeframe, which makes Blue Cross responsible for payment."

The judge eyed the papers and nodded.

"And what does Blue Cross have to say about this?"

"Your Honor, Dr. Nordella has no contractual right to be here."

This got the judge's attention. He looked up over his glasses, scowling at the Blue Cross paralegal. "Is that so?" he snapped.

"Yes, Your Honor. He signed a contract with Blue Cross holding him exclusively to arbitration. Also, these claims are too old and beyond the statute for collection for Dr. Nordella to pursue."

"He may have signed a contract to that effect, but he *does* have a right to be here," the judge rifled back, obviously not a fan of anyone telling him who did and did not have a right to be in his courtroom.

I felt a wave of relief. One point for me.

"But," he continued, his eyes once more scanning the papers, "it appears that Blue Cross is right. These claims look too old to me." His hand reached for his gavel, ready to make a ruling in Blue Cross' favor.

"Your Honor," I spat, anxious to get my point across before he dismissed the case. "I did some research on that."

The judge wasn't too happy about my interruption.

"You did, huh? And I'm sure you're going to tell me what that research said, aren't you?"

I swallowed hard and continued. "All medical claims have a four-year statute of limitations. The patient I'm advocating for had activity on their account as of six months ago, so that puts me well within the statutes, and I believe I do have a right to be here looking for judgment."

I could feel the air being sucked out of the room. The judge looked up, his mind searching his own internal legal library as he mulled it over.

"You know, you're right about that, Dr. Nordella. I seem to remember that medical bills do have four years."

"What does Blue Cross have to say to that?" the judge asked, now almost amused by this turn of events.

The Blue Cross paralegal slid an exasperated look my way before she addressed the judge. "He still doesn't have the right to be here, Your Honor."

"I already made my decision about that, counsel," he chided with a poisonous scowl. "Pay the claim."

Down came the gavel.

"Next case!" he growled, grabbing up the next stack of paperwork.

"Thank you, Your Honor," I breathed in shock.

I looked toward the Blue Cross paralegal, but she quickly turned her back and hurried from the courtroom.

I floated down the aisle toward Tris. Again, all eyes in the courtroom followed me. One elderly woman in a faded yellow pantsuit nodded with a smile as I passed. Another guy, a large weathered man in a worn but pressed work shirt actually gave me a subtle thumbs-up.

Tris smiled as he joined me to walk out. "I thought everyone was going to burst out into applause," he whispered.

"Guess I'm not the only one who's had a run in with the insurance company."

I took another deep breath as we stepped out into the grey day. I did it. I had actually won. I had beaten Blue Cross.

But it was a small victory. The war had only begun.


Months later Lindsey tiptoed inside my office. She had that look that told me something was very wrong. Again.

"We're getting hundreds of these."

She handed me a paper. "Requests for medical records?"

"It's happening on about fifty percent of all the Blue Cross claims."

It was clear what was happening.

I was on audit by Blue Cross.

Even though they never officially notified me I was on audit, as per their own contract, the audit was nevertheless happening.

The way I saw it, the intention of the audit was purely retaliatory and meant to crush my business.

Blue Cross started demanding medical records on hundreds and hundreds of claims. These medical records were then "reviewed" by a staff of medical doctors, one of them Dr. Garfinkle, the same medical director who had hung up on me months ago. The same medical director I accused of caring about profits rather than their own subscribers. After these claims were reviewed, what happened?

**Denied.**

Claim after claim was denied, most of them being denied on the grounds of being "not medically necessary." I thought back to Garfinkle's staunch contention that his only objective was "quality healthcare." Denying patients' claims? What kind of "quality care" was that? But it just kept happening. Like a big automatic rubber stamp falling from the Blue Cross heavens: *Boom! Boom!* No, not medically necessary. Over and over.

These denials were as infuriating as they were outrageous. First of all, per Blue Cross' contract, all emergency care is automatically considered medically necessary because it is an emergency. In other words, if you go into an ER, whether it's for a sore throat or a gunshot wound, you will be treated and your insurance company will pay because you, as the patient, have deemed it to be an emergency health situation. Because I had an urgent care and the majority of my patients were walk-ins, they were also deeming their medical situation to be an emergency. Most insurance companies understand this and honor all claims, even though they also discourage their clients from visiting the emergency room by saddling them with high fees and co-pays.

Secondly, the claims Blue Cross continued to deny as "not medically necessary" were absolutely ludicrous. For example, they denied an EKG on a twelve year old patient with chest pain—very, very rare for a young child, *and* the EKG was ordered by his pediatric cardiologist. They denied throat cultures on people who had pus on their tonsils. They denied X-rays on a patient unable to walk after suffering an ankle injury, and a patient complaining of neck pain after a car accident. They denied antibiotics for a patient with a dental abscess, a pregnancy test for a woman who had pelvic pain and breast tenderness, and a fracture boot for a patient who had a foot fracture. The list went on and on. One denial more ridiculous and unfounded as the next. It was crazy. And all these denials came from a "peer reviewer" who never saw any of these patients face to face, and never examined the patient, but yet made the determination from reviewing a piece of paper.

It was my opinion that Blue Cross actions were purely vindictive and violated the "standard of healthcare." They were most definitely out to get me.

The additional paperwork necessary, all the copying and mailing of medical records, was a huge burden on my staff. As for me, I dove in writing appeal after appeal on behalf of the patients, explaining the plainly obvious reasons why I had ordered each medical service on case after case after case. As soon as I got home after doctoring all day, my new job became writing these appeals. In the meantime, while Blue Cross was putting me through the wringer, all the other insurance companies I worked with never questioned me. Never audited me. Nothing.

I wasn't the only one who was reeling from the audit and avalanche of denied claims. Of course, the patients were just as angry but confused as well. While some sympathized with my predicament and knew the care I had given them was obviously medically necessary, just as many were understandably angry and they directed it at me. All they knew was what Blue Cross was telling them, that I was giving them care and prescribing treatment that was not necessary. They thought I was doing something shady or wrong.

But I hadn't changed the way I treated my patients. I was the same doctor who never had a problem with any patient or insurance company. But that was before I ruffled Blue Cross' feathers. But, in my opinion, the worst part of it all was that Blue Cross placed the patients smack dab in the middle of their fight to destroy me. With each denial, Blue Cross sent letters out to the patients. The letters basically said that a retrospective review showed that I provided medical services that were not medically necessary. But, it continued, the good news is, you don't need to pay for it!

But that was a lie.

The truth was, under the contract, doctors can bill for non-covered services, which include "medically unnecessary" services. But what Blue Cross was doing by sending out their letter was telling the patients, "Hey, Dr. Nordella treated your ear infection, your fractured wrist, your fill-in-the-blank medical problem, but don't worry about it. It's not medically necessary because we say so, so you don't need to pay for it." So, bottom line, the medical practice would be paid nothing for services rendered in good faith. How about that for getting screwed?

Even still, I refused to bill the patients for anything. I didn't think it was fair they should pay out of their pocket what Blue Cross should have been paying me. My patients paid an exorbitant amount of money for their insurance premium and the insurance company shouldn't be putting them in the middle.

Not getting paid was one thing, but even worse, the letters Blue Cross sent out were effectively and systematically destroying my business, creating a tremendous amount of bad will within the community. Santa Clarita is a small town. Just as the good word spread across the community when I started my practice, the bad word was spreading like a firestorm and my practice was soon in flames. The waiting room started to empty out and the phones stopped ringing. My bank account was plummeting. Before long, I was forced to use my own personal savings just to keep the practice afloat.

Going to the market was no longer fun. Before the audit I used to enjoy running into patients and sharing a friendly chat. After the audit

I'd see patients but didn't get the same enthusiastic hellos. I started to wonder, what did they think of the letters they were getting? What did they think of me as a doctor? Did they think I was a crook, a quack, or both?

My business continued to take a nosedive. I knew I had to do something. This could not continue or I would lose everything. Again, I went to Tris.

"What do I do? Do I take all of these claims to small claims court?"

"No, that doesn't make sense. You could set up a meet and confer with Blue Cross. You've got to hope they want to work this out with you instead of just continuing to piss on your boot and tell you it's raining."

"What's a meet and confer?"

"Basically, it's going to give you a forum to work this out. A way to talk to them."

"Talk to them? They haven't reversed one appeal I've filed. They think they're gods."

"But if you play their game and go through this meet and confer and it's unsuccessful, it'll set you up to litigate."

"Litigate? I don't want to have to go there."

"I know, but a billion dollar company like Blue Cross isn't used to backing down, especially for one measly doctor. This is the classic example of the 'tail wagging the dog.' You might have no recourse *except* to litigate."

"You just finished pointing out that they're a billion dollar company. How am I supposed to take them on?"

"Carefully?" he tried to joke. But we both knew it wasn't funny.

This whole situation burned me. I hated the idea that they knew they were harassing me unfairly and had no intention of stopping. I knew this problem wasn't isolated to only me. Many of my fellow doctors had complained about the insurance companies deciding what was best for their patients while the payouts to doctors decreased and premiums rose. The insurance company had slithered in between the patient and the doctor and the patients were suffering. In the meantime, insurance company profits were increasing to obscene levels.

"What they're doing isn't right. They're lying to the patients and making it seem like I'm the bad guy."

"I know. And I would guess they know that too. But the question is, how far are they willing to go to put you in your place? If you'd just shut up and walk away, this all might end, you know."

"You know me, Tris. I don't have those kind of genes."

"Okay, but I want to tell you something. Litigation is like dipping your hands into the bucket of tar, you will never get it all off."

He was right, but I never knew just how right he was. Regardless, I was going to move forward. I had too.

* * * * *

Arriving at Blue Cross headquarters for the meet and confer in Woodland Hills, California, was like approaching Emerald City. Surrounded by sprawling lawns, trees, and perfectly manicured gardens, the towering cement and glass edifice distinguished itself from other surrounding skyscrapers, proudly standing alone like the crown jewel of corporate greed.

Winding our way through the pristine grounds, I turned to Tris. "I wonder how many denials it took to build this place."

"And they say there's no money in healthcare," he smirked.

We arrived at the only public entrance to find it manned by a stone-faced guard. *What exactly are they guarding against?* I wondered. Disgruntled subscribers? Angry doctors? Now it became evident why they don't release their last names. Entrance into the building was limited to only the chosen. The receptionist found our names, checked our ID's, called into the corporate brain, and finally allowed us access. I felt as if I was walking into CIA headquarters rather than an insurance company.

The offices were plush. The workers bent silently over their work like drones inside the mother ship, almost invisible behind mountains of papers and files. Tris and I were led through a labyrinth of hallways to a spacious boardroom where Dr. Garfinkle and Dr. Spaulding were already seated at one end of the long, polished table along with the paralegal I recognized from the small claims court.

Dr. Garfinkle, a lean, straight-backed man with well-groomed white hair, slacks, and a perfectly pressed button down, nailed me with a quick stare before he looked away, almost as if he was reacting to some noxious fume that had just entered the room and invaded his precious space. Dr. Spaulding, short, balding, and portly, in a slightly crumbled grey suit, reminded me of a grumpy grandpa, complete with a few pesky hairs growing out of his ears and a permanently taciturn expression stamped across his wrinkled mug.

The legal rep nodded to us. "Good morning, if you're ready, we'd like to begin."

No pleasantries. Just the thinnest scrim of civility. *Let the games begin.*

"Since you have denied us the use of a third party court reporter, we would like to tape these proceedings," Tris announced without skipping a beat.

"No," said the paralegal. "I'll take the minutes."

"Alright. I'm sure you won't mind if I take my own notes as well," he said pulling out a pad and pen. "And what is your name?" he asked, nodding toward Garfinkle.

"Dr. Garfinkle," he sniffed, obviously put off.

"And you?"

"Dr. Spaulding," Spaulding snapped, already fed up with the proceedings.

"How do you spell that?"

"Like it sounds," he growled.

"Well, I could spell it with or without a 'U.' Which is it?"

"How it *sounds*," he barked, as he and Tris traded poisonous stares.

Dr. Garfinkle turned toward me. It was a silent challenge. The look told me that they would not tolerate this meeting, but they are in charge. Say what you will, but we run the show.

Straightening in his chair, Dr. Garfinkle began to orate, "The purpose of this meet and confer is to bring together Blue Cross and Dr. Nordella in the hopes of establishing common ground. Surely a reciprocal relationship built on trust is the benchmark we are all striving toward and to that end we find ourselves in a position that demands authenticity."

*What the hell is he pontificating about?* I wondered. Garfinkle continued to drone on and on. A lot of words, but not a lot of meaning.

"Can I just stop you for a minute?" Tris interrupted. "Can we just talk bottom line here? No sugarcoating? How can we get Blue Cross to stop with the denials of *necessary* medical treatment?"

Garfinkle cleared his throat, and proceeded like the king casting pearls of wisdom before swine. "Blue Cross would disagree that the treatment is necessary."

Just then Spaulding blurted, "Dr. Nordella's an over-utilizer."

"Really? And how is that?" Tris questioned.

"Well, our information indicates that he provides general medical exams," Garfinkle continued, "which, for the layperson might be known more simply as a physical examination, to an excess of thirteen hundred percent."

"Wait a minute," I said, quickly doing the mental math. "Are you actually trying to tell me that for every one physical the 'average' doctor performs, I do one in thirteen hundred? How is that possible? I must be one hell of a busy guy."

"Our evaluations are based on an extremely sophisticated matrix of medical data that is then computed with the most efficient and cutting edge technology," Garfinkle preached.

Tris and I studied the printout the paralegal had handed over. At the top of the printout under the Blue Cross heading was the number 225 and next to it the words, *family practitioners.*

"So did you compare him to the 225 physicians or is 225 the code number you use to signify a category for family practitioners."

Garfinkle stared, puzzled. "I don't know."

*Well, if you don't know, who the hell does?* I wondered.

"I don't see any evidence of over-utilization," Tris said, trying a different tact. "Just the numbers. Where does it show the over-utilization on Dr. Nordella's part?"

"Excuse me?" Garfinkle sniffed.

"The proof. Where is that?" Tris said between clenched teeth.

"We don't need proof. You have the numbers right there."

It was obvious to me they had no intention of telling the truth. There would be no airing out of differences. It didn't matter what Tris or I said, this meeting was pure artifice, or better yet, a witch-hunt.

This was my mock trial before they burned me at the stake.

For the rest of the meeting they focused on one of the denied cases, a woman I treated for pneumonia. She was a mother of three children and had begged me not to admit her to the hospital because her husband couldn't take off work to care for their kids if she were to be hospitalized. So, per her wishes, I treated her without hospitalization with daily antibiotic injections and her pneumonia had cleared up nicely. However, Blue Cross had denied her treatment as "not medically necessary." The woman was appalled and had written Blue Cross telling them how happy she was with her care and how effective my care was.

But that wasn't good enough for Blue Cross.

Dr. Garfinkle had still denied her claim calling it "not medically necessary."

To make matters worse, Tris asked them what course of treatment he would have prescribed. His suggested treatment was not only archaic, it appeared to me to be wrong. But they were correct on one point: their treatment was certainly cost-contained. It was *cheaper.* Something upon which Blue Cross apparently thrived.

As I listened to Garfinkle lecture me on how to be a doctor, I could feel the flush start to creep up my neck. I knew my diagnosis and treatment were spot on. In fact, I had an outside specialist confirm that I had taken the right course of action. And I had sent them that proof months ago.

"What about the intensivist's records I sent you?" I asked.

"Oh, we never received that," Garfinkle replied.

I had anticipated that lie and was ready to counter. "Good, I brought you a copy, here you go." I passed the evaluation down to both the doctors. They traded a look and Dr. Spaulding waved his hand dismissively over the proof.

"I'll look at that later," he sniffed.

That's when I lost it. "It's very clear that there's not a 'meet and confer' going on here."

"I don't know what you're trying to insinuate, Dr. Nordella," Dr. Garfinkle said.

"I'm not insinuating anything. I'll tell you in plain English. You're falsely accusing me of over-treating patients through unfounded statistics. You're unethically denying patients the care they need and deserve through your medical necessity reviews. You clearly are not up-to-date on the standard of healthcare in our community. Bottom line, you're figureheads for the insurance company. The only thing you care about is keeping your master happy by making them money." I stood to my feet, Tris quickly following my lead. "This meeting is over."

As we walked down the garden path of the Emerald City for the car, Tris just shook his head.

"Corporate America, dude. At its finest."

"Yep. The true power of Blue. Just like the commercial says."

Weeks later, the audit escalated to 100 percent. Every single Blue Cross patient was placed under medical review. I guess I didn't make a good impression.

I started talking to other doctors I knew and later did the research. I came across some testimony from a former medical reviewer for Humana who testified at the House Oversight Committee during the health care reform debate. She talked about a "hassle factor" employed by insurance companies to get their doctors to adhere to cost-effective methods of healthcare. She actually attended a company meeting in the mid-1990s which she called a "lecture on the psychology of physician behavior." She said, "The idea was that if we just kept grinding them down and fighting tooth and nail for everything, they would get either too busy or too hassled or too beaten down, or just wouldn't care. That's exactly what happened over the years."

I couldn't believe what I was reading. Was I caught in the cross-hairs of a nationwide crusade to indoctrinate doctors to provide less healthcare, which means more profit for the insurance industry? Not only was this unethical, but potentially disastrous for the health of the American public.

Over the past few years there's been a dramatic rise in incentive-based medicine. My research showed that doctors receive bonuses for providing care recommended by insurance companies and Anthem Blue Cross also incentivized medicine as well. Just recently, Anthem offered a program that rewards oncologists with $350 *per month* for *every cancer patient* they treat using the insurance company's recommended standardized chemotherapy formulary. Considering that a good oncologist could treat up to a hundred patients a month that equals serious money. It could make even the most ethical doctor think twice about the value of using the insurance company's incentivized chemo regime. But what happens if the treating physician thinks this care doesn't apply to each patient? Will the insurance company harass, audit, or even kick these doctors out of their networks just because they might deviate from the insurance company's standardized, cheaper care program?

Additionally, some insurance companies now rate physicians in their networks based on their claims data. They profile physicians on the basis of how much the doctor bills the insurance company. The less expensive physicians, meaning minimal billing to the insurance company, are given a higher rating and are highly recommended to the public via the computerized provider finder. So who's really practicing medicine here, the physicians or the insurance company?

And where is the patient in all of this? A patient almost inherently trusts his doctor to give him the best care possible. But nearly no one in the general public understands just how linked insurance company profit is to each individual decision a doctor makes for his patient. Little does a patient know if a doctor is being molded by the insurance company to give out inferior medication, or is secretly holding back on ordering that CT scan, MRI, X-ray, or even worse, avoiding prescribing treatment at all, all so he or she can rise further in the insurance-driven rankings and thereby increase his own profits by receiving more patients.

The result? Insurance companies were essentially forcing doctors to be insurance company men rather than patient advocates.

And I was in the middle of their indoctrination program. They had one objective: wear me down until I bent to their will.

Up until then I hadn't asked one dime from the patients. Like I said, it wasn't fair that the patients suffered the fallout from the bomb Blue Cross had detonated. But by then I was really scraping bottom. I felt helpless. Frustrated. Depressed. Pissed. I tried to compartmentalize as much as possible and not bring my worry about the business home to Carole and the kids.

Everything I had I had by busting my ass to get it. I'd always believed if I worked hard enough I would be rewarded, but now...? No matter how hard I worked, no matter how many appeals I wrote to Blue Cross justifying the care I was giving patients, it didn't matter.

One night, lying in bed staring at the ceiling for yet another sleepless night, Carole's voice cut through the darkness.

"Honey, what's wrong?"

"Nothing. Go back to sleep."

"Jeff…" She rolled over, laying an arm across my chest. "Talk to me."

I lay there for a long while. I didn't want Carole to worry. But I didn't know how much longer I could go on shouldering this kind of weight. I decided to come clean. "I don't know what to do. We're losing the business."

Carole was quiet, then, "How long has it been since you've been fully paid on Blue Cross claims?"

"To the best of my knowledge, almost two years."

"You need to go to your patients. Tell them what's going on."

"I can't."

"Why?"

"I hate putting them in the middle. This shouldn't be their fight, too."

"They know you're a good doctor. They know you treated them. They've got to know you deserve to be paid. If not by the insurance company, then by them."

"They shouldn't have to. It's not—"

"—right. I know it isn't. But what other choice do you have?"

She was right about that. What other choice did I have?

I went to Tris the next day.

"I can't keep going like this," I told him over a cup of Starbucks coffee. "I've taken out all my personal savings just to support the practice."

"Is there a question wrapped in all of that?"

"Do I have a right to bill the patients?"

"Absolutely."

"You think I should send a letter to them explaining what's happening?"

"I think it's a good idea."

And we did. It was a bitter pill to swallow, but I just told them the truth of what was happening and asked them to reimburse me for the basic fee the insurance company allowed for the care I'd given them. I'd also done a little maneuvering and managed to get Dr. Lester Garfinkle's direct phone number at Blue Cross. Not only did I draft a letter telling my patients about what was going on with Blue Cross, but I also told them if they wanted to know why Blue Cross was denying all their claims, calling their treatment "not medically necessary," they should give Lester a ring. I sent the letter out to over a thousand patients.

Oh my God, Lester got inundated with phone calls. But did he ever tell them the reason for the denials? Not that I was aware of. No, he just slandered me, insisting the care I was giving was unnecessary and informing the patients that I was being investigated and that legal action was going to be taken against me.

The letter to my patients however, understandably generated a lot of questions. Many patients wanted to know why I was billing them when they had just received a letter from the insurance company saying they didn't have to pay at all. One afternoon a patient marched right into an exam room, bristling.

"I don't care what's going on. Just as long as I don't have to pay for it."

"Well, then if you don't want to pay for the care I'm giving you, you'll need to stop coming. If you want to call somebody, call Garfinkle," I told him.

Some did, some didn't, but in the end, it was all a hot, steaming mess. I could feel everything slipping away.

Jamie: *Dad did a really good job, even in the really busy days of the practice, coming home and leaving work at work and being present. We'd always watch Dodger games at night and eat Rocky Road ice cream and he was always very much like, "Okay, now I'm home. I'm in Dad mode, husband mode." But when everything started happening with Blue Cross it was the first time I saw him really stressed out. I remember my mom and dad were just talking in the kitchen after dinner and we were just kind of doing our thing, but I looked over and my dad just kind of lost it for a second. It was the first time I'd ever seen my dad cry. He would have never let us see that, but it he knew it was getting really bad.*

Kristen: *My dad started going through a really big change. When I was little he was fun and funny and would wrestle with us, and was laughing all the time. But as we got older he was so concerned for our safety that he was worried all the time for us. He just wasn't the fun playful dad anymore. He would go to work, and then he'd come home and be stressed—and just not happy. I'm sure a lot of that had to do with the lawsuit. I started walking on eggshells all the time. It was just tense. "Is he in a good mood? Is he in a bad mood? Can we ask him if we can do this?" Nope, forget it, just don't even try.*

After I sent out my patient letter requesting payment I followed up with another letter, or more accurately, an invoice, this one to Blue Cross. It itemized all the expenses I had incurred because of their audit: time, paper, stamps, extra personnel hours for the two-year period they had me on audit.

I'm not sure if my invoice was the last straw, but in November Blue Cross hammered the final nail into my dying practice.

They terminated my contract.

# Chapter 12

## The Storm Within the Storm

Before Blue Cross had reared its ugly head, I had promised the kids, Carole, and Mom that we would take the trip we'd all been dreaming about for years: Hawaii. Unfortunately, I had originally planned the trip for soon after the 9/11 terrorist attacks. Like so many other travelers, I felt uncomfortable about flying, so I postponed the vacation. Finally, about a year after the attacks, I went ahead and purchased plane tickets and made hotel reservations. The problem was, when the time for our Hawaiian vacation arrived, I had just been terminated by Blue Cross.

"To be honest, going to Hawaii is the last thing I want to do," I told Carole one morning over coffee when the kids were off doing their lessons.

"I know, but they're going to be crushed if you cancel again. All they can talk about is going to the beach and playing on those water slides. And I know your mom was really looking forward to it, too. She was just talking about what she was going to wear yesterday."

"How can I justify living it up in Hawaii when the practice is in turmoil? I can't even make payroll."

Carole and I sat with that for a bit, and then Carole shrugged.

"It's completely up to you. But everything's already paid for. If we don't go, we'd lose the money and a lot of memories, too."

She had a point and family first was always the bottom line.

She took a sip of coffee, smiling over her cup at me. "Besides, it might be good for you. Get your mind off all the bad stuff for a while."

She was right. I needed a break. The problems with Blue Cross and my failing business had been consuming me. I felt like I wasn't nearly as present for the kids and Carole as I'd wanted to be. Maybe Hawaii would be the perfect remedy, even though it did seem counterintuitive to leave in the midst of everything going on.

"You think I could learn how to hula?" I joked.

"I'd pay big money to see you in a grass skirt," Carole said, laughing.

"Ok, stop right there."

We started packing.

The morning of the trip, after Mom had begun the drive to my house, my brother, who was living with my mother at the time, called me.

Sounding panicked he blurted, "You can't go."

"What are you talking about? We're waiting for the airport shuttle now."

I turned away from the family so they wouldn't hear the conversation.

"Listen, I know it sounds crazy, but I had this feeling for the last couple of days."

I was annoyed. Was he really calling me an hour before we were supposed to leave? "What kind of feeling?"

"I don't know. Like a premonition. Like something bad is going to happen."

No one likes to hear something like that before going on the vacation that's been planned for three years. Even if it *did* sound a little crazy.

"What do you expect me to do?"

"I think she should stay home. You guys can still go, but mom should stay behind."

I looked over as my mom arrived. The kids welcomed her with open arms, a blissful scene. She'd never been on a trip like this, at least not since her stint in the USO, which was a lifetime ago. Plus, my brother had been very sick lately, though he certainly was able to stay by himself for a short time. He had become very dependent on Mom. Was his unconscious whipping up some phantom traumatic scenario just so he wouldn't be alone for the week?

"Everything's going to be fine. She deserves this trip. It's going to be fun for her. We'll be back in a week."

"I don't know, man. I don't have a good feeling about the whole thing."

David wasn't the only one with misgivings. I thought the kids would be excited to get on the plane and fly off to a tropical paradise, but when we arrived at the airport, Jeffrey, who was always the most sensitive of my kids, balked.

Jeffrey: *I don't know what it was, but I had this weird premonition. If we got on that plane, if we went to Hawaii, something terrible was going to happen. I didn't know what it was, but the feeling was overwhelming. I was beside myself. "We can't go to Hawaii. Something bad is going to happen. I know it," I told my parents. "I'm not going to get on that plane." My parents were like, "What is wrong with you? Why are you acting like this?"*

I wrote off Jeffrey and my brother's fears as irrational rather than prophetic. I wish I had listened to both of them.

The plane ride to Waikiki was uneventful, but the moment the wheels touched down on the runway, everything just felt off. I wasn't sure why exactly, but the bright skies and sandy beaches did little to allay a sense of unease that swept over all of us, settling into the corners of our minds like a fine, unshakable dust. The beaches were packed with tourists and after fighting for a place on the sand we opted to take a tour of Pearl Harbor. I expected it to be a great history lesson for the kids, as I'd become a WWII buff, but it just left us all feeling drained and depressed.

The next day I went to the beach with my mom while Carole stayed back at the hotel. I looked around at the sand, disappointed. It wasn't nearly as clean or pristine as the photos had portrayed. Maybe that was the Hawaii of fifty years ago, but not now. Mom didn't seem to mind, however. Going back to her Ester William swim days, she still loved to swim, even at seventy-nine. It was fun to see her swimming and diving in the waves, even if it was mobbed with tourists. But before long, a fight was breaking out on the beach between a tourist and a small gang of locals. This Hawaii seemed closer to the seedier parts of downtown LA rather than the Waikiki paradise I'd envisioned. I waded out into the ocean and took my mom's arm.

"C'mon. I'm not sure it's safe out here," I said, nodding to the scuffle on the beach.

"We could get some lunch," she suggested.

"Good idea."

We gathered Carole and the kids and popped across the street to a Subway. Everyone was inside ordering sandwiches while Jamie and I sat waiting on the bench outside holding down the table. Suddenly, a dirty, strung-out looking couple who appeared to be homeless got off a bus.

"What's he saying to her?" Jamie said as she watched, wide-eyed.

The young man went nose to nose with the frightened looking woman. "You bitch! I know you got with him! Don't lie to me!"

He raised his hand to her, ready to smack her. I felt myself tense and started to leap up to stop him.

"Dad, don't!" Jamie said, grabbing my arm.

"Jamie, just stay here."

"Dad, no! Don't leave me here!"

The guy continued to scream at her while she walked to her left then to her right trying to avoid him.

*Great. My family's in Subway and I'm going to get in a fistfight with a piece of shit.*

I couldn't wait any longer. I had to help her.

"Jamie, go inside and tell Mom to call 911." I took one step into the street and a cop cruiser pulled up. The couple spotted him and suddenly dropped their abusive couple act. They split up and ran for a departing bus. As quickly as they came they disappeared from view.

It dawned on me that this could have been a dog and pony show to attract a naïve Good Samaritan tourist like me, only so they could rip off whoever tried to help. It was just strange. Unsettling. I tried to let it go as we all headed back to the hotel pool. The only thing I did know was it was an ugly counterpoint to the perfect weather and the sound of my kids' laughter as they splashed in the pool. The kids waved to me and I waved back, unable to give them my full attention. It was a surreal feeling. Almost like I was in two places at once, yet nowhere all at the same time. Hawaii was turning out to be anything but paradise.

Kristen: *The first half of Hawaii was awful. It was bad. I was like,* Why is this so stressful? Does it have to be like this? We're supposed to be on vacation having fun. *We had this great picture of what Hawaii was supposed to be like and it was the opposite. It was just stressful and tense and dirty. And my dad doesn't like to be surrounded by crowds of people like going to Disneyland. It's not fun for him. He likes wide-open spaces. We just kept thinking,* We've just got to get to Maui. Everything's going to change once we get to the Grand Wailea.

The next morning, I announced, "Let's get the hell out of Waikiki." We flew to Maui and wound our way in the shuttle past the open landscape of foamy white waves and lush tropics on our way toward the Grand Wailea. Arriving on the island I took a breath of relief. This is what we'd come to Hawaii for. The Grand Wailea is a true five star resort filled with famous water slides, stunning greenery, and beautiful private beaches. What a difference from the gritty, tourist-choked streets of downtown Waikiki. This place catered to families just like us. Now we could finally relax.

"Let's get up early and go straight to the water slides," Carole suggested that night as we crawled into the clean, plush bed. "If we stay on LA time, we'll be starting before everyone else."

"Sounds good to me. Now our vacation can really start."

The next morning I got up at the crack of dawn and met with the concierge. She helped me lay out an amazing trip full of whale watching, paragliding, sailing, swimming with dolphins. *To hell with Blue Cross. I'm going to treat my family to the time of their lives,* I determined. Since it was 11:00 A.M. LA time, we were ready to hit the waterslides at 8:00 A.M. Hawaii time. But when we arrived poolside we found a sign. Closed until 9:00 A.M.

"Wanna hit the beach, guys?" I asked the kids, undeterred. Everyone was all for it. I rented some boogie boards and the kids and I raced out into the warm water. It really was paradise. Just me, Carole, the kids, and Mom, my heart's posse. We had the beach all to ourselves. Carole and Mom watched from the beach while I took the kids into the water. My mom gazed out toward the waves.

"It's so beautiful. Heaven can just wait," she said.

Carole wasn't sure if she was even talking to her. It was an odd, out of the blue, slightly ominous statement.

Kristen: *it was early and it was like baby waves and it was calm and peaceful. I mean, they were baby waves. Grandma came into the water with us and we took a wave together. We all came out of the wave and we couldn't find her. I turned and that's when I saw her floating. I thought she was joking. Playing a prank. I ran to her and picked her head up and found out that it was very much not a joke.*

Over the lazy crash of waves, I heard the kids' distant screaming. That's when I saw my mom floating face down near the beach. In that one instant everything froze and a thought materialized in my head stating, "Here we go." Like some level of my subconscious expected all of this and now I was started on a long torturous pathway. My dad had once told me about how he'd found his mother when she'd drowned, and this seemed eerily similar.

I started to run, the chest-high water like a liquid quicksand, dragging down at my limbs, my entire body moving in agonizing slow motion. It was like a nightmare, the ones where you have to run, but you can't, the effort leaving you panicked yet helpless. By the time I got to her and scooped her limp body into my arms, I knew it was bad. All I could think was I hadn't gotten there in time.

Kristen: *I was crying on the beach, like, "What just happened?" And there were people strolling by on the walkway right next to us. A complete stranger, a woman and her husband came up and were just staring at us. It was very uncomfortable. In a very poor attempt to comfort us the woman said, as if demanding it to be true, "It's fine! It's going to be fine! You're fine!"*

*I remember thinking,* I don't know you, and it's very much not fine. *I remember thinking,* What are you looking at right now? Like, go away. I don't know you. *It was all so harsh.*

On the sun-washed shores of Maui, Carole and I performed CPR on my mother because she was in full cardiopulmonary arrest for twenty minutes until the paramedics arrived. Mom was intubated and loaded into an ambulance. I rode with her, caught between feeling like a trained doctor and a terrified son. I kept an eye on the monitor; she now had a pulse and a low blood pressure. I held her hand, the muffled wail of the siren bleeding through my consciousness as if from another faraway universe. I continually talked to her.

Her eyes slowly opened.

She blinked.

"Can you squeeze my hand for me?" the paramedic instructed. She blinked, but remained perfectly still. "How about your foot? Can you wiggle your toes?" he tried. I could see the look of panic in her eyes. She glanced toward me, a tear sliding down her face.

"It's okay, Mom. We're gonna get you to the hospital," I said, trying to hold my voice steady, still winded from the marathon of CPR. Carole had been right by my side. We had worked like a finely tuned machine, keeping Mom alive until the paramedics arrived. I had forced myself not to think. *Just do what you were trained*, I silently instructed myself as we worked on her. But now, seeing my mother's still body, the plastic tube in her mouth forcing air into her lungs, I found it difficult to digest what was right in front of me.

As the ambulance sped its way toward the hospital, the paramedic continued through each diagnostic checkpoint, assessing damage, just as I had done with so many other patients that had come into the ER. A dull ringing sounded in my ears, blocking out his instructions as the reality crept over me.

She was paralyzed from the neck down.

She could no longer breathe on her own.

The paramedics whisked Mom into the ER. But this time I wasn't the doctor. This time I waited, just like so many frightened, shocked loved ones before me, in a small barren waiting room with the chaplain while the hospital staff finished my mom's workup. Standing there in my still soaking trunks, no shirt, and bare feet, my mind whirled.

*Why didn't I watch her better?* I chided myself. *Why didn't I give her my boogie board? Why did I take her to Hawaii to begin with? This is all my fault.*

I felt the cold breeze of the air-conditioner blow past my naked shoulders.

I began to shake and I couldn't stop.

"I'll get you a blanket," the Chaplin offered before he slipped out the door. I stood alone in the room and continued to tremble. There was nothing I could do but wait.

Finally, the doctor stepped inside the quiet room. He didn't need to say a word. The look on his face told me everything I needed to know.

Kristen: *Dad came back to the hotel. We were all there waiting in our room. "She broke her neck," he said. He cried very briefly, but then he just went somewhere else. I know he'd always been really close to his mom, but it was weird for me to see him in that state because that wasn't the dad I knew. I was twelve years old and it was the first time I'd ever seen my dad cry. I didn't think boys cried... ever. It was so weird for me, like, "Oh my gosh, he's crying!" My world was rocked.*

Mom was transferred to the ICU later that afternoon where she remained for four days. I couldn't bring myself to leave her side. Carole did her best to keep the kids distracted at the hotel, swimming, eating out, and exploring the island while I sat in the ICU, losing my mother.

I called UCLA Medical Center and arranged for a fixed-winged ambulance to fly from Santa Monica to Maui to pick Mom up and transport her back to UCLA Hospital. Her MRI confirmed that her second cervical vertebrae was fractured and unstable. It also confirmed that her spinal cord was partially torn. Realistically there were no treatment options for my mom.

When she had made her last dive in that Hawaiian ocean, she either hadn't known how shallow the water was or there was a sandbar just beneath the foamy surface of the wave. She dove head first into the sand and snapped her neck.

A tracheotomy was performed, replacing the tube in her mouth with a smaller, but more permanent tube through her neck. She couldn't eat or drink, so a gastrostomy tube was also placed directly into her stomach for nourishment. The neurosurgeon attempted to stabilize her neck by placing her in a halo, a monstrous steel apparatus that immobilizes the head with a series of screws drilled into her skull. The scalp was the only place she could feel and that was penetrated by steel rods. She looked so helpless, so small, trapped inside that steel halo, enveloped in a web of tubing, surrounded by whirling, beeping machines all working to just so she could take one breath, then another, then another.

I was approached by the social worker. "You know what her condition is, don't you?"

I nodded, knowing where she was going with this.

"I'm so sorry, Dr. Nordella. But the doctor and I have talked, and we both believe at this point, given the severity of her condition... given the quality of her life, well, we would recommend you might consider discontinuing her life support."

I steeled myself against the words that fell like hard stones into a bottomless well of pain. I remember leaning against the wall of the hospital corridor looking down at my shoes, unable to lift my gaze to meet the eyes of the social worker. It was impossible to think I was even having this conversation. She was talking about my *mother*. She was talking about *letting my mother die*. On one level, as a doctor, I agreed with the social worker. Her opinion made medical sense. As a doctor I would have recommended the same thing to a patient's loved one.

But as a son?

I couldn't let her go.

Mom was so much a part of me. She was my model of strength. She was the only light I had in an otherwise dark childhood. She was the woman who gave me her last $25 just to keep me going through school so I could reach my dream of becoming a doctor and save lives.

And now I was being asked to end hers?

Maybe I was being selfish. Maybe it would have been the kinder thing to let her go immediately. But it was all too much. I couldn't imagine a world without my mom in it. Surely, she could somehow miraculously overcome this. Just as she had overcome everything else in her life. I just couldn't make sense of all of it. I needed more time to process.

"I'm sorry. I just can't."

The social worker laid a sympathetic hand on my back. "I understand. We have resources. We'll do everything we can to help."

UCLA had done everything they could for my mom. I was assigned medical power of attorney and I had moved her to a rehabilitation center in Marina Del Ray. Hoping for a miracle I intellectually knew would never come, she showed no signs of improvement. She stayed at the rehab center for a week and remained incapable of speech and movement. The only thing left for her was to think about what her life had become. I was tortured by what those thoughts could be. Was she scared? Was there something she wanted to say? What did *she* want?

Her only form of communication was blinking: once for yes and twice for no. I explained to her many times, as simply but honestly as possible, what had happened. Even though she couldn't speak, I was sure she knew what was going on. I tried to stay upbeat when I was around her. "How you doing, Mom? You need anything?"

Two blinks. No.

I'd force a smile, hoping, praying that my words, or just my presence still made her life worth living. I was determined to do anything, say anything that would give her hope or even the slightest shadow of joy.

"You wouldn't believe what Jeffrey did today. You'd be so proud," I'd ramble, hoping news of the kids would lift her spirits. She would just stare, her thoughts and intentions a mystery. But I knew she was still there, which made it even more painful.

"You want to go home, Mom?" I finally asked her.

Blink. Yes.

How could I say the next words? But I had to. I had to let her know what it meant. "If I take you back there. You'll probably... it's going to be where you'll die. Do you understand that, Mom?"

...Blink. Yes.

I set to work in the house in Simi Valley. The same house I'd bought her all those years ago. The house that had brought her so much joy. The place she loved. It would now be the place she would die.

I pulled everything out of the living room. I set up a hospital bed, monitors, IV's. Everything she needed.

I also installed a ventilator.

The machine that would deliver one breath after the other.

The machine that would keep her alive.

I bought another refrigerator to hold all of the fluids, feedings, and medications she'd need. I scheduled a series of nurses to monitor her around the clock.

I had turned the home she loved, the home she had cried tears of joy over, into a hospital ICU.

But each day she seemed to drift further and further from me.

"How're you doing, Mom? Do you need anything?"

At first it would be a simple two blinks. No.

Then she began to stare away from me with her eyes, as though she were angry.

Next she simply closed her eyes, refusing to open them. Refusing to communicate.

I took Carole and the kids to visit. The kids approached her bedside on tiptoe.

"It's okay," Carole tried to encourage them, knowing how frightening it was for them to see their grandma like this. "Hi, Barbara..." Carole said, taking Mom's hand. "We're all here." Carole would talk and talk to Mom, the kids gathered mostly silent, by her side. Mom would listen and blink. But as the days wore on, even Carole or her beloved grandchildren weren't enough.

She was tired.

She was done.

After four weeks I knew the time had finally come. She had developed pneumonia and her blood pressure was gradually dropping. She was becoming septic, a sign of the body shutting down. It would be the last time my family would see my mother. Carole and the kids circled around Mom's still body. Seeing the people I loved most gathered in one place, saying their final goodbye to Mom cut deeper and sharper than any surgeon's blade. I'd never known this kind of pain. To see tears slip down Carole's face, to see the raw grief of my kids' faces, to see my proud, feisty mother so sick, so helpless.

It was unbearable.

Mom's brother and wife where present. Everyone crowded into the living room to share stories and final words of love. Carole led us in a whispered prayer, releasing my mother from this world and into God's hands.

Carole and the kids quietly slipped out as my uncle, his wife, and I stayed by Mom as her heart rate and blood pressure dropped, leaving her unresponsive.

I made sure she was comfortable. I didn't want her to struggle in any way.

There was no more cardiac activity.

"I love you, Mom," I said and discontinued her ventilator.

I had become a doctor with the help of the woman who had borne me, raised me, and loved me. And now that doctor couldn't do anything but allow nature to take its course. The pain of that irony left me with a visceral ache I wasn't sure I'd be able to bear.

Barbara Nordella died on April 6, 2003.

# Chapter 13

## Dr. Nordella vs. Goliath

While Mom was in the hospital at UCLA, I was talking to a colleague who told me about a doctor who might be interested in moving to Santa Clarita and purchasing my medical practice. Of course, at the time of my mother's illness, I wasn't in any frame of mind to even consider a conversation. But as the months passed after her death and my business continued to take a steady dive, I decided to meet this young doctor.

"If you come on board," I told him over a lunch meeting, "you have to obtain a Blue Cross contract. That way the patients will have the ability to return to the practice, and I'll work alongside you."

I gave him the option to lease the practice for a year, and then if he liked it he could buy it. He agreed. It nearly killed me to sign over the practice I'd worked so hard for. I spent my whole life on it, but what choice did I have? I still had a wife and family to support and without the Blue Cross contract that made up almost 60% of my business, I couldn't make a living. Also I could reestablish those long-term relationships I'd had with patients.

So I sold my practice at an incredible loss.

But I'd done what I'd needed to do in order to keep my family afloat and make an attempt to move forward with my life. It was an extremely dark time.

With each blow I felt myself at a new and unfamiliar low, but I was determined to deflect the hand of fate from slapping me across the face again. The way I saw it, Blue Cross felt they were above the law. But I didn't see it that way. I didn't care who they were. The bastards weren't going to get away with what they had done. I was willing to initiate a gentleman's version of a bar fight.

I would litigate.

My first thought was to go to Tris and ask him to represent me.

"I'm not a litigator," he told me. "But I can put some feelers out and help you find someone good."

Not nearly as easy as it seemed. Tris contacted firm after firm and none of them wanted to touch Blue Cross. "Too powerful." "Too risky." Or, "Sorry. Can't do it. Conflict of interest." What I later learned was that Blue Cross hedges their bets against any potential lawsuit by contracting with hundreds of top law firms across the country, feeding them small bits of business, thereby disallowing them to work for anyone else. It was like muzzling all the dogs with the sharpest teeth so they couldn't bite.

I met Tris at our local Starbucks. The hum of activity, people coming and going with double non-fat extra hot lattes, seemed almost surreal because of the noise inside my head. *How am I supposed to take on Blue Cross if I can't even find an attorney? What kind of attorney would take on Blue Cross to begin with? Is this insanity to even consider?*

"To be honest, Tris," I confessed over our paper cups, "I don't even know where I'm going with this."

"Hang tight, there's still an outside chance."

"You found someone?"

"Maybe. I don't know if she'll take the case. But she's willing to meet with us."

"Who is she?"

"Her name's Theresa Barta. She's worked with a high profile bad faith firm by the name of Shernoff and Bidart."

"Meaning?"

"The firm did a lot of litigation against insurance companies. She supposedly worked with a lot of doctors. She went out on her own not too long ago. She's supposed to be good."

"On her own? You don't mean it's just her, right?"

"I think she might have another guy in her office who does some writing and research, but yeah. She's small."

*A single doctor and a single lawyer against a multi-billion dollar insurance company. Okay, then.*

Tris read my expression. "I think she might be just what we're looking for."

"Well if I'm taking on a Goliath with a slingshot, I hope she has some heavy rocks."

Tris nodded. "Good. I already scheduled a dinner downtown."

Later that week I gathered a bunch of paperwork, put it in a box, threw a fifteen year old Member's Only jacket on over a polo shirt and shorts, my signature outfit, and took off for downtown LA. It never rains in Southern California, but when it does it isn't kidding. It was a torrential downpour. When I reached downtown I found the address, but there was no parking. Another Southern California trademark. I finally found a metered space blocks from the restaurant. I stepped out of the car and into the storm, of course with no umbrella. Weighed down by my cumbersome cardboard box, I sprinted for two blocks before I spotted Tris standing there perfectly dry in his pressed business suit under the awning of the swanky restaurant.

"I see you dressed for the occasion," he said, smiling and giving me the once-over. There I was looking like a drowned poodle. The cardboard box was so soggy I had to hold it from the bottom for fear of it ripping.

"Is this place fancy?" I asked, suddenly feeling self-conscious.

"Don't worry about it. It's a business meeting. We're not coming here to dine."

Turns out it was fancy. Elegant would be a better word—as in four star. I felt like the red haired stepchild as I shuffled up, leaving a trail of wet in the carpeted floor as we approached the maître d'.

"I'm Tris Cannon. We're meeting a Theresa Barta?"

The flawless maitre d' cast only the most surreptitious sideways glance before checking his list.

"Yes. She's already arrived. Follow me, gentlemen."

I hitched up the sagging box and followed the maitre d' past a long row of well-groomed businessmen and women, turning heads as I went, and not because people thought I had nice legs. It was everything I could do to stop myself from blurting out, "I'm not homeless. I promise." I finally caught sight of Theresa, seated alone at the back of the restaurant; her head bent over a legal brief. She looked every inch the professional: tall, short stylish hair, a beautiful yet intelligent face, razor sharp in her business suit. Theresa glanced up, saw me, and quickly returned to her brief. Hoping, I assume, we weren't her potential clients. Or if we were, hoping we'd just go away.

"Ms. Barta?" Tris asked.

She looked up again and managed a cordial smile. "Yes?"

"I'm Tris Cannon and this is Dr. Nordella."

"Nice to meet you," she managed.

I could tell she was trying to be nice.

Theresa: *It didn't surprise me when Jeff walked in, soaking wet, dressed in shorts and tennis shoes, lugging this huge box. Doctors are their own breed. I represent doctors who are neurosurgeons. I've represented skin cancer specialists, but they're all different. It's always a whole new experience just trying to figure out what area they practice in, what their issues are, and then who they are as a person. Jeff seemed like a pretty easygoing guy, but really, really passionate and fired up. As soon as I'd ask a question and needed just a little information he was ready to pull out files while we were still sitting there in the restaurant. He had done so much homework. He had everything highlighted and indexed and notated. And he'd written about a thousand appeal letters to the insurance company. It was impressive and frankly, pretty astounding.*

We hit it off. She could tell I was just a regular Joe, and I think she knew that I had passion and conviction. I also think the audacity of Blue Cross caught her attention. After looking through some of the denials, appeal letters, and then the trumped up excuse Blue Cross used for terminating my contract, she finally looked up a little shocked.

"Wow. I mean, wow," she exclaimed.

"I know…" It was exactly how I felt.

"So what do you think? Do I have a case?"

"Absolutely. It's called wrongful termination."

"Will you take it?"

She held out her hand and we shook. "You've got yourself an attorney, Jeff."

\* \* \* \* \*

As I opened the lawsuit against Blue Cross for wrongful termination, I had the highest of hopes. I really did believe that justice did exist. And I believed justice would be served. Ever since childhood, my philosophy was, if you've done something wrong, there were systems in place that would ferret out that wrong and the perpetrator would be punished.

The only system I knew of where that could be accomplished was a court of law. I was going to have to get an impartial third party to prove that what Blue Cross did was illegal. After all, this was America. All I needed to do was allow Lady Justice to do her work, couple that with my own determination and tenacity, and I'd get the justice I deserved.

I knew I had to fight, but I was ready for that. I saw my battle with Blue Cross as yet another obstacle to overcome. I didn't care that it was a billion dollar insurance company. They had lawyers? Well, I now had my lawyer, too. I was ready to dip my hands into that bucket of tar.

But as the legal process wore on, I realized there was much more at play than justice. There were forces at work, dark forces that I had never had to deal with before: politics, money, and corruption. All of those things were the antithesis of logic.

I soon learned that during law school, students are trained to think with a mindset that seemed to defy comprehension and common sense, at least to me. Throughout the entire process, I used to tell Theresa I didn't know how she did it. I didn't understand the system she worked within. Nothing was as simple as A plus B equals C. There were twenty-thousand ways to define A, and maybe A wasn't A at all, maybe it was C, or maybe there was an M in there that nobody had ever thought about.

On top of that, an attorney's logic might be different than a judge's logic. And one judge's logic could be diametrically opposed to another judge's logic. Above all, everyone in the legal system seemed to be a spinner. I don't spin anything. I don't like it. With me, what you see is what you get. I also don't think in circles, but straight lines. I'm not used to having meaningless zig-zags all over the place.

Even the language of law confounds me. All the sentences are complex prepositional phrases almost impossible to understand, changing their meanings numerous times before concluding. All the confusion is intentional. In that regard, Blue Cross and the legal system had a lot in common. It seemed to me from the get go that Blue Cross' intention was to deceive, confuse, and cover up so they wouldn't have to own up to what they had done.

Nevertheless, the slow, fractured wheels of justice began to grind. Blue Cross hired a firm that had represented the tobacco industry, Chadborne and Park, the lead attorney hailing from Harvard, Robin Ball. Theresa jumped in and filed a total of ten claims, the major reason for our suit being wrongful termination. Blue Cross did exactly what any multi-billion dollar corporation would do.

Confuse, delay, deflect, deny.

Every legal piece of paper in the world was filed and argued. Every possible date was pushed. Every possible person was deposed for days on end. Every scrap of paper was pored through and extracted for discovery. Anything in an attempt to weaken our case, slow things down, and beat me into submission.

During all of this I was trying the best way I knew how to just keep being a decent father and husband, all while I was bleeding money for legal fees. Each time Theresa filed a motion, it cost me. But it wasn't just the motions that cost me. It was the countermotions too. Blue Cross knew this. Creating more paperwork, more mountains of motions and countermotions worked exactly as they wanted, draining my pocketbook as well as my resolution to continue. However, it never crossed my mind that the storm of my legal battle would seem like dead calm compared to the sea of personal tragedy I was soon to face.

# Chapter 14

## Carole


On Memorial Day afternoon, we were hosting a pool party and had invited some neighbors over who were grieving from the loss of their husband and father from the previous month. I remember praying prior to the feast and asking God to give the family something they could hold onto, some evidence of his presence in their time of pain and need. In an odd way I think I was asking for the same thing for myself. The party wound down, the family thanked us, and they headed home. Carole and I cleaned up, and Carole made the rounds with the kids before she crawled into bed. Before we drifted off to sleep she turned to look at me.

"Thanks for all of your hard work, Jeff," she said with a soft smile.

She didn't have to say anything more. I knew she appreciated what I was doing, even though it was hard on all of us. Her support meant everything to me.

"I think good things are about to happen," she said before we both drifted off to sleep.

\* \* \* \* \*

Jeffrey: *The night of Memorial Day I had a nightmare that my mom died. I was ten years old, but even though I was starting to get a little older, I was still very attached to my mother. I worried if she went places without me. I always wanted to be by her side, but I'd never had a nightmare like this. I woke up in the middle of the night crying. She came into my room and tried to calm me down.*

*"I don't know what I would do if anything happened to you," I sobbed.*

*"Everything's fine," she soothed. "I'm here. I'm not going anywhere."*

*That morning I was downstairs watching TV in the living room eating cereal. Kristen was upstairs sleeping in. Dad had left to take Jamie to a class with our homeschooling group. Everyone else had just finished eating breakfast and Mom was cleaning up around the kitchen, talking to Dad on the cell phone.*

*All of a sudden, the dogs started barking. We were both kind of confused. My mom walked to the doorway that led to the mudroom on the side of the house. The door was open. I looked past the kitchen where Mom was standing. A man opened the screen door to the mudroom and walked in towards my mom.*

*I could tell immediately that this wasn't right.*

*"Excuse me," my mom said, on guard. "You can't be in here."*

*We live in a gated community at the end of the cul-de-sac and we don't get a lot of people showing up at our doorstep. We both knew something was really off about this situation.*

*Something was also very off about him.*

*"You can't be in the house," Mom repeated, a thread of fear lacing her voice. "Who are you?"*

*He didn't answer.*

*Instead, he reached behind his back, pulled out a gun and pointed it at her.*

*She turned to me and gave me a look that was clear: "Run. Go!"*

*That vision of her looking at me, with him pointing the gun at her is still to this day burned into my mind. I don't think it will ever go away.*

*As I ran up the stairs she started to scream...*

Jamie: *Dad and I were just talking in the car, just another normal day of Dad taking me to my homeschooling class. We were stopped at a light, waiting to turn left. It had just been Memorial Day and we were talking about the party we'd had the day before and how my uncle was sick.*

*Then my mom called and my dad put her on speaker. "What're you guys doing?" she asked, relaxed and cheerful.*

*"Just sitting here in traffic. Again," I snipped.*

*"Don't worry," Dad said. "We'll get there on time."*

*"We never get there on time," I complained. I was fifteen years old and worried about doing anything that would make me stand out from the other kids.*

*"Hold on, the dog's barking," Mom said.*

*Then all of a sudden, her voice changed.*

*"Jeff, there's a guy in the house!"*
*A second later she started screaming.*


I was taking Jamie to a homeschool class when Carole called my cell. We were talking about ordinary things, like we did most every morning, when suddenly it all stopped. "There's a man in the house," she said before she began to order him out, her voice angry, but quickly turning to panic, then within moments... screams.

It didn't seem real. My wife telling me a man was in the house? I was hit with a jolt of white-hot adrenaline. My only thought was to get to her. *Now. Faster. Faster. Faster. I had to get to her and the kids.*

I punched the accelerator, tires squealing, jumping over two curbs to make a U-turn for home.

"Call 911!" I shouted to Jamie as Carole's screams reached a panic-stricken pitch.

I tore down the steep, windy incline into the valley, barely braking as I went, almost bottoming out as we hit the base of the grade before stomping on the gas pedal, blowing past a red light as I raced for home.

Jamie, near hysteria, cried into the phone at the 911 Operator, "She's screaming! Our dogs are going crazy! Please help her!"

Carole's shrieks continued. I could hear crashing. More screams.

"Please, Dad," Jamie begged, "turn it off! Please, I can't stand it!"

She just couldn't take listening to her mother's screaming anymore. I was desperate to stay connected to Carole, but the sound was so tortuous, I had to spare my daughter.

"Hold on," I told Jamie as I flipped the phone shut and sped up, laying on my horn and punching on my flashers, trying anything to get through the tangle of morning traffic on our small two lane back road.

All my EMT days came back to me in a sickening flash. My eyes flicked toward the speedometer. At times hitting 100 mph. I screamed down the small road swerving and honking, weaving into passing lanes, cutting across to the shoulder and back again.

Anything to get to Carole and my kids in time.

The car bottomed out on a dip then bounced up, the wheels almost losing contact with the asphalt.

For just a split second the steering was free. I thought I would lose control.

I could feel the weight of the car pulling to the side.

I grabbed the wheel tight.

The car jerked and straightened.

"Get out of the way!" I screamed to the cars piled up in front of us and slammed my foot to the floorboard once again...

Jeffrey: *I ran toward Kristen's room, when I heard a loud noise. I assumed it was a gunshot.*

*Halfway up, the screaming stop.*

*I kept going into my parents' room and grabbed a phone and punched in 911.*

*"Hello, hello? We need help!" I yelled into the receiver.*

*The phone went dead. Disconnected.*

*I sprinted for Kristen's room...*

Kristen: *I woke up to screaming. I didn't think anything of it at first. Jeffrey was always grumpy as a kid and he would get in these weird moods. In an effort to snap him out of it, Mom and Jeffrey would have these dinosaur roaring competitions. They would just roar as loud as they could at each other. They usually ended by cracking up just because the whole thing was so silly. Then everybody was happy. I remember waking up thinking that's what was happening.*

*But I quickly realized this wasn't a roar.*

*This was Mom screaming.*

*Then suddenly, she stopped.*

*Jeffrey ran into my room, terrified. "There's a man downstairs. He just shot mom."*

*He had a phone in his hand. I grabbed the phone and locked us both in the bathroom.*

*I called my neighbor, Mary Lee. "There's a man downstairs. He has a gun and he shot my mom."*

*It was then we saw the doorknob twist. First slowly, then when he found out it was locked he jerked it hard. Then... BOOM! The door rattled in the casing as he kicked the door once, then twice, then the door flew off the hinges.*

*He walked in.*

*He had the gun.*

*I screamed and dropped the phone. Mrs. Lee hadn't heard everything I said, and thought I was laughing and not screaming. She assumed it was a prank call and had just hung up.*

*He pointed the gun at me.*

*I can't remember if he spoke or not.*

*Then he hit me on the head with the butt of the gun. That was it. I blacked out.*

Jeffrey: *He hit Kristen and then he walked over and hit me.*

*I woke up and saw Kristen lying in a pool of her own blood.*

*It was so hard to see because of all the blood in my eyes. It was almost like the whole world was tinted with the red of my own blood and panic.*

*I shook Kristen awake.*

Kristen: *I woke up to see blood everywhere. I wadded up a bunch of toilet paper and put it on Jeffrey's head to try to stop the bleeding.*

*"I'm going to bleed to death. I'm going to bleed to death," Jeffrey kept crying.*

*There's a little bathroom window. We stood up and looked out the window. I could see him down on the patio. I could see the back of his head. He was standing by the back of the house. I don't know what he was doing. He was just standing there.* Who is this person? *I kept thinking.* Why did he do this to me? What just happened? Do I know him? Do I recognize him? Are there more of them? Who is still here?

*And then we heard footsteps. I told Jeffrey not to make a sound and put him in the bathtub and closed the curtain.*

*I got out of the tub and lay on the bathroom floor in that puddle of blood.*

*I put my hand over my chest and thought,* I can play dead. *I held my breath as the sounds of footstep came toward the door.*

*I was so embarrassed because during the night it was so hot and I got up and changed my pajamas. The pajamas that I put on were this little spaghetti strap top and these tiny shorts that were two sizes too small because they were old. I thought,* Oh my God. What am I wearing?

Jeffrey: *When I was still in the bathtub I remember an incredibly specific moment when I looked down at my hand. I looked at the lines in my hand, covered with blood. I had to focus really hard on the lines in my hand because it truly felt like none of this was real. I had to check these details to make sure it was all happening. I couldn't shake the feeling that I was living an actual nightmare with my eyes wide open.*

Kristen: *I laid on the floor, in all that blood, listening to those footsteps and I thought,* Okay, 50/50 chance. This is either someone who is going to hurt me, or someone who is going to help me. Do I risk it? Do I open my eyes?

*I opened one eye. It was an eighteen year old boy. I didn't know him, but I knew he was also hurt because his face was also covered in blood. It was then I knew he was trying to help me.*

*"It's okay. I'm just the pool man," he told me. I recognized him then. He was an EMT and he and my dad used to talk all the time about medical stuff as he would clean the pool.*

*"Is my mom dead?"*

*"She still has a pulse."*

*"Is the guy gone?"*

*"Yeah, he took my truck and he's gone."*

*"Is he coming back? What did he want?"*

*"I don't know."*

*I went to my dad's closet where he keeps all is guns and got down his pistol.* If he's coming back, we have to do something, *I thought.*

I skidded up to the front gate of our community, got through the electric gate, and floored it toward our home. I whipped the car toward one of the last turns before I reached our street. That's when I saw a truck coming toward us. *He's coming out from my property*, I thought. It was a little black truck with pool cleaning equipment in the back. *It's the pool guy. Does he know what's going on in my house?*

I started to flash my lights at him. I rolled down my window and stuck my arm out the window, signaling for him to stop.

He just kept driving.

But before he could pass, I yanked the wheel to the left, hoping to cut him off, and ended up headlight to headlight with the truck. But he wasn't about to stop. He whipped around me, jumped up the curb, and sped across a neighbor's lawn.

"That's him!" I shouted.

Jamie: *We came up right on him. We just stared at him for this one long second, then my dad pushed me down, yelling, "Get down! He's got a gun!"*

It wasn't the pool man. This was the man who had hurt my wife.

I threw the car into reverse, stopped, and instructed Jamie to run to a neighbor's house. I swung around and hammered it down the road, even though by now the truck had disappeared around the corner.

Jamie: *I knew Dad would do anything to catch him.*
*"Let me out, let me out. I'm going to go to the Lees' house"*
*I threw open the door and jumped out. I just ran. I got to the Lees' house and started banging on the front door screaming and crying.*
*I was still on the phone and the lady was like, "Don't hang up, don't hang up. Keep me on the phone."*
*"I have to throw up." I vomited on the front porch just as Mrs. Lee threw open the door.*
*"It's 911. You need to talk to her," I said and threw the phone toward her. I just couldn't talk to her any more.*

With Jamie gone, I threw caution to the wind.

"You fucker. You are not getting away," I said into the windshield.

I whipped around the corner and looked up to see the last bit of his taillight disappear around the corner headed for the second gate. I knew I had him because it's an electric gate that opens automatically. And it doesn't open fast.

*He's going to have to wait. It's enough time to get him,* I thought.

I was out of my mind. My whole agenda was just to get at him.

Just as I flew around the corner, I saw a police car appear in my rearview mirror. I raced down the street and made the turn and saw the gate opening barely enough for the culprit to get out.

He got through the gate, but was bumper to bumper on Santa Rosa road. All locked up. He tried to wedge himself out into the traffic. I got through the gate, jumped around him in my car, blocking him so he couldn't get out into the road.

I threw the car into park, grabbed the door to open it, and looked back over my right shoulder. I saw the guy, about fifteen feet from my car. He was standing with the truck door open using it to steady the pistol he had pointed at me.

In slow motion, I saw two blasts of smoke rise from the barrel of his gun. There was no sound. Only smoke.

The back passenger window exploded with gunfire and I dove across the console. Just then the police officer rolled through the gate and behind the perpetrator. He turned and opened fire on the officer as he bailed from his car and headed to the trunk. Thinking I was going to be in the middle of a gun battle, I dropped the car into gear and rolled forward out of the line of fire. I turned to see the cop drop to a grassy knoll near the gate, later finding out he was shot through the shoulder.

The guy jumped back in the truck, and pushed his car though the traffic as everyone started to pull off to the side of the road. He swerved into the center passing lane and peeled out down the road.

I floored it, right on his tail.

Both of us went flying down the center passing lane, cars swerving to the side of the road, now realizing this is no normal traffic dispute. *I'm not gonna let this asshole get away.*

I mashed the gas pedal to the floorboard, flying toward him—

*Bang!* I rammed the back of his truck. He accelerated, but the little truck wasn't a match for my car. I hit the gas again. And... *Boom!* Smashed into the back of the truck. *Bang! Bang! Bang!*

I slammed into his car at least five times.

I don't remember seeing his face. I just remember he had long hair. Every time I rammed him, I could see his head whip backwards and his long hair flying up almost in slow motion. It was such a surreal picture.

I don't know why he didn't fire at me as he drove. I don't know if he was out of ammo or if all he wanted to do at that point was to escape.

Overhead I heard the familiar *whoop, whoop, whoop* of helicopter blades.

Within seconds, two unmarked cars came flying down the road in the opposite direction. The cops got one look at us and locked up their brakes, tires burning, squealing into a U-turn.

They were on us within a half a mile.

I motioned out the window, pointing to the truck and pulled over as they took over the pursuit. I spun my car around, continuing to honk and flash my lights as I headed toward home again.

I tore up to the gate and saw another cop on one knee next to the other officer who was still lying in the grass, wounded. The moment I stopped to get inside the gate, the officer rushed my car, weapon drawn and pointed at me. I rolled down the window and held up my hands.

"It was my house. Has anybody been back there yet?"

"No." He holstered his gun and ran back to his fellow officer.

I ripped up past my gate, through the streets of our community, and back the long road toward our property. As I pulled into the driveway I saw that the side door was wide open, the four dogs running around the front lawn barking.

I ran inside.

The first thing I saw was Carole's motionless feet poking out from behind the kitchen island.

I sprinted in and dropped down beside her.

She was unconscious, lying in a pool of her own blood. She was still breathing, but each breath was slow, irregular, labored.

*Agonal breathing.* A sign of deep brain injury.

It was the only sound inside the house.

*Oh my god. Where are the kids?* I suddenly thought.

"Kids!" I screamed, rising from my dying wife.

Nothing.

I raced for the stairs and called out again.

Kristen: *It was then I heard him.*
*"Kids!" he shouted.*
*It was my dad.*
*"Dad!"*

*Jeffrey and I went for the stairs. There was Dad. Standing on the landing.*

*"No!" he said, putting out a hand.*

*"Stay upstairs!"*

*He didn't come up for a long time.*

The kids and the pool guy both came out. Everyone was covered in blood. The moment the kids saw me they started crying, desperate to know what was happening.

"Where's Mom?"

"Is Mom okay?"

"I want to see Mom!"

I didn't want to tell them. I didn't want them to see their mother like that.

I grabbed a couple of towels and told them to stay upstairs. I ran down the stairs to tend to Carole just as the cop who pulled the gun on me came through the side door. I just snapped into ER mode.

"I need an RA here! I need two units! We can air-vac! Get them here! Where's the fire department!"

"I don't know; I don't know!"

My neighbors rushed in and suddenly the place was filled with people, police, and fire rescue units.

"Get an air unit in here! You can set down in the field."

They did.

While they were loading Carole into the chopper, I told the pilot, "I'll be back in a minute." I rushed to the ambulances that were loading my kids, making sure they were going to go to the same hospital as Carole.

But then I heard the chopper lift off.

I dashed over to the battalion chief.

"What they hell are you doing? They just left me. What if she has a brief moment of lucidity?"

"I totally understand. Let the paramedics take care of your kids, get in my car and I'll get you to the hospital," the chief said.

Jamie: *I just watched fire truck after fire truck, after cop car, after ambulance drive back to the house. I couldn't get in touch with Dad. I kept calling the house phone over and over and over. Just constantly. Just redial. Sometime after about a half hour, Kristen answered.*

*"Hello?"*

*"Kristen! What's going on! Is everyone okay!"*

*"Jamie, you just need to stay calm."*

*And she hung up the phone.*

*Not knowing who was in the house, if there were more people, I just stayed at the Lees' house for what felt like forever. Mrs. Lee started making calls. We were all on our knees praying. Then my dad showed up on the way to the hospital and told me to stay there.*

*"Is everyone okay? Is everything okay? Is Mom okay?" I pleaded.*

*He looked at me. "Everything is going to be fine."*

*I knew my dad so well. I really thought I could have told if he was lying, but the way his face was, I totally believed him. I remember taking a sigh of relief. Everything was going to be okay.*


We finally got to Los Robles Hospital in Thousand Oaks. Carole was critical. Still unconscious.

They had intubated her, but her vital signs varied.

She went into CT. Her skull was fractured.

A lot of bleeding and a lot of swelling in the brain cavity.

A special line was placed to monitor her intracranial pressure, which was elevated.

I stood at Carole's bedside unable to make sense of where I was. Everything seemed so far away like it was happening to someone else, the definition of the word surreal.

The ambulance was now unloading the kids. I tore myself away from Carole as they were moving her to the ICU to check on Kristen who was vomiting continually from the severe blow to her head. It turned out her skull was fractured and she had an intracerebral bleed. Jeffrey had a huge laceration on his scalp.

*This is not happening,* I kept telling myself. *This cannot happen.*

"Doctor Nordella," I heard over the PA system. "Dr. Jeffrey Nordella. STAT to the ICU."

*Oh God. Please. No.*

I raced up to the ICU.

The intensivist caught me in the hall. "I don't think she's going to make it," he said passionately.

I couldn't quite understand what he was saying. He continued talking, but I couldn't hear the words over the dull ringing inside my head.

"I'm sorry, Dr. Nordella, but I need to talk to you about organ donation?"

*Organ donation?* I wondered. *Carole? This can't be happening to my wife. This isn't real.* "No," I reacted as rapid as a knee-reflex. "She's not going to die," I stammered. "No organ transplant."

I ran to the bedside. Her blood was pressure dropping despite being on every medication attempting to support it. She just wound down.

She was leaving us.

I held her hand, her wedding ring pressed against my palm. I kept apologizing to her. "I'm so sorry," I told her. "I love you so much. I'm sorry."

Carole never regained consciousness.

I watched as her blood pressure could not be measured and her heart rate dropped to nothing.
She was pronounced dead.

I sat on a chair in the ICU, bent over, head in my hands as I desperately tried to understand, to process, and then collect myself. Just as I was getting up to head to the ER, the social worker approached.

"I'm so sorry for your loss," she quietly muttered before she reached out and pressed Carole's wedding ring into my hand.

I stared at Carole's ring as it lay in my palm. *What an ugly symbol of finality... till death do us part.*

Alone inside the elevator, as I rode down to the ER, I realized the first thing I would be forced to do in this new living hell of mine was to tell my children their mother was dead. How could I do that? They were still all so young. Jamie was fifteen and Kirsten was thirteen. They were just entering those confusing and tender years of adolescence when they desperately needed their mother's advice and support to negotiate the world of first dates, proms, and Sweet Sixteen parties. Jeffrey was just ten. I'm sure there were mothers and sons who were closer than Jeffrey and Carole, but I had certainly never known them. Carole and Jeffrey went everywhere together. Carole had a way of securing Jeffrey and bringing out the best in him and Jeffrey worshipped her. I wasn't sure how he was going to sustain her loss.

The thought panicked me.

When I first got to the emergency room, Jamie was sitting in a chair outside of her brother's and sister's room. She'd had the chance to see her mother in the emergency room before she passed and had prayed over her, despite the fact that Carole was unconscious and unresponsive. I stepped to her now, and our eyes met for a moment before I had to look away, but she stood and hurried toward me.

"How is Mom doing?" she asked, her voice desperate.

"I'm so sorry," I choked out. "But Mom didn't make it. There was just too much damage."

I held her as tightly as I could as she broke down and sobbed into my chest.

Now I needed to tell Jeffery and Kristen. I had to be careful. Not only had that bastard hurt them physically, but they were also dealing with the emotional devastation he'd heaped onto both their small backs. I spoon-fed both of them the truth in increments, giving report after report of the bad news, until finally I delivered the worst news of all.

Their mother was gone.

I remember Jeffery repeating over and over as he cried, "It's so unfair."

He was right. Everything about this was unfair.

The only thing I could do was hold him and tell him I would always be right there for him. What else could I say to reassure my son whose world had been destroyed at the tender age of ten?

Kristen was moved to the ICU where her aunt stayed by her beside as she continued to vomit repetitively because of her head trauma. When I told her that her mom had died, she broke down and wept uncontrollably before she drifted off to sleep.

While the horrible news of Carole's death spread like an unwanted cancer, and the hospital filled with a mob of friends and family that spilled out of the ER entrance, I was left to tell Carole's parents that their daughter was gone. They were elderly and feeble and didn't want to believe any of this was happening. "Oh, no. Oh, no..." Carole's mother kept repeating over and over, while her father reached out to hold his wife, his frail body shaking as tears streamed down his stunned face.

That night I slept on the floor in Jeffrey's hospital room. He didn't want me to leave his side. Having difficulty sleeping, they gave him something to relax. Finally he drifted off. That's when I turned on the news.

The first image I saw was Carole's face—a photo from her driver's license. Our tragedy had now become national news.

I listened as the newscaster reported that the gunman fled to a nearby Walmart where he shot into the ceiling of the store, terrorizing customers and staffers before dashing into the sporting goods section for more guns. But when the SWAT team surrounded the building, he shot himself with his own gun.

I stared at the television set in disbelief. *All for what, you piece of shit?*

I woke early the next morning. It was June 1st. It hit me like a wrecking ball.

Today would have been our 17th wedding anniversary.

# Chapter 15

## The Aftermath

After Carole was pronounced dead, life turned into a strange state of slow motion.

I repetitively kept taking inventory.

My medical practice was gone; my mother died from a horrific trauma on my watch; my children were brutally beaten by another man in my home; and now, worst of all, Carole had been murdered in her own sanctuary, beaten to death by the same strange asshole.

And I hadn't been there to stop it.

The litany of all that had gone wrong circled around inside my head in a slow motion loop, over, and over, and over again.

But as much as I tried to suppress my feelings, I couldn't help constantly questioning, *Why God? Why had all this happened? Carole was the last person this should have happened to. She was good, she was faithful, and she was obedient to you.*

*So why?*

Of course, there were no answers.

And we still had a funeral to endure.

Carole's family had decided they wanted a viewing of her body. As numb as I was, I conceded. The kids, however, didn't go. The idea of seeing their mother's body frightened them. They didn't want to remember her that way and I completely agreed.

The viewing took place in a small mortuary chapel. I hung back as Carole's parents entered first, followed by her brother and sisters. I waited. Somehow, I just wanted to see Carole alone. They emerged one by one, some weeping freely, other's choking back their grief.

It was my turn.

I stepped inside the dimly lit chapel to see her coffin up front near the altar, illuminated by a soft light. I moved slowly down the aisle toward her body, the only sound being my reluctant footfalls on the carpet. I braced myself as I looked down at my beloved wife. The sight of her hit me.

I felt physically ill.

She was not Carole. She was simply a shell. An empty figure of the woman I had so dearly loved for the last twenty-one years of my life.

It was evident Carole was not occupying her body any more.

I had seen death more times than I could count. But all that experience in the ER, my desensitized attitude toward death, was shattered the moment I laid eyes on my wife's body.

I stumbled backward and collapsed into the empty pew. Reality circled around me.

Carole was dead.

There was no way around it. Nothing would change that fact. *There's nothing I could do,* I thought. *Nothing.*

I glanced up toward the front of the little chapel towards the stained glass window, the sunlight streaming though the colored glass, illuminating it as if from the hand of God. But rather than being a comfort, a sign of God's presence in this untenable time of grief, it felt nothing but empty. Dull. Cheap. A sham. *How could God let Carole die? Especially like this?* I wondered. There was no point. No message. No meaning in any of it.

I felt a rip in the very fabric of my tenuous connection to God. Not only had I lost Carole, but I could feel myself losing my sense of God. I realized that my faith, sitting there in that small house of God, was evaporating into the heavy silence of Carole's loss. My veil had been reestablished. That faith, the faith Carole had staked her life on, was replaced by the now familiar anger.

As Jamie and Kristen each placed a single rose on Carole's coffin the next day at her burial, my anger only morphed and grew. But it was Jeffery, so painfully thin and frail after what he had suffered through, the stitches poking out from the top of his small head, his dress shirt three sizes too big, looking so out of place in his little tie as he tentatively placed his rose on Carole's coffin that put me over the edge. There was no relief in any of this. The fact that my children had to go through this filled me with nothing but rage. A rage that had no outlet; a rage that would never find justice. The man responsible for all this was dead. He could never pay us back for the damage he had caused.

Over time my anger festered like an infection, a corrosive toxin that had no antidote. How was I supposed to act like a normal loving father and yet have that kind of hatred occupying almost every waking moment? What would it do to me? Who would it turn me into?

Denial was the only way. If I got pissed, I would quickly distract myself, get up, and move away from the situation. If I felt overwhelmed, I'd just stop what I was doing and start a different project. I knew denial might not be the best strategy, but I knew of no other. I had to disguise these emotions as much as possible because I knew they weren't healthy. I found myself constantly trying to reign in all this vitriol I felt inside of me because the kids didn't deserve to be exposed to it. They were deeply suffering as well and there was no way I would allow them to be involved in my hell.

I was grateful that both Jeffrey and Kristen had made a full recovery, at least physically. Emotionally, it was a different story. They too were being hunted down by their own separate demons, as was Jamie. I used to believe in the saying, "Time heals all wounds," and I would try to imagine what life would be like in a year, two years, then five. But time moved painfully slow and I knew my children were relying on me to get them through to the other side. After all, I was a dad and a doctor. I should be able to relieve pain.

I had to somehow find a way to claw myself to the surface and bring my kids along with me. But the thought of that seemed as impossible as a paraplegic willing himself to walk. And in the midst of all this personal tragedy I found myself still fighting for my professional life as well.

Theresa was outstanding, taking on the battle without blinking an eye. She knew I needed time to heal, take care of my kids, and get my head right. And that's exactly what I did with the time. But there did come a day when I had to put the suit of armor back on and reengage in the fight.

As for my battle against Blue Cross, my grief for Carole settled like a hard pit at my very core, serving only to fuel my anger toward them. Like Carole's killer, there was no way to make sense out of what was happening to my family and me. What had happened to Carole, the kids, and me was wrong. What was happening with Blue Cross was wrong. And yet, the fact that it wasn't right didn't stop the reality of being forced to live with the consequences. I couldn't accept the fact that evil could prevail. Yet, I had no evidence, at least at that point, that evil was anything but the victor in my life.

I took off work. The kids didn't want to go back into the house, so we parked the motorhome in our driveway and lived out of it for two months. I was trying to distract them, trying to figure out how to get them into school, get them back into life. *How was I going to flip all of these pancakes?* I constantly wondered.

My first priority was to make sure I could house them, feed them, and make sure that they felt protected. I couldn't hire anyone to help. Not a maid or a cook or a gardener or a pool guy. Nobody. The kids were too afraid to have anyone except friends and family anywhere near the house. I was just trying to monitor and deal with their grief and their anxieties. Trying to talk and trying to communicate with them.

Jeffrey: *Everything after my mom's death was like a weird fever dream. Time was not linear. We lived in a sort of hazy daydream. We were constantly with people. Distraction was our biggest ally. I just wanted to be outside, surrounded by people. Five or six families lived with us in our backyard for those first few weeks. They were our core support, and they're still very close friends today. When we were by ourselves that's when the wheels fell off.*

*I remember one day not soon after Mom died, when we were still staying in the motorhome, our friends decided to leave so they could give us "family time." We had dinner at the kitchen table just like we used to, but it wasn't anything like family time.*

*Nobody spoke. We just ate.*

*It was so weird because it was the first time we'd sat down together as a new family without Mom. It all felt so sterile. I had the sensation that I was miles away, watching my family and myself.*

*Our mom was gone.*

Jamie: *I can't describe what a weird time of life it was. It was pure survival. I'd wake up and for a second I wouldn't remember, and then it would hit me, and I'd realize what I would have to face that day. I would* walk into my parents' bedroom and imagine my mom's face and even hear her voice, but at the same time I knew I'd never see her again.

My sister and brother were so emotional and so open about how they felt. But it made me uncomfortable. Everyone was crying around me and I couldn't cry. I needed to be the strong one. But then I'd break down by myself and call my friend, Elizabeth, while I sat in my closet because someone had to be strong.

I mean, I knew my dad was strong, but he was just so sad. And to see him so sad and lonely and not knowing what to do as a single parent with two teenage girls and a son who had so much anxiety he had to work through…. Well, someone had to not cry. Someone just had to get stuff done because otherwise there wouldn't be groceries in the house, the laundry wouldn't be done, and life would just stop.

I remember my dad didn't know how the laundry machine worked so I was doing the laundry and was ironing his polo shirts for work. Our laundry room faced a back road, and I heard my friend out there. So I called out to her and she came inside. "What are you doing?" she asked. "Just ironing my dad's shirts," I responded. I tried to make light of it, like it was normal. She looked at me and was like, "Do you need help?" Then both of us just broke down.

Jeffrey: *We slept upstairs in my dad's room all together for the first few weeks. I stayed in his room for six years. Until I was sixteen. I'd like to say that after a while that sleeping arrangement was out of habit, but it wasn't. In my mind, if I didn't have his protection, if I wasn't right by his side, I wasn't safe.*

*My immediate fear and the core of my anxiety was that something was going to happen to my dad and I would be left with no parents at all. I didn't leave his side for years. I went everywhere with him. Even when he went back to work, I'd go with him and sit in his office. The only exception was when my mom's brother-in-law would come out once a week to watch me. Even then, if I called my dad and he didn't answer, I'd go from fine to having a full-blown panic attack. I'd imagine him having gotten into a car accident, something, anything had happened to him and he'd be gone… and I'd be left to live without him. As morbid as it sounds, I've told him so many times, if he wasn't here, I wouldn't be here, either. He was my security.*

*To have a son who was constantly attached to him…. It was his entire job for years, trying to help me feel secure. Trying to convince me that everything was all right.*

*I couldn't get past the idea that if the worst happened once, it could happen again. My mother had been murdered in our own home. Someone tried to kill my sister and me in my own bathroom. For me, unspeakable tragedy was a reality. To me, logic didn't exist. It didn't matter that statistically speaking the odds of something happening to my father were almost infinitesimal. The worst had already happened. My heart told me it was likely to happen again.*

Jeffrey would get so sick to his stomach that he would almost pass out from the pain. At three in the morning he'd be deathly pale, and I'd be giving him smelling salts, wetting cold cloths and putting them on his head, all while he was just screaming in pain. He suffered from "Irritable Bowel Syndrome" and would have abdominal cramps. It was diagnosed by two different specialists after a complete work up. His symptoms would occur, two, three, four times a month. He was already thin before Carole's death, but afterwards he dumped ten pounds, leaving him little more than skin stretched over bones. *What am I going to do?* I wondered. I was a doctor and I had no idea how to help my own son.

Because Jeffrey slept next to me, I heard his every movement. If he as much as rolled over in his sleep I was instantly awake, ready to kill off the demons, even though I never really could. For the first year after Carole's death I never had a full night's sleep. I walked around at home and work in a sort of half-life, a numbed out zombie-like state, just going through the motions necessary to keep my family and myself just above the waterline.

Jamie: *I was the first to go back into my room because I hated sleeping in Dad's room with everyone else. I hated how weird it felt. Obviously I had a different experience than Jeffrey and Kristen, not being at the house when it happened. But my coping mechanism was to pretend like everything was fine.* Why is this all so abnormal? Let's be normal again, I'd think. *I just wanted to sleep in my own bed and have it be a normal thing.*

Carole's death had raised questions. Hard questions. Questions no one could answer to my satisfaction. I found myself challenging friends and family who tried to offer platitudes. I wanted answers. I wanted to understand. I read the entire Bible. I had gone to church. I was a good person. I had devoted my life to Christ. And *this* was what I received?

I took stock of my life. First my mom's death, then my wife's death, and then six months later, my brother died in the same ICU where Carole died. How could I reconcile my experience with Bible verses like, "God knows about every hair on your head. He cares about every sparrow?" Why would a loving father, who was supposedly in charge of the universe, allow this to happen? How could he stand by to see his children tortured like this? It didn't make sense. It didn't add up.

No one had the answers. Not even the pastors. And sadly, they weren't around long enough to give any answers either. Looking back, even a simple "I don't know" would have helped. I was hurting. My children were hurting.

My pastor came over once, but mainly just to discuss the funeral arrangements. The only other time he came I was so hurt, so angry, and in so much pain. I asked him question after question, and I think it just blew his doors off. I had one friend, a pastor from a church Carole and I used to attend, that I thought would stand by me. Walk through the fire with me. But he came out one time and offered nothing but a string of half-baked spiritual clichés. He never came back.

I was carrying my pain alone. And I was also carrying my children's pain.

There were times it hurt so badly I just wanted it all to stop. The idea of death often seemed like it would be a much-needed respite from the constant current of pain. Not as a solution, but just as anesthesia. I just wanted to go to sleep without dreaming.

In reality, I just didn't have the time to break down. I had children and I had to be strong and there for them.

Jamie: *A longtime friend of my mom's, Di, would give us recipes that were easy for Kristen and I to cook. We had a lot of moms who came alongside and helped out. But a lot of the people in the church just went* away. Our pastor was horrible. He told my dad, "This all happened for a reason."

My dad would just be like, "Bullshit. You're coming into my house and telling me that? You don't understand anything that's going on. I would never tell you that if you'd just lost your wife at the hands of a madman."

I think the pastor realized there was nothing he could say or do that was going to help the situation, so I think he did the cowardly thing and just stayed away from us.

My dad took his anger and very vigorously began to research the Bible, trying to understand Revelation and heaven and God's involvement here on earth. He started to truly believe there was no God, or if there was a God, he was completely uninvolved in everything that happened here on earth.

Jeffrey: *My dad had a lot of anger against God and the church. He just recently told me, "I was so angry that everybody else wasn't as angry as me." I think so many people tried to make what happened to us fine, but rather than helping my father it just hurt him further. It made him feel very isolated in his anger, which only caused him to become even angrier and cut him off from his friends in the church.*

*He also inadvertently threatened to tear down all the walls they'd constructed their whole lives, using religion and God as a barrier against all the bad things that can happen in the world. Without realizing it, he was asking them to question their own beliefs in the same way he was questioning his. He never would have guessed how defensive his friends would become when he tried to poke holes in their carefully constructed concept of life and of God, a concept that had kept them safe from uncertainty about how the universe operated. To these friends, if evil existed, then there must be good in that evil, or else that meant that God wasn't in control. And if God wasn't in control, then what was the point of having a God at all? And if there wasn't a God... well, none of them wanted to even entertain a concept as earth-shattering as that.*

*So, ignorant to what the consequences might be, he started an open forum where people could bring their questions, doubts, and concerns about God. They'd meet at night in our family room, everybody sitting around in a circle talking and debating. The invitation spread and by the* end we had the head pastor from every church in the area attending, along with dozens of other parishioners. It just turned into this massive deal.

I remember one particular time sitting there watching everyone, feeling the tension in the room constantly increasing. There were two guys who started to answer almost every question: One guy was very aggressive and rigid about his beliefs and his faith. His delivery was naturally aggressive, his theology filled with legalistic rules and the flames of hell. Another guy, until that night, was pretty mild-mannered, the father of a friend of mine. But that night they both took an extremely dogmatic viewpoint of God's purpose in our own personal tragedy from the start.

It started to become very argumentative and quickly became people attacking one another rather create a safe place to discuss ideas and differences. There was no, "Hey, let's collectively see what we think." The one guy actually started yelling at Dad, "Well, you're just going to have to get over what happened!" This was just a few months following my mother's murder.

I remember being so angry at him. I remember thinking, you have ruined religion for my dad.


Jamie: *That night at the meeting my dad said, "Here we are, living in paradise in a gated community and the worst of the worst happens." And this guy had the guts to say, "This was going to happen. And it happened for a reason. God did this." That's what he truly believed.*

*"I think you should go," my dad said.*

*We haven't talked to that guy or that family since then.*

*Really, something that I've learned from this is, you cannot understand anyone else's life or their grief. You cannot tell anyone what to feel or how he or she should be feeling. You can't tell anyone what it's like to suffer great tragedy. All I can say is it's different with every person and in every situation.*

*People did mean to say the right things, but I was horrified by how many people tried to push their views on us about what happened. I understand that people don't know what to say, but they should just say that, that they don't understand. I understood why Dad was angry. If that was the way he was going to grieve, then that's how he was going to grieve. And he didn't take his anger out on us. Ever.*

Jeffrey: *Soon after that night when it all went wrong with the church friends, my dad just stopped asking questions. Before that he was reading the Bible and underlining everything. Asking questions. Taking his anger and pain to other people and asking, "What happened?" But all that just stopped after that night.*

Kristen: *I think my dad is someone that cares very deeply. What happened isn't just a tragedy. You couldn't have attacked his core any more than what happened. It challenged everything that he valued, his security, his safety, his need to protect, his need to care for and be present for his family, his need to control.*

*All of these things are my dad.*

*That was what rocked his world the hardest. It wasn't just that his wife passed away. That would have been hard. But not as hard as what happened. If she had died of cancer, or in a car accident, that wouldn't have encompassed the horror of what actually happened. Those wouldn't have been the invasion of his entire security. Every which way he looked at it he could blame himself. "I should have been there, I shouldn't have left when I did, I shouldn't have moved the family here, we should have built the house fifty feet away, I should have had a faster car, I should have, I should have, I should have... whatever that looked like that involved that day.*

*He's a great dad. He really tried in every way he could to fill the holes. But there are some holes you just can't fill. But he tried.*

Like emotional amputees, we very slowly learned how to move forward without that lost limb. We had to.

Carole was gone and we would forever feel the ghost of her absence. But we did have each other. At least that had not changed. If we had any rudder, that was it. The sea was still uncharted, but we would be forced to sail toward an unknown horizon whether we liked it or not. And we would navigate the journey the same way we always had—as a family.

# Chapter 16

## The First Case

Shortly after our tragedy I received notice for a deposition from Blue Cross. My entire world had been blown apart and now I was left struggling to survive with my children. Jeffrey was suffering from anxiety and wouldn't leave my side. Kristen and Jamie were battling depression, trying to be strong, but I knew they were in pain. Nevertheless, I went to Westlake Village, about thirty minutes from home to give testimony. Only one of the attorneys off-handedly said he was sorry for my loss, but the others remained mute, carrying on business as usual. I got the feeling like I was a weakened animal and they were biding their time until they could finish me off. Their indifference had unexpected results.

It galvanized me.

I would never get justice from the man who killed my wife. I could never get my hands on him. I could never let him know what kind of chaos and searing despair he had created. But it still wasn't over with Blue Cross. I'm sure some people were judging me for not dropping the lawsuit in light of Carole's death. I could almost hear their silent criticisms. Didn't I have enough on my plate just trying to deal with my family's grief? Why didn't I just stop everything and take care of my kids?

The answer was I couldn't stop. This fight had become about more than just me and my case. It had become about principles. It had become about others who also suffered at the hands of Blue Cross—my attorney, the patients, and other doctors who were caught in situations similar to the one I found myself in.

But perhaps my lock hold on Blue Cross was more than standing up for my principals. Blue Cross gave me something to hold on to in the midst of my grief. Blue Cross gave me something tangible to fight against, a target for my helplessness and anger. There was absolutely nothing I could do about the injustice of Carole's death. But I could do something about Blue Cross.

I really believe that being a doctor was something I was born to do. I was a doctor who had done nothing except care and advocate for patients. I knew that. It was wrong that Blue Cross could tell me I didn't have the prerogative to continue being a provider for their subscribers. Especially after everything I had to overcome to have the honor of putting M.D. at the end of my name.

If they wanted to turn an indifferent eye to my grief, if they thought they had the right to cripple my business and make it improbable to make a living as a doctor, if they wanted to continue to drag me through the alligator-infested waters of the legal system, so be it. My attitude was: Bring it on!

My deposition dragged on for two days. I was determined not to let the Blue Cross attorneys twist what I knew to be the truth. They had fabricated a bogus reason for my termination. If I told the truth, that truth would surely rise to the surface. I let them interrogate me taking one question at a time. I could feel each question firing me up, the anger burning white hot inside me, but I was also careful to maintain my composure. I could play their game if I had to. And I did.

On some unconscious level I believed I was fighting for my life. I was fighting for something to make sense of the world. In some ways I was still that boy born into the chaos. That same boy was desperately searching for some sense of security. If there were any chance that right could prevail, I would do anything to make that happen. If I could defeat Blue Cross, if I could prove just how evil and intentional their actions were against me, maybe the world would start to spin once again on its axis.

Night after night, after the kids were in bed, I found myself poring over thousands of Blue Cross' denials, rifling again and again through reams of paperwork, searching for anything that might help my case.

One late night, as the kids slept, the house shrouded in an eerie quietness, I came across what I was looking for. I read through one denial letter, then quickly switched to another, then compared a third to the first two. *What the Hell?* I thought. This couldn't be. I checked it over and over, dumbfounded by the findings. But the more I looked, the more

I realized I just might have stumbled upon that single piece of incontrovertible evidence against Blue Cross...and it came in the form of a denial letter.

What I found was this: It seemed that Blue Cross had merged two different letters, creating a hybrid, which documented the reasons for denials. I wondered if it was part of Blue Cross' own policies and guidelines?

Or was this letter created for me and me alone?

I didn't know whether to be enraged or flattered. The only thing I knew was that I was excited about the discovery.

Why? I thought this could prove Blue Cross had targeted me. This was the letter sent out to my patients stating that their claim had been denied because my care had been determined to be "not medically necessary" *and* the patient did not have to pay.

The constructed letter's language was vague and convoluted, but it essentially enabled Blue Cross to deny literally any claim they wanted. It was written in such a way as to make it impossible for me to perform any medical service without being subjected to their unethical medical necessity evaluations and my ever getting reimbursed for performing medical services. It had torpedoed my goodwill and financially strangled my practice.

This letter was Blue Cross' big stick they used to attempt to beat me into compliance with the hopes that I'd play by their rules. But that's not who I am. It was time to use their own weapon against them. These letters were exactly the proof I needed!

Depositions, motions, oppositions to motions, oppositions to oppositions, delays, stays, and all the legal maneuvering finally came to the point I had been waiting for. After three years, after a small lifetime of personal grief, it was almost over. On the eve of trial, a Friday afternoon, literally one week before we were to go to court, Theresa called me with another unexpected dividend.

"Jeff, you're not going to believe this. Blue Cross has just hung themselves." I'd never heard Theresa this excited. She was almost breathless with enthusiasm.

"You're kidding, what happened?"

"I was deposing one of Blue Cross' middle management types, who I think inadvertently exposed something. The attorney was literally kicking her under the table. I thought he was going to break her ankle!"

"Whoa, whoa, slow down. I still don't know what you're talking about."

"Okay, okay," Theresa said. "But before I say anything I need to do a little research. But if this holds true it will be great news for our case. "It's a little complicated. It has to do with what kind of things Blue Cross will pay for and what they won't, prospective verses retrospective review, and a bunch of missing and inconsistent documents."

"Don't lose me here, Theresa," I said, wanting to get to the heart of the matter.

"Bottom line, I have a feeling we're on to something big. I think we might have caught them trying to cover it up. And it's all in regards to the denial letters."

Yes, the pieces of the puzzle were starting to fall together.

It was almost too good to be true.

I should have remembered what Mom taught me: If it seems too good to be true, then it probably is...

On Monday night, just two days after Theresa had called me over the moon with happiness, I got another call. Only this time her tone was very, very different.

I was in the kitchen cooking dinner, or at least attempting to cook dinner, for the kids, still buoyed by Theresa's Friday phone call. But the minute I heard her voice, I knew something was wrong.

"Jeff, I've got some bad news..."

I turned off the burner and slumped against the kitchen table. "What...?"

"It looks like Blue Cross had an emergency meeting over the weekend."

"What do you mean?"

"They know we were on to something and that I'm going to keep digging until we expose it, so they had to do something to derail us."

The moment stood suspended in the silence between us. "What did they do now?"

"I just got a certified letter demanding that we cease and desist from our California lawsuit."

"Cease and desist?"

"Meaning there will be no trial, at least in California. Instead, Blue Cross is filing a motion for an injunction."

"What does that mean?" I asked, not sure if I really wanted to hear the answer.

"It means Blue Cross' attorneys are asking to have our Wrongful Termination case enjoined."

"Wait, slow down. What do you mean 'enjoined'?"

"They want to sweep our case into another class action lawsuit that has already been settled."

"Wait, what? What case? How the hell can you do that? Is our case like the other one?"

"No, but that's almost beside the point. The concern is, they're going to try to make our case look like the other one."

"What case it is?"

"There was a federal class action lawsuit in Miami that involved several hundred thousand doctors that claimed the insurance companies were using something called "edits" in their computer programs to improperly deny, delay, and down code claims."

Down coding is when the insurance companies change medical procedural codes after the doctor had submitted the billing forms, relabeling them into less expensive procedures, thus lowering the payouts. How ethical is that?

"The insurance companies, including WellPoint (Blue Cross' parent company), were sued for conspiracy, racketeering, and violating state and federal statutes."

"But what does racketeering have to do with our case?" I asked her.

"Nothing that I can see right now. I think it's just a Hail Mary and I'm going to fight it, Jeff. But I have to warn you—"

"I don't think I want to know," I interrupted.

"That case was settled and it's too late to get paid anything from it."

"What? Wait, so you're saying that I could never be made whole again. And let me guess, the insurance companies never admitted wrong doing by screwing the doctors."

"Exactly. The doctors just took a payout, a small percentage of their losses. If Blue Cross can convince the judge that our case fits under this lawsuit, it could be their get out of jail free card. There will be no wrongful termination case and they won't have to pay you a dime because they capped their payout to those seven hundred thousand doctors. Even if the court finds you to be part of that case, you'll never see a dollar."

It was hard to believe this could even be happening. Like I told Theresa, our case didn't have anything to do with that case. I remember prior to retaining Theresa I'd made a call to the California Medical Association, CMA, and after paying my dues I spoke with their attorney. I explained my situation to her in depth and after her analysis she explained to me that my claims were not part of this action. In the end she advised I get an attorney and file my own lawsuit. And that's exactly what I did.

Nevertheless, there we were—Blue Cross had figured a way out of going to trial, at least for now. Our judge put a hold on our arbitration trial here in California known as a "stay" and moved it to the Miami Federal Court with a new judge.

Theresa: *I think that the Blue Cross attorneys thought this was a way to delay the case. They thought they'd just throw this up and see if it stuck. In the meantime, maybe Jeff would give up. Maybe he wouldn't have the fortitude or the money to continue to pursue the case. So the Blue Cross attorneys purposely confused the language of our case and mixed it around enough to make it sound like it was the same as the RICO case so it would be enjoined.*

The fight became about trying to convince the Federal Court why we weren't "in any way related" to the class action lawsuit that WellPoint had already settled. In order for a case to be enjoined, it needed to be obvious that the cases were the same. The cases must be based on the "same factual predicate" for one case to be enjoined with another case. And Theresa attempted to show the judge just how different our wrongful termination case was from this case.

Motions were filed, then countermotions, and then countermotions to the countermotions and on and on. The federal judge who ruled on the case, Judge Moreno, now had to decide if my case was to be among the hundreds of thousands of doctors across the country that were damaged by the computer scam. The process was slowed down even more when Moreno handed the case down to his Magistrate to recommend a ruling. The Magistrate wrote a "Report and Recommendation" and sent it back to Judge Moreno.

When we saw the recommendation we were appalled. What did it say? "Nordella is a Class Member that has initiated litigation concerning Released Claims in violation of the Court's Order."

How was it possible? Our wrongful termination case had nothing to do with a computer software scheme. When we looked at the recommendation it was filled with errors, one of which even referred to Health Net insurance instead of Blue Cross. Health Net? The magistrate couldn't even get the insurance company we were suing correct!

Theresa immediately filed objections to the recommendation. Even though I was devastated by the magistrate's decision, I still felt confident that Judge Moreno would see all the differences in our case, as well as all the errors on the part of the magistrate. He was, after all, a judge. He must be able to think and to read at the very least. We waited, then waited longer, hoping Moreno would make his ruling and overturn the magistrate's recommendation.

Theresa: *The bottom line was, when Moreno sent the motion to enjoin to a magistrate for a "recommendation" as to how to rule, there were many other cases also under consideration for being enjoined and I think ours got lumped into that pile.*

*I think that the fact that the words "down coding," "not medical necessity," and "denial" all showed up in my complaint, led the magistrate to believe, "Look, it's the same as this case," even though they were clearly two separate kinds of lawsuits.*

*I filed objections to the magistrate's recommendation and I said, "It was in error as a matter of law. The recommendation means, in essence, that because a nationwide class of doctors sued WellPoint in Florida concerning billing practices, Blue Cross was free to do whatever it wanted to a California doctor in order to drive him out of business. Does that mean, for example, that Blue Cross could have committed arson, burning Dr. Nordella's records, in order to drive him out of business? The question is absurd, but it illustrates the profound illogic of the magistrate's conclusion."*

*I knew I had a really strong argument. I knew I could prevail. The only problem was, now it was sitting on Moreno's desk for him to affirm or deny.*

*And it sat there for almost* two years...

So now we had a whole other problem besides the possibility of being enjoined to a case that had nothing to do with our case. We had to worry about getting Moreno off the dime to make a decision. As Theresa pointed out, judges aren't the kind of people you push. If you do get in their ear and bug them, you run the risk of pissing them off. And you really don't want a pissed off judge when he's ruling on your case.

Theresa: *Our trial judge here in LA had stayed the case, but she hadn't dismissed it. They only thing she'd done was tell us we had to wait for the federal judge to decide what he's going to do with the case. Was he going to enjoin and say we can't sue, or would he decide not to enjoin so we could continue to try our wrongful termination case?*

*I'll never forget when we went to sit in her court to give her an update of what was going on with the case. We sat down at the counsel table next to the Blue Cross lawyers who acted as if they had no real idea of what was going on at all.*

*"What's going on with this case!" the judge demanded.*

*This was my opportunity, right? I said, "Your Honor, it's been sitting there for two years."*

*"Two years?" the judge repeated. I could see she was outraged.*

*"I can't do anything about it. My hands are tied, Your Honor."*

*As for Blue Cross, they were happy to just let it sit there. So they said to the judge, "Well, we don't have any information. We don't know what's happening."*

*The judge was livid. "Well, I'm going to get to the bottom of this. I'm going to go back to my chambers and call Moreno right now. Does anybody have the number to his chambers?"*

*"I do!" I chirped.*

*She went back into her chambers right then and there and called Moreno.*

*She came back out and said, "Well, I got his voicemail, but I left my number and I asked him to call me back today."*

*By the time I got back to my office from Los Angeles, Judge Moreno had issued his ruling. It said, "The recommendation is affirmed and adopted."*

*He had enjoined the case.*

*It was like he said, "You want your ruling? Here's your ruling."*

*I think that Moreno didn't want to open the door for other doctors across the country to sue and argue that their claims were not governed by the class action settlement. In other words, if he made an exception for first one doctor, then another doctor, then maybe hundreds or thousands of doctors would start saying, "Wait, this case doesn't apply to me," and pretty soon the floodgates would open and the integrity of the entire settlement would be put into question.*

*I don't think it was so much a conspiracy as it was going to open a can of worms. Almost every major insurance company was named in that case and there was this snowball effect where the insurance companies kept settling. AETNA had settled first, then another, and another. And then WellPoint settled. Only one or two were left. The case had been going on for years. All of these companies nationwide had settled with hundreds of thousands of doctors. I don't think Judge Moreno wanted to undo what had taken so many years to put together.*

Theresa, Tris, and I sat at my kitchen table looking out at the ranch, the same kitchen table where Carole and I had shared endless cups of coffee, made plans together, and shared a life together. Now Carole was gone and it looked like my battle against Blue Cross had been lost. Although it had been three years since Carole had died, the kids and I still felt like gossamer replicas of the people we once were. The legal loss only added to my sense of cynicism. I was exhausted financially, emotionally, and physically. But Tris and Theresa had come with an objective—they wanted to take the case to the next level, the appellate level. Still processing our loss, I wasn't so sure.

"I still don't understand. A second grader could see the differences between our case and the class action case," I said, still trying to compute the lunacy of Moreno and the magistrate's decision.

"Judges get it wrong all the time, Jeff," Theresa said, meaning to sound encouraging.

"And that's supposed to make me feel better?"

"The system's not perfect," Tris interjected. I tossed him a look. "Okay, the system sucks, but it's the only system we have."

"Do you really think if we bring this to the appellate level we could win?" I asked Theresa.

"I think we have a very strong case. If we can just get someone to give the court's ruling a really close look I'm sure I can make them see the differences in our case."

"You just said you're sure."

"You know as well as I do that nothing is one hundred percent. There are no guarantees in life."

She was right about that.

"But the RICO case was in Florida, right? That's where it was venued?"

"Yes, the 11th Circuit."

"Don't you have to be admitted to that court or something?"

Theresa nodded. "I'd need to have a local appellate lawyer who is a member of the bar on the case with me. Or you could hire an attorney from the 11th Circuit and I could step down."

"No. That's one thing I know I don't want to do." Nobody knew the case like Theresa. Hiring someone else wasn't an option. "So I'd have to hire another attorney, but you'd be the one arguing the case, right?"

"Yes."

"You'd have to learn a whole new set of procedural rules, and you'd have to do it fast," Tris reminded her.

"I know. I'm a quick learner." Theresa was clearly up for the challenge, but she also wanted to be honest with me. "I won't lie to you, Jeff. Florida is a very conservative venue. It's the South."

"And they're very pro big business. Including insurance," said Tris.

I looked to Theresa for confirmation of this.

"He's right. Let's just say the 11th Circuit isn't exactly the kind of place I'd choose to practice."

"I'm glad you guys are attorneys instead of salesmen. You're doing a rotten job of convincing me to move forward with this thing."

"It's up to you, Jeff. But I wouldn't drive three hours in traffic to try to convince you if I didn't think we had a good shot. I just want to tell you what we're walking into."

"What about you, Tris? If it were you what would you do?" It was a question patients used to pose to me whenever facing a particularly difficult decision about their health.

"If it were me?" Tris said, a small grin growing. "I'd get back in there and kick their ass."

"If we win this, we send a message not just to Blue Cross, but to all the other insurance companies," Theresa reminded me.

"And doctors too," Tris added. "You told me yourself how fed up they are. The tail wagging the dog and all that."

Before they'd arrived I'd wanted to quit. I just didn't think I could muster the necessary energy to go another round with Blue Cross. On the other hand, I had come this far, and I believed in Theresa. We'd traveled through several circles of hell together already and I knew she'd be an invaluable partner if we journeyed deeper into the pit. By this point she didn't manage my case simply as a professional, but as a friend who really did want the best for my family and me. She wouldn't encourage me to take the case to the next level just so she could make a buck. She knew how much I needed justice.

There was something else at play in this decision as well. Someone had to stand up. If nobody fought them, the insurance companies' hold on doctors and patients would only get worse. People would continue to get less and less care as they paid out more and more for the favor. Doctors would become nothing more than puppets dancing on the insurance company's strings. The healthcare system, like the legal system, were both badly broken. There needed to be a paradigm shift. If I walked away, I'd be like every other doctor who wanted to see a change, but in the end had lost heart in the heat of the battle.

"How much of my money are you going to spend this time?" I smiled at Theresa.

I forked out a flat $10,000 fee for a new attorney. Theresa buckled up and started to prepare. She flew to Florida to discuss the case with her brand new co-counsel.

Blue Cross hired another top-level team of attorneys but this time, out of Washington D.C., which sounded suspicious to Theresa and me. Were they about do the Potomac two-step? Like they say, everyone dances with everybody in Washington D.C.

I mentally prepared for round two.


Theresa: *I went to Florida to meet with the lawyer we had to hire to sit at the counsel table with me. We met at the usual attorney's watering hole not far from court.*

*We settled in at the bar and he turned to me.*

*"You realize I don't know California law and your case is all California law."*

*"Yes, I realize that."*

*"You also realize your case has nothing to do with this class action case."*

*"That's why I'm here arguing it."*

*"And there's a statute that you're arguing, that Business and Profession Section 2056. I've never even heard of it before."*

*"Don't worry. I have."*

*"If you don't mind me just sitting here, then I don't mind doing it."*

*"I get it. It's fine. I'm prepared to argue the entire thing."*

*He nodded, then gave me a not too quick once over. I was dressed in my usual business suit and simple silk blouse. "Okay, but one thing. When you come out here to argue it, remember you're a woman in a Southern court."*

*"What the heck is that supposed to mean?"*

*"First of all, you might want to wear a dress. Not a pantsuit. And it should be something frilly and very ladylike."*

*"Thanks for the tip," I said, trying to be more amused than offended. Yes, we really were in the South.*

*In the end, when I showed up to court I didn't take his advice. I didn't wear a frilly dress. That's just not me. I'm just no Southern Belle.*

*But I also didn't wear a pantsuit.*


*The appellate courtroom was huge. Straight out of the kind of courtroom dramas we've all seen in television and film. Two polished oak council tables were positioned on either side of the podium facing the stately bench that stretched across the room.*

*I stepped into the room to find my place among the dozens of other attorneys who were arguing their separate cases that day. I'd argued at the appellate level plenty of times before, but it never failed to send an electric jolt of energy straight to my heart whenever I stepped inside the courtroom.*

*I would argue to three men, two of whom were Appellate Justices on the Bush/Gore election during the "hanging chad" controversy. I had been warned how very conservative this court was and I had also been told that at least one of the Justices had a reputation of being fairly liberal. I knew when I was called up to argue Jeff's case that I'd be timed. I'd be given fifteen minutes.*

*Because I'd brought the case appealing the lower court's decision to enjoin, I was the moving party, or appellant and would argue first. Then the opposing party would respond. After that I'd get to go one last time since we had the burden. The opposing party would get fifteen minutes too, but I'd have to split my fifteen minutes total between my initial statement and response. I had told myself, "Okay, I'm only going to use ten minutes initially, then save five minutes for the end." But the problem is that on the appellate level, you might start to go down the points on your little spiel and all of a sudden the judge might interrupt you. "Council, I have a question. This is California law so can you tell me a little bit about it?" So pretty much on the appellate level you can count on not giving some sort of canned speech.*

*When I got to court there were three other appeals on the calendar. I listened to them to get the lay of the land. As I said, I've argued to different appellate courts out in California and they're always filled with questions from the Justices. I'm comfortable with that. But this was Atlanta, Georgia. As I'm listening I'm realizing these Justices just sit and listen while the lawyers argue their cases. So I'm thinking, "Oh, I'm going to get to say everything I want because they don't interrupt."*

*"Why aren't they asking any questions?" I whispered to my co-attorney.*

*"It's pretty typical. They don't interact very much."*

*"Why not?"*

*"Usually they've already sort of made up their mind before they hear the arguments."*

*I didn't know if that was a good or bad thing. I tried not to think about just how pro-big business I had heard this place was.*

*My case was called.*

*I took a deep cleansing breath, gathered my papers, and approached the podium. I'd rehearsed my speech like I always do, over and over in the mirror until I didn't even need my notes. But I'd prepared to be interrupted. I'd need to stretch this if I didn't get any questions.*

*I started.*

*I talked for maybe twenty seconds, just setting up the basics of the appeal and I got interrupted. Then another interruption. Then another. Two of the three Justices started to almost argue between themselves as if I wasn't there. One was obviously in favor of my appeal, the other wasn't. I watched my clock tick down. Then the other Justice asked questions.*

*The big issue they kept trying to figure out: How can this be a class action case? Isn't this a wrongful termination case? I was just standing there, letting them go at each other.*

*I'm thinking,* Yeah! they get it.

*Then it was all over.*

*I collected my papers, slipped them into my briefcase and walked out alongside my co-counsel. I floated out into the sweet smelling humidity grinning ear to ear.*

*"Wow," said my co-counsel. "I've never seen three 11th Circuit Justices that involved in an oral argument. Ever. That was amazing."*

*"I know. I have a really good feeling about this."*

*"Are you kidding? You totally got it."*

*When I boarded the plane and settled into my seat for the trip back to California, all I could think was,* Okay, this is it. Jeff is finally going to get some good news.

This time Theresa came to my office. I didn't like the look on her face. Or the fact that she had traveled all the way from Orange County to deliver a single envelope that she handed me without saying a word.

Inside there was one piece of paper. Unlike that single sheet of stationary from USC announcing my acceptance into medical school all those years ago, I knew this letter would contain anything but good news.

I unfolded the letter. It was from the 11th Circuit Court. There was no reasoning, no explanation. All it said was, "We AFFIRM the judgment of the district court based on the well-reasoned Report and Recommendation of the Magistrate."

The 11th Circuit Court had upheld the lower court's decision to enjoin our case to the RICO case.

*What? We lost?* I tried to reason.

Again.

Speechless, I turned to Theresa. I'd never seen her like this. She was fighting back tears. "I thought we'd won, Jeff. I really did."

Suddenly, I wasn't thinking about myself. I felt worse for Theresa.

"It's okay. I know you did the best you could."

"No, it's not okay. I hate it when they make decisions based on factors other than the law. It's wrong." As difficult as it was for both of us, I knew that now Theresa understood exactly what I'd been feeling all these years. I hated to think she was in the same camp I'd been exiled to, but I'll admit it was sort of comforting to have some company.

"What do you think happened?"

Theresa, always the professional, even if she had now become my friend, pulled herself together. "I could go for a caramel macchiato. How about you?"

We sat over our coffee drinks, the sun on our backs.

"I think what happened was the 11th Circuit didn't want to undercut Moreno's authority," Theresa theorized. "His decision on the RICO case was meant to continue into the future and have breath. But if all of a sudden it didn't, if it had big gaps and holes all over the place that was going to create issues."

"So two wrongs make a right. Makes perfect sense. If you're a judge," I quipped.

"I'm really sorry, Jeff. I am. It shouldn't have happened."

"It feels like the ultimate screw," I said, beginning to fume. "I feel like I'm flushing my kids' inheritance down the toilet."

Theresa sat quietly. Now I felt bad again.

"I'm not blaming you."

"I know." She looked up at me, concerned. "How are the kids?"

They're doing okay," I hedged. I didn't want to get into it, but it was very rough at home.

The truth was I had told myself the pain would be more bearable as time went on. The visceral ache of Carole's loss wouldn't consume me quite as much. The kids would be able to better get on with their lives. But the pain was every bit as fresh as the day of her murder. For all of us. I'd gone to war with Blue Cross hoping for some kind of remedy for the pain. To try to reclaim sanity and safety in a world that seemed to be devolving into a sea of chaos. And now this? If I stopped fighting, what was I saying to my kids? To myself? That there was no hope? That evil would always race past the checkered flag in first place? Despite how many times they kept knocking me down, no matter how grim my personal life had become, I still just wanted to get those bastards.

"What if we took them to the Supreme Court," I asked.

Theresa looked surprised, then doubtful. "I don't know, Jeff."

"Why not? Somebody somewhere has to see what's happening."

"But the Supreme Court isn't there to correct bad decisions, it's there to create law."

"Well, is there a way to do that with our case?"

Theresa sat with that for a minute. "There might be."

"What would you say my chances are?"

"Not great. But there's always a chance." She took a long sip of her coffee, thinking. "You know, if our case ever made it to court in some other iteration, we could get some mileage out of the fact that we had taken the case all the way to the Supreme Court."

"I don't want to talk about some case in the future. Let's talk about now."

"Okay."

"You know what I want. I want my day in court. I want justice. If this is my last shot at it, I want to do it."

Theresa's lips formed a thin line of determination. "Then that's exactly what we'll do."

So she did.

Theresa filed with the Supreme Court.

By then I was accustomed to the basic machinery of the legal system. Whenever Theresa filed a motion it was followed by a flurry of paperwork, calls, delays, arguments, depositions. This time? What did we hear from Blue Cross?

Crickets. Nothing. Nada.

Blue Cross never even submitted a response to our filing at the Supreme Court level. I don't know if it was their Washington connections or what. I'm thinking, *How can that be?* We file a motion. They were supposed to answer. Were they cocky, sticking out their chests from all the previous wins? Did they think the case could never merit the value of writing new law? Were they trying to be cost-effective? Or maybe it was a conspiracy. Politics. Connections. My mind continued to reel—were their Washington lawyers in collusion with the powers that be at the top level of the legal system?

I'll never know the real answer.

I thought back to all those years spent in the court or trying to get there. All the depositions. All the worrying. All the sleepless nights. All those thousands of letters I'd written to Blue Cross advocating for my patients.

Justice? None.

Got my ass kicked? Big time.

Lost $150,000 in legal fees? Yep.

The Supreme Court's response: not interested.

I felt like I was done.

That night Theresa told me it was over. Long after the kids were in bed I wandered out into the backyard.

I was utterly broken.

I'd lost my practice, my wife, my mom, and my brother. I'd lost every which way we could lose in court. And I'd lost a great deal of money. And on top of all that I was still trying to be a dad. Dealing with my kids' depressions. Fears. Nightmares. Therapy. The laundry list of pure bad seemed to have no end.

I walked out into the deepest part of my property. It was pitch black. Utterly still. I dropped down on my knees in the damp grass. Gathering the last delicate threads of faith that remained, I lifted my gaze to the stars.

"God please. If you're here, if you're real… give me something. No one else is here. Give me a sign. Appear to me somehow. Let me know I'm not alone."

I waited, hoping, searching the night for something. Anything.
There was nothing but silence.
And with that, I realized, I had lost my faith as well.
I was completely on my own.

# Chapter 17

## Just When I Thought it was Over...

During the battle with Blue Cross, I had been approached by the Providence Healthcare Group, a hospital holding company that operates hospitals nationwide. They were interested in opening a full service urgent care and wanted me to be their lead tenant in a large medical building just west of Los Angeles in a new preplanned community called Porter Ranch. Providence's Holy Cross hospital ER was continually packed, and having an urgent care nearby would help the constant quagmire inside the emergency room. Also, they had seen just how successfully my Santa Clarita urgent care model had worked, as well as my ability to build on goodwill within the community before Blue Cross had brought down the hammer that destroyed my business. They believed I could create another thriving business if given the chance, as well draw patients to the other specialty doctors who would soon fill their medical building. Their offer presented an enticing opportunity.

I knew that if I accepted the offer, I'd have to build another business from the ground up. The idea of being involved in the construction and implementation of a new urgent care would be exhausting, but I also knew it could potentially be the prescription for getting me back on my feet both emotionally and financially.

In the midst of the legal battle with Blue Cross, I had accepted the offer.

At the time I decided to move forward with Providence, I was sure we would win the case against Blue Cross and I'd get my contract back. It seemed inevitable that the courts would see the logic of our case, my wrongful termination suit would prevail, Blue Cross would pay out, and I would be automatically accepted back into the network.

Of course, none of that happened.

Instead, I had hit rock bottom. I could see the toll Carole's death and the lawsuit had taken on my family and me. I'd dropped a lot of weight; I'd developed dark shadows beneath my eyes, and I felt constantly fatigued. When I looked in the mirror I saw my dad looking back at me.

I had to come back to the living. I had to try to begin again. I refused to die defeated and broken like my father.

I was a doctor. Just because the world had brought me to my knees, that fact hadn't changed. My love for medicine, despite what had happened with Blue Cross, remained intact. I still very much wanted to practice medicine. That meant one of two things. Either I could become an HMO employee doctor, or I could continue with construction of the Porter Ranch urgent care and start my own business again. I knew myself too well to think I would never be accepted within the HMO system, getting a salary and bonuses for giving cheap care or no care at all. I was far too much an advocate for patients to survive within that unethical Ponzi scheme. That left me with Porter Ranch. Besides, not only had I broken ground on the Porter Ranch space, I'd also signed a ten year lease. I had made an obligation. I wasn't about to walk away from that.

But I also knew that making this business work would mean I'd have to reapply to Blue Cross.

If I didn't reapply, the business wouldn't even survive, let alone thrive. The fall of my Santa Clarita urgent care had taught me that much. I couldn't ignore the fact that Blue Cross made up to sixty percent of my Santa Clarita practice before I'd gotten into this whole mess.

Theresa and I met halfway between Orange County and Los Angeles for our typical Starbucks.

"What do you think I should do?"

"You've got to reapply, Jeff."

As much as I hated to hear her say it out loud, I knew she was right. But I felt like a Nazi sympathizer. How could I beg for permission back into a system that I so loathed?

"I know you don't like it..." Theresa said.

"... But what other choice do I have, right?"

To say it was a bitter pill to swallow would be a gross understatement. However, even though I knew I was *persona non grata* with Blue Cross, I believed I'd have no problem reapplying and getting back into the network. Surely they'd see I was someone they had to reckon with and would just leave me alone this time. Or, perhaps they thought they had beaten me into submission and believed I'd finally fall in line like all their other trained monkeys who heard no evil, saw no evil, spoke no evil.

Whatever the reason, as humbling as it was, I wouldn't go away. I just didn't know how to do anything different than to keep going. Why should I cower or curl up into a ball and shuffle off into a corner? That's exactly what the insurance company wanted. Just for me to go away. Change the kind of doctor and person that I had always been. I don't think so.

Now all I needed was to get back into the lion's den.

I started reapplying to all the health networks, Health Net, United Healthcare, Blue Shield, on and on. One of the requirements for reapplying is to fill out a questionnaire regarding training, where I did my residency, specialties, where I did my internship, where I practiced, where I worked, etc.

However, there is also this question: Have you ever been terminated by an insurance company before? I wondered if this might be a sticking point, even though I'd been unfairly terminated and never had a ruling on the legitimacy of that termination. I had Theresa help me with an explanation of this, making this very clear in a letter she sent to Blue Cross.

I got a quick response from every other insurance company except for Blue Cross. Not even a question. I even qualified with federal government's healthcare program, Medicare. They all said the same thing: We need primary care and urgent care centers. In fact, even Blue Cross was running a campaign at the time to educate their patients about when to go to an emergency room and when to go to an urgent care. Emergency rooms were many times more expensive than urgent care centers and the insurance companies were really pushing the growing phenomenon of urgent care facilities. It was cost-effective for them. Even though I was well aware Blue Cross and I weren't on the best of terms, I assumed my qualifications and their need for urgent cares would assure my entrance back into their network.

But I should have known better than to hope Blue Cross was guided and fueled by logic or ethics.

When I applied to Blue Cross as a family practitioner and in emergency medicine I got a response that I couldn't apply as a family practitioner because I didn't have my board certification in that specialty. However, they informed me I could apply as a general practitioner. I found their response to be pretty nonsensical and also confusing. How was it that I couldn't apply as a family practitioner? As Theresa pointed out, I met their requirements whether or not I had board certification in that specialty. I just needed past certification with ten years' experience practicing medicine and I had done both.

But what I really wanted was back into the network. It didn't matter to me under which specialty I applied as long as I could get into the network, so I checked the general practitioner box as suggested and mailed it back to Blue Cross. I also sent my own letter to Blue Cross clarifying that my practice was "neither a general practice, nor just a family practice, but rather an urgent care. The office is a brand new state of the art facility that provides urgent care services, family services, and occupational services all on a walk-in basis." I searched how many urgent cares there were within a ten-mile radius. There were only two, which told me my practice was very much needed. I was sure to point this out to Blue Cross in my response letter as well. Finally, just like Theresa did before, I reiterated that I met all the eligibility requirements set forth in the Blue Cross manuals.

Soon after, I received their response to my letter and application.

Their letter was simple, but as crushing as it was confounding. Their response to my request to be accepted back into the network?

Rejected.

Their reason? There was no network need for a general practitioner.

"What a bunch of crap. You don't need primary care?" I blurted out.

I jumped on my computer and looked at their provider finder, a simple computer software program for patients listing how many and the specific specialty of the doctors in every area based on zip code. I looked up all general practitioners within the Blue Cross network in a ten mile radius of my Porter Ranch zip code.

How many general practitioners were listed? Two.

I grabbed the phone and called Theresa. "Oh my God, how stupid do they think I am? Or maybe how stupid are they? No network need? Blue Cross is begging their patients to go to urgent cares. It's all over their literature. And to add insult to injury, just the other day, they invited the doctor that I'm working with at Porter Ranch to join the network!"

"Jeff, did you really believe they would let you in?"

"Yes! I'm qualified. And every other insurance company welcomed me with open arms. Didn't you think I'd get in?"

"I knew they wouldn't accept you."

"What! Why didn't you tell me that before I applied?"

The phone line nearly crackled with silence, then, "Have you ever heard of the old saying if you give somebody enough rope they'll hang themselves? I knew if they intentionally blocked you from the network we could possibly go at them again."

Now it was my turn to let the silence slip between us as I put together what she'd just said.

"You're not talking about another lawsuit, are you?"

"That's exactly what I'm saying. They can't reject you just because they don't like you. They can't just make up a bogus reason to keep you out."

"You knew this was going to happen all along, didn't you?"

"I had a pretty good idea," Theresa admitted. She let me think about that for a moment or two before she added: "You'd have another bite at the apple, Jeff."

The tone of her statement was as though she was dangling a carrot in front of my face.

*Wow. Another lawsuit? Could I really stomach it?*

Theresa read the stillness on the other end of the phone. "Look Jeff, this is up to you. But here's the good thing: since you're not under contract with them, you don't have to go to arbitration. There would be a trial with a jury, twelve human beings to hear your story."

I chewed on that for a minute. "So I'd finally have my day in court."

"If you can take it, I can," Theresa said. "What do you think?"

What I thought was, it wasn't as simple as it sounded. I had been dragged through the deepest, darkest, thickest mud imaginable for the last nine years. Simply standing upright took Herculean effort at this point. And I knew firsthand all the possible pitfalls involved in the legal system.

But I thought again. I'd never gotten justice with Carole, my mother, my practice, or the first lawsuit. But now, Blue Cross, out of their arrogance and stupidity, had given me a fresh new chance. That apple was starting to look awfully juicy.

It didn't matter how slim my chance was. I had to try.

"I'm in."

# Chapter 18

## Pretrial

Jamie: *When the second lawsuit started against Blue Cross it was the same stressful time as before with the other lawsuit, but times a million. It was all he talked about. It was all he focused on. It took all his energy and then some.*

Kristen: *When they started back with the depositions and the boxes all over the house filled with paperwork, that's when I got more involved. I remember long hours and long strategies with Theresa talking about game plans and details of the case... I remember praying, "Don't let this be in vain. He's got to get a win out of this. Because if he doesn't... his whole faith in humanity is riding on this. Please, Jesus, let this be a win. Not for money, not just for justice, but for my dad's heart."*

The second lawsuit would be different from the first wrongful termination suit. This case would be for violation of fair procedure, and specifically the statute, Business and Professions Code Section 2056. Theresa explained it to me over yet another Starbucks Frappuccino.

"If the insurance company has only a small percent share of a doctor's practice, they don't have to provide fair procedure when they exclude a doctor from a provider network," she said.

"So how much do they need?"

"A substantial market share. So in trial, I'll be sure to establish that."

"So what's considered substantial?"

"It depends. The actual number can be all over the place—as low as 15% and as high as 60, maybe 70%. It all depends on the jury. The point is I'm going to have to establish that Blue Cross made up a substantial amount of your business."

"Which is true. I can't see convincing the jury of that being a problem."

"Exactly. But the next part gets a little trickier. There are two parts to violation of fair procedure. One part is almost like due process. The insurance company has to give you notice, and the doctor needs to be given an opportunity to refute or defend him or herself."

"But they did do that." It was true. Blue Cross had followed procedure to the letter of the law.

"So," Theresa continued, "I'm not going to contest the procedural fairness. What I *am* going to go after is the substantive part."

"Which is what?"

"When Blue Cross excluded you, the reason for the exclusion needed to be *substantively rational.*"

"You know I hate it when you talk lawyer to me, Theresa," I joked.

"Okay, substantively rational as defined by case law means it cannot be arbitrary, capricious, discriminatory, or defy public policy. If they've done any of those things, they've violated fair procedure."

"Okay, that I follow."

"Good. So the claim is that Blue Cross excluded you for being an advocate for your patients. There's a sentence in the statute that reads, 'The decision to terminate or penalize a physician who advocates for appropriate medical health care violates public policy in California.'"

"And public policy is the fourth prong of that substantively rational definition, right?"

"Exactly. So I'm going after violation of public policy. I'm saying the reason why you were excluded from the network was because you advocated for appropriate medical healthcare for your patients."

"Meaning all those letters I wrote, right?"

"Yep. So if we can show that Blue Cross made up a substantial amount of your business, which I know we can, all I have to show is they excluded you because you had advocated for your patients."

"And if we do that, we'd win?"

"Well, in theory. As you know, anything can happen."

I smiled, undeterred by her warning. "I love this. Blue Cross is so stupid for not letting me back into the network. They know I'm qualified. They know they don't have any real reason for excluding me except that I spent their money and stuck up for my patients. But they're so big they think they're above the law."

Theresa smiled back knowing exactly where I was going with this. "And because they're so big they made up more than half of your business."

"Which is exactly why we can nail them for violation of fair procedure. That in and of itself smells like justice to me."

"Let's not count our chickens, Jeff," she warned again, always the voice of reason. "I've still got a problem."

"What's that?"

"I need to make this case about you advocating for patient care, right?"

"Right..."

"But I can't bring up the old case. Those facts are inadmissible."

"So what are you going to do?"

"I have to get their attorneys to talk about that first case. I can't do it, but if *they* bring it up, then it's fair game."

I wasn't sure I liked the sound of that. We'd have to hope Blue Cross brought up our first case, but we knew that case made them look bad, so what would compel them to bring it up? It seemed like a hope and a prayer that they would voluntarily refer to the case so we could jump all over it and show how devious their practices were. Nevertheless, this was exactly what we would have to bank on if we were to fully reveal their deception and illegal dealings. Quite the task.

And so it began.

Theresa hit a major obstacle even before preparing for the second case. Her partner who had been helping her write and research the first case had a sit down with Theresa.

"I'm sorry," he told her. "We've been doing this for nine years. I can't throw any more time and effort into this."

"Why would you quit now?" Theresa wondered.

"The truth?"

"Always."

"I just don't see the case going anywhere. And it's been so long. I just can't keep going over the same material. I need to move on."

Now, not only was Theresa facing the titan legal force hired by Blue Cross, she'd have to do it alone.

Just like before, albeit one lawyer short, we began to push the boulder of justice up that very steep legal hill. And just like Sisyphus, just when we'd get to the top of the mountain, that rock would come rolling back down. Depositions, calls, more depositions, delays. Blue Cross hired yet another team of top tier attorneys and the pretrial scuffle began all over again. While none of the Blue Cross attorneys were exactly warm and cuddly, this team, or at least one of the attorneys, seemed to take on the case with supersized tenacity. I think there might have been the smallest power struggle between her and Theresa.

Theresa: *Junga, one of the Blue Cross attorneys, is just this arrogant little thing. Petite, and wore a pantsuit every day with six-inch heels. She's probably only about 4'10, but she had a huge attitude, which was, I work for a great big firm and you're just on your own. I'm better than you.*

*Word got out that this woman hated my guts, and it became really personal. I didn't care. I was like, I'm just doing my job, but I think that blinded her in ways.*

*One of the strategies attorneys employ to try to win a case even in the pretrial portion of a case is to exhaust the other side. This was certainly true for Junga. She called me one day, I'm sure thinking, we are going to bury this woman. Just make her life miserable. She informed me in no uncertain terms that I had to make sure I produced all of the files from the underlying case, the first wrongful termination case for discovery.*

*I found this strange, since she also recently informed me they weren't going to retry that case, so I asked her why they would want all that documentation.*

*Junga didn't give any other reason except that they were entitled to at least see them for discovery purposes.*

*Fine.*

*The problem was the sheer volume of files that the wrongful termination case involved. Twenty boxes worth. There were copies of correspondence, requested discovery, discovery from Blue Cross, pleadings, medical records for Jeff's patients, deposition transcripts, all the filings, research and writing, on and on. About ten to twelve of those boxes were denial letters and letters from Blue Cross telling Jeff they needed medical records.*

*But the worst part was that my work product was in there as well, meaning that all my notes and little stickies, basically all my thoughts and legal strategies, were scattered through those boxes. Legally, no one was allowed to have access to that, and the last people I wanted to know how I was going to try this case was the Blue Cross attorneys. If I gave them access to those boxes, that meant I'd have to go through it myself and remove my entire work product. I was upset, but I did it.*

*But for now, I knew if Junga was requesting the material, I had to provide it. But I didn't have to provide it in a way she might have liked.*

*"Fine," I told her, "but I'm not paying to copy all this. You bring a copy service to my office. I'll put you in the conference room and you can copy whatever you want."*

*At first I think she couldn't quite believe it. Maybe she thought I was kidding. But I wasn't. I knew she wouldn't like the sound of it. But there wasn't anything she could do. If she was going to bury me, I'd bury her. And on my own turf. And at her expense.*

*My partner and I drug out all twenty boxes one by one and stuck them right into the conference room. Junga and a couple of wide-eyed bushy-tailed law clerks arrived at the office.*

*I very cordially ushered them into our conference room. Why didn't I have a video camera when she stepped into that room and saw the entire thing piled high with all those boxes? Her look was priceless.*

*I told her there was a Starbucks across the street if she needed it, smiled and walked out.*

*You're going to need it, I thought.*

*I don't know what they ended up copying and what they didn't copy because that's their work product, which made it their problem.*

As Theresa moved forward with the trial, I was still trying to manage the home front. For the last several years, inch by painful inch, the kids were beginning to get their feet under them. We all still desperately missed Carole, but no matter how deep your grief, life has a way of rolling forward. Jeffrey was making plans for college hoping to become a dentist. Kristen was starting her own floral arrangement business, and Jamie had fallen in love with someone she'd had her eye on since she'd been a kid. In fact, it was a young man Carole used to tease her about.

"You kind of like Gregger, don't you?" she'd ask Jamie.

"Mom!" Jamie would whine. "Stop!"

But when Gregger arrived on a warm December evening without Jamie to "talk," I had a sneaking suspicion I knew what was on his mind. As he respectfully requested if he could have a Coke out of the fridge, I knew I was going to be asked the impossible: to let my little girl go. Popping the top of his Coke can he sat down on the sofa. He managed some small talk for a bit, ending in a very pregnant pause. I knew what was coming next.

"Sir," Gregger said. "I think this is a long time coming."

"Yeah?" I asked, smiling knowingly. "What's up?"

"Jamie's awesome. You've done a helluva job raising her."

I stared, not helping him out in the least, sadist that I am.

Gregger swallowed, then took a deep breath. "I, uh, I came over to ask you a pretty big question."

I let the silence hang there, waiting for him to fill in the blank.

"I'd like your permission to marry Jamie," Gregger stated with confidence, obviously following his rehearsed script. Then he threw in, "I mean, if that's okay."

I took a long beat, pretending to be thrown off guard, drawing the moment out just a little longer. Gregger patiently waited. Finally I couldn't make him suffer any longer.

"You're a good man, and I know you will take care of her well. I'd be glad to give you my permission, Gregger."

"Awesome," he laughed. "You really scared me for a minute."

A wave of memories flooded past. Holding Jamie for the first time, Carole's face lit with love. Jamie's first steps, her little cheeks pink with pride as she toddled between Carole and me. Carole sitting at the kitchen table going over Jamie's lessons, Jamie in braids. Carole's firm, calm voice convincing me to let Jamie go to her first sleepover. Carole had poured her life into Jamie, into all of us. I couldn't think about Jamie, so much like her mother that it almost hurt, without thinking of Carole and our life together. *She would have been thrilled to know it was Gregger,* I thought. *It would have meant everything for her to know our little girl was going to be happy after all. It was proof that life moves on, whether you want it to or not.*

I would have traded literally anything to have Carole at my side just then. Just for a few minutes.

The words were out of my mouth even before I knew I was going to say them. "I still have Carole's ring. If you want, I know she would love for you to have it when you propose," I told Jamie's future husband.

That ring meant so much—the joy it had brought to Carole when we were first engaged, the searing pain of accepting it from the social worker when Carole had died, and now the hope and future it would represent to our first child and her soon to be husband. All the love, all the pain, and all the hope. The cycle of life continued. It was an honor to offer it to Gregger as a seal of our blessing, as well as a symbol that Carole's spirit would never die.

Gregger stood speechless, his eyes clouding over with unshed tears. I stepped to him and pulled him into a hug. "Congratulations," I managed, my voice cracking with emotion.

"Thank you. I promise to make her happy."

"I know you will, son."

There I was, in the middle of a titanic legal struggle, still picking up the pieces of my fractured practice, but in the months to come, my home soon became a whirlwind of activity, long days spent with Jamie picking out wedding dresses, flowers, addressing invitations. And thank God for Kristen, an incredible maid of honor, the go-to person. I was not just a fish, but more like a whale out of water as I took on the role that Carole should have filled. But like the entire experience of Carole's death, it drew us even closer together as a family.

Another thing happened as well. Jamie's upcoming marriage to Gregger showed me that in the midst of all the ugliness, something beautiful had been planted and started to grow. Love could and would still flourish. It was proof that good could exist. Jamie's happiness gave me the much-needed perspective necessary to press forward and fight for what I believed was right. But even armed with this newly minted resolve, nothing is as capricious as life itself, and I was soon to face another one of its temper tantrums.

Three months before trial, Blue Cross deposed me. Every word of my deposition was videotaped and they lasted for five days total, spanning over several months. It was utterly exhausting. Blue Cross nitpicked every detail of my life and business. Never knowing where they were going with each question I knew they were attempting to undermine my credibility so they could play it back to the jury at the time of trial. I negotiated each question as best I could, and whatever I did I refused to get angry and lose my cool. It had been nine years since Theresa had signed on, and a total of thirteen years since my initial small claims suit against Blue Cross. It seemed like a lifetime, but I could see the finish line just up ahead. Now was not a time to get comfortable and inadvertently let my guard down.

We were in the middle of the fifth day of my deposition when Theresa's phone rang. Strange. Theresa never had her phone on her, nor took calls in the middle of our business. Something wasn't right.

She looked down at her phone, then said, "Ugh, sorry, I need to take this," and quickly stepped out. The videographer shut off the camera and we all just sat there in silence staring at each other.

Awkward.

Theresa was my only ally in the room. I looked out the window, trying to pretend the downtown Los Angeles landscape was incredibly captivating. Junga and Ken whispered a couple of words to each other and took notes on their yellow pads. No one wanted to leave, thinking Theresa might be back at any minute.

We waited for forty-five minutes.


Theresa: *I had gone in for my mammogram in December. I've had lumps removed before, and every time I would freak out that I had cancer. So when I had lumps this time I told myself there was nothing to worry about because it would turn out to be nothing just like before. I had a mammogram and then they did a biopsy, but the whole time, I'm like, "It's just the calcification from that one breast because of all the lumps that were removed." I was like, "Whatever."*

*I stepped out of the deposition and told an assistant, "I need an office where I can talk. It's a private call."*

*I was led into a small dark room and closed the door. "Sorry," I said into the phone. "I can talk now."*

*"Yes. Ms. Barta, we're sorry to tell you this, but it's cancer."*

*The first thing I thought was how am I going to tell my daughters? They knew I had all these aunts with breast cancer. It turned out that it was DCIS, not real invasive, like the best kind of cancer you could get, but I was going to have to tell my daughters.*

*The second thing I thought was,* I'm going to have to tell Jeff, 'Guess what? Your trial is not going to go in three months like we thought.'

Finally, realizing this was no normal call, I excused myself and went to find Theresa. The assistant showed me to the room. I knocked and Theresa cracked the door, her face stained with tears.

"Are you okay? Are your girls okay?"

"Yeah," she managed.

"What's going on?"

She hesitated, as if deciding what to say. "It's personal. It's a family thing."

I believed her. I never for a second thought it was about Theresa.

"I'll go back and call off the deposition for today," I said as I turned back to head for the conference room.

"All right, but give me a minute," she insisted, wiping the tears away. "Let me tell them." That's Theresa for you. Always shouldering the burden.

I didn't hear from Theresa for another week. Whatever it was it was bad.

Theresa: *I decided almost immediately that I would have a double mastectomy. I wasn't going to wait it out and see if the cancer would come back in the other breast. I have a really strong family history of cancer. But I didn't know if I was going to need chemo. It was all a big question mark at first. Was I going to be out for two months, four, five?*

*And then there was Jeff. Three months away from court. Finally, finally he's going to have his day in court. All I could think about was everything he'd gone through, the death of his mom, his brother, Carole's murder, the whole debacle of the first case.*

*It was like, what next?*

*But one thing I have learned because I'm constantly juggling so many cases is to focus only on what I need to do today. Because tomorrow? There's going to be all kinds of other new problems. Everything that I worry about today might not even happen tomorrow. It's happened so many times in my life that I just go, "I'm not even going to worry about that because it may never happen. I'm just going to worry about today."*

*But I was really concerned about my daughters and I was really concerned about Jeff. His case had been going on forever and now on the eve of trial, it was one more thing. It was like, "Oh my God, how am I going to tell Jeff?"*

*I decided to call my mentor, Mike.*

*"Oh my God, Mike, I have this case and I have cancer. I'm up in L.A. Can I stop and see you because I don't know what to do with this and I cannot have this case go on forever."*

*"Do you need me to try it?" he said, immediately understanding.*

*"I might. I just don't know how sick I'm going to be or for how long."*

*"You just do what you need to, Theresa. I'll talk to my partner."*

*He called me back within ten minutes.*

*"We'll step right in."*

*I trusted him with my life. Mike's firm specializes in suing insurance companies. They taught me how to try cases. I knew they'd get Jeff's case. I felt like Jeff would be in good hands, but still. We had been through nine years together. It killed me to walk away when we were so close. It didn't matter how good my mentor was. Nobody knew the ins and outs of this case like I did. It could mean the difference between winning and losing.*

*Now that I had a game plan, I realized I couldn't put off telling Jeff any longer. Finally, when I was with my daughter at a water polo tournament in Santa Barbara, I realized it couldn't wait another day. I remember it being on my mind constantly and all I could think was,* Ugh, how am I going to tell him this? *I was getting ready to go to dinner and I was sitting in the hotel room, and I was like, "Okay, I'm going to do it today." I've tried tons of cases, stood up in front of the Supreme Court and it doesn't make me nervous, but needing to talk to Jeff, I was like "Ugh..."*

*I'd just told my daughters and they'd taken it really hard. I was so emotional myself. It's just a tough thing to talk about and live with.*

*I picked up the phone and punched in Jeff's number. I could barely choke it out.*

Jamie's ring glittered in the sun streaming through the window as we sat at the kitchen table and went over her wedding list, another task that left me feeling lonely for my partner in crime. My cell phone rang.

"Sorry, honey," I said to Jamie. "It's Theresa. I haven't heard from her in a week. Do you mind if I take this?"

"Sure, no problem."

I stepped onto the patio to take the call.

"Theresa. How are you? Everything okay?" The hesitation on the other end of the line told me no.

"Jeff, I'm so sorry...?"

"What is it?"

"I have breast cancer."

*Cancer? Theresa?* My heart broke for her, but I quickly slipped into doctor mode. "What is the cell type, do you know?"

"It's DCIS," she said.

"Okay, if you're going to have it, it's the one to have."

"I know, but I'm going to have a double mastectomy because of the family history."

"That's really smart. I think it's a good idea."

"I don't know about the chemo and the radiation... I'm not sure how long it will be."

It killed me to hear she was thinking about me in the middle of her own crisis.

"Don't worry about that. The case isn't important."

"Yes it is."

"Not compared to your health. You just take care of yourself. We'll figure out the rest when you get better."

"My friend Mike has agreed to step in and try the case. He'll do a good job for you."

"No, we're just going to wait this out."

"But you've already waited fourteen years."

"I'm young, what's another one or two," I joked. "Theresa, you're going to be fine. It will be good. You'll see. I'm not getting another attorney. We're a team."

By that time Theresa and I had become very close. We'd been through the wash, rinse, and spin cycle together and back again. You don't go through that much with a person without developing your own sense of humor, or in our case, gallows humor.

"I hope you don't have Blue Cross insurance, do you?" I quipped.

It felt so good to hear her laugh. "I used to, but not anymore. Thank God."

Theresa: *Honestly, I think what happened was that I just went on autopilot. I just wanted to do the double mastectomy and get it over with. A lot of people would want to delay or they'd get scared and put it off. I was like this: I found out January 16th and by January 25th I'd had the surgery. I just kind of compartmentalized it and had it done. The surgery was scheduled on my husband's birthday. I tried to use my sense of humor about the whole thing. I told my husband, "That's okay, everybody in Newport gets new wives with big boobs and you're going get the same wife with new boobs."*

We both decided it was best if Theresa didn't say anything to the court about her condition. Theresa just said that she had a medical condition and needed to have surgery.

"We can't stop the case, Jeff."

I wasn't quite as sure about it as Theresa. The last thing I wanted was for her to do anything to compromise her health for sake of the trial. "Are you sure, Theresa? Don't make me worry about you."

"Then don't. I'm having the surgery. I'm going to be fine, just like you said. And we're going ahead with this trial. If we don't, it could be disastrous for us."

"You're the boss," I smiled. I'd learned never to argue with Theresa. She was an awfully good attorney after all.

During Theresa's two-week medical leave, the judge on our case was moved to another court. So without doing anything, we fortuitously ended up being kicked from his courtroom into another judge's courtroom which gave us the extra time we needed for Theresa to recover enough to try the case. I couldn't believe that for once I was thankful for all the legal mumbo jumbo delays. But eventually, a judge was assigned, and a court date set. Finally, after fourteen years we were finally getting down to it. It was time to select a jury.

I was like a kid watching Perry Mason. This is something I hadn't experienced in the first case. I liked to be involved in every aspect of the trial and this was no exception. The potential jurors filed into court and we started the process, Theresa, Ken, and Junga firing a round of questions at a cornucopia of men and women. Theresa had warned me beforehand that trials are often won and lost in pretrial proceedings, so I was all ears as the day wore on. At day's end Theresa and I retreated to our unofficial office: a Starbucks not far from the courthouse.

"We're going to have a problem picking a good jury," Theresa told me.

"Why?"

"All of the jurors who would be best on the jury for you are going to be the worst jurors for me."

"What do you mean?"

"Think about it. Look at you, Jeff. You are an attractive man. Who am I going to put on the jury for you?"

"Women?"

"Exactly. And women about your same age."

"I'm flattered, but what's the problem?"

"I do fine with women as long as they're really, really young or they're really old. But there's a certain age that I don't do well with. The same women who would like you best."

"How do you know that? That those women wouldn't like you?"

"It's just my perception, but I'm pretty darned sure I'm right. I know who I get along with in my own life. It's not much different in trial."

Theresa told me when she first started trying cases when she was young she tried to hide the fact that she was young and attractive. She purposely bought stodgy looking business suits that toned down the way she looked just so jurors wouldn't be jealous or feel competitive with her.

"There's also the relationship the jurors perceive between the attorney and the client. It's usually unconscious, but we're going to be crammed in right next to the jurors. They're going to be basically sitting right on top of us."

This was much different than what I'd seen on television. In those lawyer shows, the courtroom was cavernous. I'd soon see just how right Theresa was. I could almost reach out and touch the jurors.

"Don't talk to me too much," she warned. "You don't want the jurors to be envious of our attorney/client relationship. Jurors can become infatuated with the lawyers and their clients. The plaintiff who brings the lawsuit always sits closest to the jury. That's us."

"Sounds stressful." And to me it was ridiculous. It had nothing to do with the substance of our case.

"It is. Jurors take so many clues from what lawyers and clients do. I learned after all my years of experience that if there's some testimony that is really damaging to my case, I sit there and act bored, even if I'm dying inside."

"It's going to be hard to just sit there stoned-faced. Especially when Blue Cross starts lying."

"But you have to. Very little about communication is *what* you say. It's all about *how* you say it and your body language. Ninety-three percent is non-verbal. So you have to watch everything you do, much more than what you say."

"Wow, no pressure."

"I know, but I want you to be prepared. For instance, if all of a sudden I start writing something, suddenly the jurors start writing. They don't know why they're writing, but they think, *she's writing, so it must be important and I'm going to start writing.* If you're going to start taking notes when the person starts, then you better be doodling or writing nonstop, because if you stop the juror is going to wonder, why did he stop when the witness said that other thing?"

This was an entirely different ballgame. It sounded intense, but I'm glad she was filling me in on the rulebook.

"Remember, you just develop a relationship with the jurors. Because they're there and if they start to perceive you in a certain way, it starts to take on a life of its own."

"Let's hope they like me," I half joked, realizing I wasn't joking at all the moment the words were out of my mouth.

"Let's hope they like me, too," Theresa said.

Theresa: *I issued a notice to appear at trial for a Blue Cross Medical Director, Dr. Lehrfeld, who was key to winning our case. However, two weeks into the trial I received an email from Junga:*

"Although Dr. Lehrfeld is listed as a trial witness, we understand that he is on medical leave. We do not know any details (such as his medical condition or the time anticipated for his leave), but Blue Cross cannot compel him to appear at trial."

I immediately called Junga and told her that simply being on medical leave does not make Lehrfeld unavailable for trial. The law says that witnesses are only unavailable if they are dead or unable to attend or testify because of a physical or mental illness or infirmity.

She refused to provide any information about Lehrfeld other than repeating that "he's unavailable for trial."

I highly doubted that, so I took matters into my own hands and tried to learn what the real story was. Through a third party, I learned that Lehrfeld had "taken personal time off until August 1, 2013"—a date well after our trial would be over. This did not make him "unavailable for trial" so I brought the matter to the judge's attention by filing a motion that asked the court to hold Blue Cross and its attorneys in contempt of court.

It was quite a sight to see Theresa, Junga, and Ken face off in court in front of the judge. Theresa started by stating it clearly and concisely: Dr. Lehrfeld needed to appear on Monday morning. The judge looked over at Blue Cross and asked Ken where Dr. Lehrfeld was. I couldn't quite believe it when Ken responded that he couldn't tell the judge where Dr. Lehrfeld was.

The judge just cracked up, reminding Ken that she was the *judge.* She repeated the question—where was Dr. Lehrfeld? Ken finally gave it up, telling her Dr. Lehrfeld was on disability. When the judge wanted to know the nature of Dr. Kerfeld's disability, this time Junga spoke up— they weren't going to tell the judge that either.

This time the judge wasn't laughing.

She leaned forward, her scowl as serious as it was intimidating and informed the Blue Cross attorneys that they would produce their witness or she would put a warrant out for his arrest.

Theresa and I stepped out of court and hoofed it to Starbucks.

"We've got to find him, Jeff. We're going to put a big torpedo in his side and I want him here. I *need* him."

"Okay, hang on." I grabbed my cell phone and looked up my retired LAPD friend.

"Hey, Jeff. What's up?" he said.

"I was wondering if you knew where Joe was working nowadays."

"The P.I. Joe?"

"Yeah, that's the one."

"You want me to get in touch with him?"

"Yeah. I might have a job for him."

My friend gave me the info. I turned to Theresa. "This guy's retired LAPD. He's got his own private investigation company. I heard he's really good at his job, too."

"Okay find him, please," Theresa said.

I punched in the numbers. "Hey Jeff, what's up?"

"Hi Joe. If I send you a photo and a name of a guy, you think you can run him down?"

"Yeah, I think so."

I had a photo of Lehrfeld on my phone.

"I'm texting you the photo right now."

"Okay, got it. I'm on it, Jeff."

I knew that working with so many cops out in Santa Clarita would pay off one day.

Saturday morning, about twelve hours later, Joe gave me a call back.

"Jeff, Joe."

"Yeah, Joe, what's going on? You find him?"

"I'm sitting in front of his house. And he just walked out and got the newspaper."

"Really? Does it look like he's sick?"

"No, he just walked out and got the newspaper... Oh, hold on a minute, he's getting in his car. I'm gonna follow him."

He tailed him all around town for half a day, and then called me when Lehrfeld walked back into his home.

"He just finished running a bunch of errands," Joe told me. "The guy looks fine to me."

"Okay, good to know. You got an address?"

"Sure do."

I wrote down Lehrfeld's whereabouts.

"Good job, Joe. Appreciate it. How much do I owe you?"

"Ah, after what you did for my kids all those years, it's on the house, Doc."

I called Theresa immediately. "I know exactly where he is and what he's doing." As it came to pass we didn't even need the information, we were informed that he would be in court.

After fourteen years of going against Blue Cross I was finally about to have my day in court.

# Chapter 19

## The Trial

*February 26, 2013*

The skies were overcast, blocking out any trace of California sunshine, the air a crisp 55 degrees.

Theresa and I unloaded her stack of boxes out of her trunk and onto the dolly.

"Well, this is it," Theresa said. "Can you believe it?"

"Actually, no." It was a surreal feeling. A lot of life had happened. So much of it just to get to this point.

We strode through the courthouse doors, pushing the stack of boxes in front of us on Theresa's dolly down the long marble hallway toward our courtroom. As we pushed our way through the small swinging gates and joined the defendant's lawyers at the already crowded tabletops in the musky, overheated courtroom, I felt a surge of adrenaline. There would be no more pretrial antics to delay, and there would be no more time for coaching or preparation.

My day in court had arrived.

Theresa had prepared for this day for nine years.

We believed we had a strong case. We had done everything humanly possible to stack the odds in our favor for a win.

But when it came right down to it, we had no control over what Blue Cross might throw at us. We had no control over what the jury may ultimately think of us or our case.

But what we did have was the truth. And we were prepared to tell it.

In my view, the truth was the last thing Blue Cross wanted exposed.

Fourteen years would all come down to just a few weeks. A few days to tell my story as simply and convincingly as possible. A few days when Theresa would try to sink her teeth into the ankles of Blue Cross in hopes of bringing them to the ground. In just a matter of days, twelve people who I had never met before would apply justice. Or not.

Theresa drew a nervous breath as we sat in our chairs scanning the courtroom. "You good?" I asked her.

"Yeah, I'm good." She sounded as if she might be trying to convince herself. She knew this wasn't about money for me. She knew the stakes.

I pulled up, taking her elbow. She stopped, looking a little concerned. "Hey," I said, "Thank you. For everything."

"Don't thank me yet," she smiled, her expression still strained.

"No. Really. Whatever happens, I want you to know I appreciate all your hard work."

She nodded. My words sinking in. "You're welcome."

"You ready?"

This time her smile was relaxed. Her eyes flashed with a sudden, familiar confidence. "Absolutely."

The courtroom was anything but grand. Paneled in an out of date eighties light oak, the 50x60 utilitarian room housed six rows of squeaky theater style chairs for the gallery, a clutter of random work desks and file cabinets pushed near the bailiff's desk, a raised judge's bench flanked by the California and American flags, and two scarred oak desks for the plaintiff and defendants pushed together in the center of the room. When I settled in my seat I found myself literally shoulder to shoulder with Junga Kim and Ken Smersfelt.

I'd foregone my usual polo shirt and shorts for a suit and tie, but I could feel a thin layer of perspiration rising across my forehead. Someone had cranked the heater, amplifying the closeness of the room, which smelled slightly of old grandmother. I looked around to see the gallery beginning to fill just minutes after we'd entered. Looked like we'd drawn a crowd. I angled my chair slightly away from Junga, uncomfortable to be rubbing elbows with the enemy.

"Wow, these are close quarters," I whispered to Theresa as she and the other attorneys readied their notes for opening arguments.

Then I remembered Theresa's words of wisdom.

My eyes flicked over to the jurors. Sure enough, at least half of the jury, about half male, half female, stared at Theresa and me. They were already watching our every move.

The judge, the Honorable Suzanne Bruguera, entered the courtroom. She did not require the occupants to rise, which to me, spoke volumes to her character.

*Here we go,* I thought.

The judge, a small, no-nonsense woman with a wise, well-worn face and eyes that could drill a hole straight through steel, teetered into the room in a swirl of black robes, the hitch in her stride telling me she may have suffered from a chronic orthopedic problem. Although she was diminutive in size, in pretrial proceedings I'd seen her make mice of men and women.

"Good morning!" she announced, her voice echoing through the room, immediately establishing her domain. "I know you've all taken time out of your personal lives and I want to start by thanking you. Please, go ahead and have a seat."

I smiled to myself. I had a good feeling about this woman from the start. Then again, I suppose it didn't matter if I loved her or hated her. I buckled myself in. The rollercoaster had just started up the rickety track. The only thing I could do was hold on and, as best as humanly possible try to enjoy the ride.

After laying out jury instructions, the judge called Theresa to give her opening statement.

Any nerves Theresa showed on the way to the courtroom were buttoned up and tucked away. She strode, unhurried and graceful to the podium where she turned to the jury.

"Good morning," she said, her tone controlled and almost soothing, her smile not only perfect, but warm and genuine. I saw a couple of the jurors nod their own greeting, many of them leaning imperceptibly forward, ready to listen.

*Boy, she really knows what she's doing,* I thought.

"You will hear that this case is about a doctor being excluded from the Blue Cross network, and that's true.

"But that's not all the case is about. This case is also about Blue Cross limiting its provider network by excluding qualified doctors, primary care doctors. And that results in lack of access to health care for patients.

"You might be wondering, what is it about Dr. Nordella? It's two-fold. The reason Dr. Nordella was denied is because Blue Cross has an interest in profits, not in patients, and Dr. Nordella is exactly the opposite. He cared only about his patients.

"Let me start with the profit and explain how that works. Medical care costs money. Every time there's medical care, Blue Cross has to pay for it. Less medical care means less money going out and more profits. Blue Cross is a for-profit company.

"So how does that relate to Dr. Nordella? He is an advocate for his patients. He's a fighter, that's what I mean by advocate. He wants his patients to have the care they deserve. And he didn't like Blue Cross' business practices. He didn't like them putting money before health care.

"Blue Cross would deny claims for his patients saying the care was not medically necessary. When that would happen, Dr. Nordella wouldn't just say to the patient, 'I'm sorry, Blue Cross won't let me order that. He fought for his patients. He wrote letters, he picked up the phone, and he called the medical director, multiple medical directors. In one letter, Dr. Nordella wrote, 'Blue Cross' decisions seem to be driven by the cost of a procedure, rather than medical necessity. After that particular letter, Blue Cross terminated Dr. Nordella from its provider network.

"After a lawsuit for wrongful termination that lasted about six years, Dr. Nordella knew he could reapply to Blue Cross' network, and he did. But Blue Cross denied his application. And here we are.

"So that brings us to this lawsuit, which is a claim for violation of fair procedure. What does that mean? The law says that physicians cannot be excluded from provider networks unless the decision was fair or rational. Was the decision fair? Did it meet the standard of rational? It will be up to you to decide on what Blue Cross' decision was."

Theresa then proceeded to lay out the whole chronology of what had happened and how Blue Cross had unethically and unfairly excluded me from the network. But what I knew was this: The jury would never hear any direct evidence that proved Blue Cross excluded me because I was a patient advocate.

As Theresa had explained it to me many times, Blue Cross isn't stupid. They were going to make sure they didn't leave a trail of breadcrumbs. It would look very bad for them if that trail of breadcrumbs led to evidence that showed they excluded a doctor for being a good doctor. They are a healthcare company, after all. They are *supposed* to take care of their subscribers.

In one of our many Starbucks breaks before the trial, she explained it this way: "When somebody does something wrong intentionally, they're never going to walk into court and say, 'We did it!' Blue Cross is going to get on the stand and say for the entire case, 'Ms. Barta has no evidence whatsoever that we intentionally did something wrong.'"

That didn't sound particularly reassuring. "So you don't have any direct evidence to show the jury they intentionally tried to exclude me?"

"Of course I don't have any direct evidence. Blue Cross has made sure to cover its tracks as well as possible," Theresa told me as she sipped her latte.

"But remember, the jury is going to receive a very important jury instruction. And that instruction is this: Circumstantial evidence is just as strong as direct evidence," she said.

"What you're going to hear in the trial, what the jury is going hear is circumstantial evidence, Jeff."

"Which is what, exactly?"

"I'll use an analogy I like to pull out in court," Theresa said. "Let's say you're at the pond. You can hear the duck quack. You can see the duck prints. You can see the feathers, but you're never going to see the duck. Ever. That's circumstantial evidence. You can't prove it, but you're sure a duck had been there.

"Now Blue Cross will try to tell the jury that they can only find against us if they see the duck. But that is incorrect. What I will make sure to make the jury understand is that what they'll be looking for is circumstantial evidence. In other words, what is inconsistent? What doesn't make sense? What evidence or testimony is contradictory?"

I thought about that. "So what you're telling me is I'm not going to see that theatrical moment you always see in the movies when the bad guy cracks on the witness stand and blurts out, 'You don't understand! She deserved it! I killed her, and I'd do it again if I could!'"

"Exactly," Theresa said.

As Theresa wrapped up her opening argument, I sat back and reminded myself not to look for the duck. Theresa was doing her job. She was setting the groundwork and I needed to trust her.

She concluded by bringing the jury back to two simple point she had made earlier in her statement: "What we have here is a case about profits—which is why we say Dr. Nordella was excluded—versus patients, which is why we are here."

Theresa smiled to the jury and returned to my side.

"You nailed that," I whispered.

She allowed me the smallest of grins, sliding her eyes across to the jury. I followed her gaze. Several of the male jurors were smiling at Theresa. *Wow. She really is someone to be reckoned with,* I thought.

It was Blue Cross' turn. Ken, trim and confident, took his place behind the podium. He began immediately, not even pretending to engage with the jurors. His approach seemed much more about, "I am the expert and you need to be educated," rather than Theresa's approach, which was all about respecting and relating to the jurors as intelligent equals.

"Let me start my presentation by telling you what this case is *not* about. Several things it is not about, the first of which is that it's not about access to health care. There will not be a single patient who comes in here and testifies that they were unable to see a doctor. There will not be any evidence that there was less care provided to anyone as a result of anything that happened in this case. It's just not there.

"Also, this case is not about all doctors, and it's not about all patients, and it's not about all of Anthem Blue Cross' business practices. The case is simple and discrete. What it involves is one doctor, Dr. Nordella, who demands that Anthem Blue Cross enter into a contract with him, whether it wants to or not, so he can be part of an Anthem Blue Cross network.

"He makes this demand even though he is not board certified in any specialty, and he makes this demand even though the evidence will show that within ten miles of where his office is, Anthem Blue Cross has more than one hundred, about one hundred and thirty-seven, primary care physicians back in 2010 that would, could, and did provide exactly the type of care that Dr. Nordella wanted to provide to Anthem Blue Cross members."

*Lie,* I thought. *There were two general practitioners; the specialty that you told me you had plenty of. I looked. And I can count. And by the way, do any of the jurors actually believe that you can have one hundred and thirty-seven family practice doctors in a ten-mile radius? How could any of them make a living?*

"And I want to underscore this," Ken continued. "I need to make this crystal clear to you now. This case has nothing to do with putting profits before the health of Anthem Blue Cross members. You will see no evidence about that. There is no evidence about that because it's not true.

"In addition, there will be no evidence, not a shred of evidence, that anyone who had anything to do with the decisions here retaliated in any way against Dr. Nordella. It's supposition. It's his hypothesis. It's his conjecture, but there's going to be no evidence."

Yep. Just like Theresa warned me. The Blue Cross attorneys would tell the jury they had to see the duck, when in fact all they needed to do is hear the duck and see the feathers. Circumstantial evidence.

"What's the evidence going to show you? The evidence will show you that everyone who touched this file from Anthem Blue Cross had never heard of Dr. Nordella before. They certainly never dealt with him before, and they didn't know anything about Dr. Nordella other than what was on the application and applying the rules, procedures, and guidelines of the company to what was on the application.

"There also will be no evidence that anyone at Anthem Blue Cross lied to Dr. Nordella, tried to defraud him, tried to cheat him or tried to trick him. It's just not there.

"So as much as counsel wants this case to be one of corporate intrigue and a conspiracy to retaliate against Dr. Nordella and to harm him, to ruin him, there's just simply no evidence, ladies and gentlemen.

"What's the evidence going to show? Again, it's simple. It will show that Dr. Nordella applied to be part of the Anthem Blue Cross PPO network. The evidence also will show that the company was under no obligation to accept a contract with him. It could have just said, 'No thanks,' but they did more than that.

"They didn't make it up on the fly, ladies and gentlemen. The company did not. The people who made this decision didn't make it up on the fly. They followed established policies and procedures of the company.

"Ladies and gentlemen," Ken continued, "the evidence will show that your job here will be easy. It will show that Anthem Blue Cross denied Dr. Nordella's application for rational business reasons.

"The theme of the case that will come out loud and clear is that the case is about freedom of choice. It's about the freedom to contract with someone that you want to contract with, not to have a contract forced upon you, but to choose who you wanted to do business with."

Theresa and I grabbed a quick sandwich at a café near the courtroom and carried it to Grand Park. We sat down on the edge of the spouting water fountain to eat.

"Good God. I didn't think I could bite my tongue for one more second listening to Ken get up there and lie like that," I complained in between bites of my turkey and Swiss. "What was that crap? Nobody knew anything about Dr. Nordella, 137 doctors, rational business reasons? I guess greed is rational to a 'for-profit' corporation."

"I loved it. We have evidence to show just the opposite on each point. They just gave me something else to go after besides the public policy part of the fair business statute."

She took a dainty bite of her sandwich as we both watched a toddler hold a hand under the splashing water, much to his delight. "And remember, I still need to get Blue Cross to talk about that first case. That's what our case is really going to be based on."

We both watched the mom of the toddler sit down beside the boy and start to play as well. "Remember when your kids were that age?" Theresa asked.

"Like it was yesterday," I admitted, memories of Carole and the kids flickering across my mind like an old Super 8 movie.

Theresa caught my eye. We both knew I was thinking of Carole. She didn't need to say it.

"You ever regret coming this far?" she gently asked.

I thought about that, measuring my answer. "Not long before Carole died we had some friends over to the house. She got up after dinner and read me a letter. In front of everyone. It was actually sort of embarrassing."

"What did it say?"

"Just that she was proud of me. How I always did everything I could to provide for the family. How much she appreciated that."

"She was right. I know it's been hard, but you're a good dad and husband, too. I mean that."

I waved off the compliment, embarrassed again. "She ended the letter by saying she was behind me. That she knew the lawsuit was taking a toll, but she was glad I was fighting for what I thought was right."

Theresa turned to watch the little boy take the hand of his mother and walk off. "You're going to do great on the stand, tomorrow, Jeff. People like you. Just stay with the truth and leave it to the jury."


The next morning, the judge settled herself into her seat and nodded to Theresa. "Okay, counsel. It's your case. Please call your first witness."

"Dr. Jeffrey Nordella," Theresa announced to the court, and then turned to me as if to say, "You're on."

This moment was epic, no words, just nerves. I stood and strode toward the witness box, as if in some kind of dream. My stomach twisted with low-grade nausea, yet a simultaneous wave of relief washed over me, leaving me focused and resolved to speak the truth.

Finally, *finally*, after all these years I could tell my story.

The clerk swore me in as the first witness of the case.

"Good morning, Doctor," the judge smiled.

"Morning, Your Honor."

"Okay, Dr. Nordella. Don't be afraid to turn your back to me and face the jurors. And please, for goodness sake, don't talk too fast. "

I smiled, relaxing just a bit. A couple of the jurors smiled along with me. *A good sign.*

"Ms. Barta, anytime you're ready."

"Thank you, Your Honor."

After covering who I was, and how qualified I was, Theresa focused in on what was the heart of our case.

"After you conducted the search on the Blue Cross provider finder, what did you conclude with regard to their denial letter to you?"

"They didn't want me in their network. It was personal."

"What do you mean by that, 'It was personal'?" Theresa asked.

"Well, it was targeted against me. I had given them information that I was an urgent care and we were practicing in urgent care. Six, seven days later, they write this letter inviting my associate at the same address to be listed in the directory."

Ken leapt up. "Your Honor, I move to strike the testimony as speculative."

"As *what*?" the judge asked.

"Speculative," he reiterated, then threw in, a little flustered, "Lacks foundation."

"That's overruled. The answer remains. Go ahead."

"Did you think Blue Cross had lied in its denial letter dated March 25th, 2010?" Theresa asked, not skipping a beat.

"Yes."

"And why is that?"

"Because when I went on the provider finder, I found no general practitioners in Porter Ranch and they just stated that they had no network need for me as a general practitioner."

"Why do you think Blue Cross denied your application?"

"Objection! Speculative and irrelevant," Ken shouted.

"That's overruled. You may answer."

"Because I advocate for the patients and I spent Blue Cross' profit."

"What do you mean by that?"

"Well, patients come in, they need health care and if they're assessed and evaluated and they need testing to come to a conclusion on a diagnosis, I've always fought for them and have written letters and had phone conversations and peer-to-peer meetings over the phone with their medical directors to try and get the care that people need."

Theresa nodded to me, giving me a silent *atta boy*. "That's all, Your Honor," she said. Then she turned to Ken and Junga and added, "Your witness."

Ken nodded, adjusted his perfectly knotted tie, and took the podium.

"Doctor Nordella," he began, his voice nearly dripping with contempt, "you believed that Anthem Blue Cross retaliated against you prior to 2003? Is that accurate?"

"Correct."

"And that led to your termination in 2003. Is that correct?"

My eyes shot to Theresa and then quickly back to Ken. *Did I just hear what I think I heard?*

They knew as well as I did that they terminated me for advocating for patients, but as Theresa pointed out, that termination was part of our first case and not this one. It was inadmissible in this court.

"Correct," I energetically answered.

"And you believe that Anthem Blue Cross terminated you because you disagreed with its medical necessity determination regarding treatments for some patients, correct?"

Yes, it appeared I had heard correctly.

"They terminated me because I was advocating for patient care," I said, still not quite believing what was happening.

Ken paused, looking for his next question.

I nonchalantly looked over at Theresa again, both of us holding our poker faces.

She'd done it. By drilling me on the issue of being a patient advocate, Blue Cross had taken the bait and brought up the first case.

Theresa had knocked and Blue Cross had opened the door. Now for the rest of the trial, Theresa simply had to walk into their house of lies and expose the truth.

Ken continued grilling me about the first case. How it went all the way to the Supreme Court and how it had ended up terminating our ability to move forward with our California litigation. I guess he was trying to prove to the jury that the case had been settled and I had lost. But what he was so painfully overlooking was that my first wrongful termination case had *not* been settled. By bringing it up, Theresa could have a field day by reexamining all the ways that Blue Cross had screwed me.

After two days on the stand, finally, my time as a witness was over. I returned to my seat next to Theresa. She leaned in and whispered into my ear, just loud enough so Junga and Ken could catch wind of what she was saying, "You did great."

I glanced over at Ken and Junga. They had heard, but the moment my eyes met theirs they quickly looked away and began to scribble on their legal pads.

That night I took the kids, plus Jamie's fiancé, for pizza.

"What was it like testifying in front of all those people?" Jeffrey asked. He was developing a love for film and television, and courtroom dramas.

"Nerve-wracking. I was sweating like crazy."

"Why?" Jamie mused. "Did you mess up?"

"No, because it's so stinking' hot in that courtroom."

"Why didn't you ask the judge to turn down the heat?" Gregger joked.

"I wish. But the judge isn't exactly the person you want to talk to about her court room temperature."

"So, how do you think you did? You think the jury's on your side?" Kristen asked.

"It was weird. I couldn't really read the jury. Sometimes I thought they were with me, other times I wasn't so sure."

"But you were telling the truth. That had to come across."

"That's the hope," I said. "But at least Blue Cross brought up the first case. One of their medical directors, Lehrfeld, is on the stand tomorrow."

"The one who tried to ditch you and Theresa?" Jeffrey asked.

"Yeah. Theresa has a fun day planned for him. It should be pretty entertaining."

Theresa called Dr. Lehrfeld to the stand. He stared out at the court, his face set in a permanently pissed off scowl.

Theresa: *Blue Cross thought I was calling him because he's co-chair of the committee that admits doctors into the network. They think I was going to ask him why he didn't let Jeff in. But what I was after was their lies.*

Theresa moved to the podium and calmly turned to Dr. Lehrfeld, polite as could be. "You have conducted numerous medical necessity determinations on appeals by Dr. Nordella, correct?" she asked.

Lehrfeld remained as calm as Theresa did. In fact, he straightened himself in his seat and looked at me dismissively, wearing the fact that he held a M.D. and J.D. degree like a badge of not only honor, but also superiority.

"I have no memory of that."

Theresa asked him again after showing him his prior deposition testimony, "Have you conducted a medical necessity determination as to any appealed claims by Dr. Nordella?"

Lehrfeld's response: "No, I have not."

Lehrfeld shifted nervously in his chair. You could almost hear him thinking, *is there something I'm missing here?* Beside me, Ken started to jot down notes on his legal pad. Junga saw that, grabbed her pen and followed suit.

Theresa stopped looking confused.

She dropped the disguise and grabbed a document from her table, asking to have it marked as an exhibit. "It is a letter from Blue Cross."

At the same time, Theresa delivered a copied set to Junga and Ken.

Suddenly rigid with panic, Junga and Ken looked at the papers, then at each other.

"We object, Your Honor!" Ken yelped.

The judge responded, "The objection is overruled. The letter is signed by the witness and it says, 'Dear Provider Nordella.' You can provide a copy to the witness."

"Does that refresh your recollection now, that you made medical necessity decisions on appealed claims by Dr. Nordella?" Theresa asked.

"It appears I did, yes," Lehrfeld admitted.

"You did it more than once, didn't you?"

"I have no memory of other ones," Lehrfeld retorted indignantly.

"You Honor, I would like to mark another letter as the next exhibit. It is also to Provider Nordella and signed by the witness."

"There are objections, your honor," shouted Ken.

"I know you object, just like you did the first time," the judge responded.

In response to Theresa's question about the letter, Lehrfeld had to admit that he had signed it. The letter said, "Blue Cross' decision is to uphold the denial of laboratory tests because they are not medically necessary."

"Does that refresh your recollection now that you had handled more than one medical necessity review and determination on appealed claims by Dr. Nordella?" Theresa asked.

Lehrfeld stood his ground. "Again, I have no recollection of these. I don't know if there are more or not."

"I have more, Your Honor," Theresa smiled. "I can continue, but I don't want to waste time."

Theresa produced yet another signed Lehrfeld letter, but that didn't stop him from remaining indignant. Even with yet another letter, he maintained his position as if saying again made it true. "I've seen here three letters that show I have reviewed appealed claims. Again, I have no recollection."

By this time, even some of the jurors were trying to hide their looks of disbelief.

As Theresa continued to cross Lehrfeld up, Ken became more desperate in his objections: "Your Honor, I object. It's not been produced in the case. It's irrelevant and 352 and lack of foundation."

The judge scolded him, "Just say 'I object,' okay. Because when you give all of your reasons, it appears that you are making a statement about the evidence in front of the jurors and to the witness. So it could appear as though you're giving the witness a hint, because he's a lawyer, or that you're trying to tell the jurors something. So just say you object." She then turned to the jurors. "The jurors are not to take any direction as a result of the objection of any lawyer."

When the door closed after the last juror left the courtroom, Ken and Junga went ballistic: "We've never seen these letters, Judge!"

The judge turned a stern eye toward Theresa. "Counsel, let's all talk in chambers."

Theresa: *We go back into chambers. The Blue Cross attorneys are livid. Ken and Junga kept on continuing to pitch a fit about never seeing the letters I had just used against Lehrfeld, claiming that they should have been a part of discovery!*

*The judge looked at the letters and asked* how *the Blue Cross attorneys could not have seen them. After all, they were on the Blue Cross letterhead...their own client.*

*It was everything I could do just to keep a straight face, but then the judge turned on me and asked where I got the letters.*

*I played it as cool as possible. "I got them from Blue Cross," I told her.*

*The judge took a good look at the letters, noting that they were dated back in 2002 and 2003.*

*I reminded her about the first wrongful case and how Jeff wrote all those letters to Blue Cross advocating for his patients. "That advocating," I told the judge, "was the very reason Jeff was terminated in the first place. Because he kept appealing denied claims. Dr. Lehrfeld was one of the doctors who was on the credentialing committee and decided Dr. Nordella should be excluded. He also knew Dr. Nordella had appealed claims and advocated for his patients, because Lehrfeld had personally denied Dr. Nordella's appeals."*

*Ken started spouting objections, saying all this was completely irrelevant!*

*The judge flatly disagreed.*

*Now it was Junga's turn to object, her voice getting louder with each syllable. She insisted Blue Cross had specifically asked for everything from the first case.*

*I didn't flinch—instead I simply reminded Junga that I had given her everything. In fact, she had access to every one of all those twenty boxes. Those boxes included those letters. If she missed Lehrfeld' s name, that wasn't my fault.*

*Now the judge turned on me, her face deadly serious. She wanted to know if those letters were turned over.*

*I told her in all candor there would be no reason for me to withhold the letters. Certainly Dr. Lehrfeld knew he wrote letters and had dealings with Dr. Nordella. It wouldn't even make sense that I'd withhold them.*

*There was nothing Blue Cross could do.*

*Ken's claims to the jury in his opening statement that "Everyone from Blue Cross who touched Dr. Nordella's application never heard of him, certainly had never dealt with him before, and didn't know anything about him" were anything but true. And that evidence was now before the jury.*

\* \* \* \* \*

Theresa and I convened at our new courtside Starbucks "office."

"I think I've pretty much nailed Lehrfeld," Theresa said. "I'm hoping the jury will see no network need and board certification was just pure crap. I mean, he had admitted that you met Blue Cross' alternative to board certification."

It was true. Not only did Lehrfeld have to admit he had dealings with me before, but Theresa also got him to admit that Blue Cross has alternatives to the board certification requirement that allow doctors into the network. I met that standard, thus rendering their claim about excluding me because of board certification pure artifice.

"And I loved the way he couldn't remember anything. Even the Judge pointed that out," she added.

"What about their proof about the 137 doctors?" Blue Cross had produced "evidence" of their mythical 137 doctors in the form of a suspicious one-page document. The document had only seven doctors listed on a single page marked one of two. As for the rest of the 130 doctors? Well, they couldn't produce the second page or the names of the other doctors, which seemed to really get on the judge's nerves. She didn't seem to take too kindly to what looked like very thinly veiled lies and manipulation in her courtroom.

"I don't think any of the jurors bought the idea that 130 doctors could be crammed onto the second page," Theresa said.

"I still don't see how they ever thought that would work."

"They had to come up with something. So I think we're good on network need and board certification."

"So what's left?"

"I really want to set them up for punitive damages. I want to show that they *knew* you were a patient advocate and that's why they targeted you. You can't retaliate when a doctor advocates for his patients. You're the insurance company. You're supposed to be helping your subscribers."

"Are you going to be able to do that?"

"Well, I have to show malice, oppression, or fraud and the evidence needs to be clear and convincing. I have to show that when Blue Cross violated fair procedure they did so with malice, oppression, or fraud, and the law specifically defines each of those. Basically, I have to show intent, intent to cause injury, intentional misrepresentation, or despicable conduct. And even despicable conduct is defined. The law says it means conduct that is contemptible, looked down upon, and despised."

"But do we have any direct evidence of that?"

"No, just circumstantial evidence. That's why I went after their lies about no board certification and no network need. And we also know they lied about what Ken said in his opening..."

"About how it wasn't personal and nobody at Blue Cross had heard of me or had dealings with me?"

"Right. And the fact that they keep producing different documents and changing their definitions of what their qualifications are for their doctors and why they excluded you."

"Plus, it seems like every time Ken objects the judge shoots him down."

Theresa nodded. "The jurors will see right through all their maneuvering and shading of the truth. At this point we're the ones with the credibility."

"Is that enough to show malice?"

Theresa shook her head. "I don't think so. We need something more."

"And how are we going to get it?"

"There's still one guy, Ben McLane."

"The Blue Cross guy who makes the decision of who gets in the network?"

"Yeah. I like him as a witness."

Theresa had something up her sleeve. I just hoped she could pull it out when she had him on the witness stand.


Theresa: *Ben McLane was in charge of the entire Southern California Network of Physicians that Blue Cross contracts with. He helped decide which doctors are in and which doctors are out. He went to Boston University, and looked to me like he had played football there.*

*I love football. My brother was with the Vikings for twenty-five years. Football players can be really nice guys, but they're not always the brightest. After McLane graduated he worked for a restaurant as a manager, then he worked at a bar, then he came out here and managed apartment buildings. Suddenly he went from that to managing the entire*

*Southern California Network of contract physicians. Tens of thousands of doctors. He's got to know somebody, right? Maybe family money or connections?*

*The point is that I planned to ask him questions and get him to go along with me. I was hoping that he'd be not quite sure where I was going. Hopefully he'd start to agree and I could lead him where I wanted him to go without him realizing it*

Ben fidgeted nervously, his large frame filling the witness box. Theresa smiled, wordlessly inviting him to relax, as if he were her new best friend. Feeling more comfortable, Ben smiled back.

"So, you wrote an email on March 23, 2010, correct?" Theresa asked.

"Yes," he easily agreed.

"Why did you do that?"

"I was asked to review the network for adequacy and physician coverage and see if we can make an exception to bring Dr. Nordella into the network."

"And you wrote, 'At this time, we will not be issuing an ANW waiver for Dr. Nordella,' correct?"

"Yes," said McLane

"Doesn't ANW actually stand for Access Need Waiver?"

"Yes, it does stand for Access Need Waiver."

But McLane's email made no mention of any review of network adequacy or physician coverage. Instead, the email said, "This provider was terminated from our network in 2003 under Code 35."

It referred to another document, which was now displayed on the courtroom screen. It also made reference to a Code 35. "That's a code number for the reason why Dr. Nordella was terminated, correct?" Theresa asked.

McLane shot a look toward the Blue Cross attorneys.

"Yes," he mumbled.

Theresa: *Now this part I didn't know. I was fishing and I just hooked a big one. This was one of those times I was going to have to ask questions on the fly without knowing what answer I would get. I needed to think in the moment and follow up. Most attorneys feel like they have to depose everybody, ask every single question at a deposition. Half the time I depose someone simply to get a feel for them instead of gaining a bunch of information. In fact, my best witnesses are usually the ones I've never deposed and have never even met. They're the ones I'm forced to question on the fly. And even if I do depose them, I won't ask all the questions I'm going to ask them at trial, and I never ask the* big *question in a deposition. If I did that, the witness would have time to figure out how to reconfigure their answer in front of the jury. You want to ask the big questions right in front of them. And that's exactly what was happening right now.*

"Next to Code 35 it says, 'REFER TO PB VP,' what does that mean?" Theresa innocently asked.

"That says Refer to Prudent Buyer Vice President."

*A list?* I thought. *Another thing I was unaware of. This was something Blue Cross definitely didn't produce in discovery. Boy, whatever was on that list must have some pretty damning information. But I at least had gotten him to agree that the cryptic "REFER TO PB VP" meant that he had gone outside the normal guidelines and gotten additional information from another source about whether or not to terminate Jeff.*

"Okay, thank you," Theresa concluded. "That's all, Your Honor."

Theresa smiled her thank you to Ben McLane as he visibly relaxed, smiling back.

"What was that all about?" I whispered to her as she took her seat next to me.

"Don't worry. Be patient. You'll see when I do my closing, but it has to do with Lehrfeld's previous testimony."

The next day, I felt jittery with nervous energy. I trusted Theresa, but I still knew there were lots of hanging threads she'd have to tie up before closing, which was just around the corner.

Lehrfeld didn't look happy the first time he was on the stand, and even less amiable now. None of it seemed to make a dent in Theresa's easy calm.

"Were you Co-Chairman of the credentialing committee of Blue Cross in 2010?" Theresa asked.

"Yes, I was," Lehrfeld answered, his tone dismissive and clipped.

"And you hold several different positions there, correct?"

I knew where she was going with this line of questioning. Theresa had done her research and found out that Dr. Lehrfeld was not only co-chair of the credentials committee, but he was also a vice president. He was an officer. The reason that was important was because in order for punitive damages to be awarded against a corporation, the wrongful malicious conduct must be perpetrated by an officer, director, or managing agent.

Theresa was gracefully circling Lehrfeld like a self-contained cat waiting to pounce on her unsuspecting prey. She wanted Jeff's application to be denied by a vice president, an officer.

"You were also a vice president of Blue Cross, correct?" Theresa questioned, almost casually.

"No, I was a medical director."

"I think I have seen documents showing you as a staff vice president. When did you earn that title?"

"There was a merger and during that merger, titles changed."

"When was that?"

"I believe in around 2005."

He was almost twitching with discomfort. Was he lying? The information was public knowledge. In fact, Theresa told me she had just looked it up the night before on the Internet.

"Well, currently on the Blue Cross website, it shows your title as Blue Cross Credentials Committee, Richard Lehrfeld, M.D., J.D, Staff Vice President. Is that not correct?" Theresa asked.

"I haven't checked the website in quite some time."

His evasion was almost laughable.

"Okay. So you lost the title of vice president, is that what you're saying, before 2010?" Theresa innocently asked.

The lines of Lehrfeld's well-defined scowl deepened as he glared at Theresa. "After the merger in 2005, I believe, there was a rearrangement of the various titles within the company," he barked.

*How convenient. He was vice president right before he excluded me, then he wasn't vice president exactly during the time he excluded me from the network, then he was magically vice president again after I was excluded.* I thought. It all sounded deliciously fishy.

When Theresa finished with Lehrfeld and took her place at my side I leaned in to whisper into her ear. "What just happened?"

"Be patient. We've still got closing."

I rocked back in my chair. *Be patient? Really?* A lot seemed to be riding on Theresa's closing. But as usual I chose to trust her. In reality, there wasn't much more I could do anyway.

Theresa: *One of the hardest things about this trial was the amount of time it covered.*

*Fourteen years.*

*And I had to condense all the facts from those fourteen years into nine days of testimony. That was just one problem. The other was that those nine days of testimony were spread out over a four-month period. So not only did I have to make sense of a mountain of facts and material, but also I honestly thought we might lose the whole trial, because of the amount of time that had passed since the trial began. I knew we had a really good case, I knew that we should win, I knew that the facts would be really clear, but my problem was I didn't think the jurors would remember my case since it had been stretched out so long. I started putting on evidence in February and now we're in April. So many things go on in the lives of the jurors. They have their own dramas that occupy their time and minds. Any little "ah-ha" they might have had during the first days of trial? They're not going to remember those. It all was going to come down to my closing argument.*

*From the time I finish the first part of my case and it goes to the defense, I start to think about my closing argument. What points do I want to bring back in what order, how do I say it? What's my story going to be?*

*Because the opening statement is simply evidence, you don't get to argue. You can't do anything inflammatory or fun, it's just the evidence. The evidence will show and this is what happened. And the evidence will show this and here is this document. So it's very matter of fact.*

*But in closing you can pull out the arguments. It isn't evidence. The attorney can say anything they want and the jurors have to go back and see if it's in the evidence. So there's a lot of pressure about what you're going to say, what's your story. I felt a tremendous amount of pressure to tell Jeff's story the best way I knew how.*

*But I never work from scripted notes.*

*What I do is I keep practicing it out loud until I get it down to just bullet points that I have on a piece of paper. Then, because I've done it so many times that all I need to do is just glance at the list and I'll remember.*

*On the morning of the trial, I drove up to downtown L.A. from Orange County. I got there nice and early. The last thing I wanted to do was rush. It's nerve-wracking enough to give a closing argument, especially this one, so I gave myself plenty of time. I parked over at the Dorothy Chancellor Pavilion like I usually did, loaded up all my boxes, got to the courtroom, and sat down. The first thing I looked for was my closing argument notes.*

*I couldn't find them anywhere.*

Oh my God. They've got to be in the car, *I thought. I felt like I was in a dream.* This can't be happening. Oh my God.

*I was completely freaking out.*

*I didn't want to waste time going back to my car, but time was running out, so I ran back to my car.*

*They weren't there. Anywhere.*

*I dashed back and I saw Jeff. I couldn't let him know. How was I supposed to tell him I've just lost my notes to the most important part of the entire case?*

I'd hardly slept the night before. How could I? Everything I'd fought for the last fourteen years was converging to this one day, a twenty-minute oration. It had to be spot on. Theresa had to convince every member of the jury that Blue Cross was out to get me from day one. And she had to do it with no direct evidence. In some ways, as much I knew it was true, and as good a case as Theresa put up for the jurors, it seemed almost impossible. The evidence we had against Blue Cross was technical and as the plaintiff, we carried the burden of proof.

Theresa had anticipated press. Our case had garnered a lot of attention. I was the David to Blue Cross' Goliath. Would a sole practitioner with a sole attorney be able to topple the giant? And the further I went with the case, the more I realized that almost everyone had had a bad experience with an insurance company. They were the epitome of big business and corporate greed. My story had become newsworthy.

As I approached the court I could see several news and media outlets cramming into the courtroom, almost as anxious to hear the closing arguments as I was.

As I walked into the room I noticed another gang of attorneys gabbing to Junga and Ken. *What's going on?* I wondered. *Are they already planning an appeal? Why not only the best when you're filthy rich?* My stomach churned. I turned and spotted a knot of friends and family who greeted me. I spotted Theresa, already seated at the table.

"You ready for this?" I asked, a little breathless with anticipation.

"Absolutely," she said. She looked like the poster girl of confidence.

"Anything I can do?"

"Nope. I'm great."

"Okay, I'm gonna go say hi to my brother."

"Good idea," she said and started to rifle through her boxes. She seemed busy so I left her to her work, moving off to find my brother.

Theresa: *I felt like everyone could see my heart beating out of my chest.* Where the hell are they? *I kept thinking as I continued to frantically dig through my boxes.*

*I had this young man, Josh, who is my trial tech. He helps me put all the evidence I need onto a big screen. When, for instance, there is a witness on stand, I have a big notebook and the judge has a big notebook. I'll say "Let's turn to exhibit 72," and Josh will use his computer to put exhibit 72 onto the screen so jurors can follow along. It needs to be seamless.*

*Josh is really good at his job. I never had to talk to him or correct him or tell him what to do. I finally realized we had only minutes until we started.* Oh, shit. I'm going to have to tell Josh I don't have my notes to give him for the closing.

*I rushed up to him, just as his boss walks up. This guy is sort of like the mayor of the courthouse. He knows everybody. If he finds out I've messed up, everyone's gonna know.*

"You good to go?" *the boss asked, oozing enthusiasm.* "You got Theresa's notes, Josh?"

*I just froze. I looked at Josh, who was still waiting for me to give him my notes. We locked eyes for what I hoped was one meaningful second.*

"Yep," Josh says, without skipping a beat. "We're good. She usually kind of wings it though."

I almost cried with relief. It was five minutes before we start and I haven't handed him anything.

"Okay, Theresa," the boss says, all business. "You're good to go. Go get 'em."

"Okay!" I waited until he turned and lost himself in the crowded courtroom before I bent down and whispered to Josh, "I am really sorry, but I don't have my freaking notes."

"That's what I figured."

"You're just gonna have to go with me and when I say number whatever you put it up."

"I got it."

"Sorry," I said and I walked away toward the bathroom. I'll splash some water on my face. I've got to get this together, *I thought. I step into the hall to see Jeff's brother break away from Jeff and come straight for me.*

"You know, you have to hit a grand slam," he said, his voice low and urgent. "This has to be it. Nobody is going to remember any part of your case except for this."

I didn't even know how to respond. I love Jeff and his brother is great. But didn't he think I already felt enough pressure? I was terrified the jury wouldn't remember any of the key points. And now, I've lost my outline and I'm going to have to go from nothing but memory.

I looked around and saw every top Blue Cross executive I knew crammed into the room. Not to mention the room was thick with press. The L.A. Times, Business Journal, *local newscasters, and another reporter based out of Washington.*

I stared speechless at Jeff's brother and the growing circus inside the courtroom.

Then Jeff approached, looking hopeful but terrified.

"It's time," he told me.

Then it was on...

# Chapter 20

## Closing

The courtroom was, again, miserably hot and utterly silent except for the quiet echo of Theresa's voice. The jury sat completely still, except their heads, which followed Theresa's every move. She strolled in front of them and after an uncharacteristically shaky start, was now deep into her argument, and she was gaining steam with every word.

"Let's look at exhibit 73," Theresa said.

Josh clicked away at his laptop, and exhibit 73 popped seamlessly onto the big screen for the jurors—the same document that referred to Code 35. Looking strangely relieved, Theresa gave him the slightest nod before she turned back to the jury.

"This is from Blue Cross' internal database that Ben McLane found for Dr. Nordella. Back in 2003, when his contract ended, the cancel reason was Code 35. What's Code 35? The facts are right there in front of us: 'Refer to Prudent Buyer Vice President.'

"And back in 2003, do you know who was a vice president, who dealt with denied and appealed claims and medical necessity claims?"

*Dr. Lehrfeld!* I silently screamed. The one who had tried to avoid appearing in court. I saw the ah-ha flicker across the jurors' faces.

Now it all became clear. Theresa had purposely made a big deal about when Lehrfeld was VP and all the "Refer to VP" business when she cross-examined McLane, but she had never tied the two together.

"When Lehrfeld was here, I asked him his title. He said, 'I am a medical director.' But, when I asked him about the title of vice president, he said, 'Yes, I used to have that title.' In 2005, Lehrfeld said his title changed from being Vice President to Medical Director. Why is that important?"

I looked toward the jury. Theresa had them hooked now with her question. You could see them putting the pieces together right in front of my eyes.

"This database, exhibit 73, refers to Prudent Buyer Vice President. McLane got the information that was more specific than the database from somewhere. For example, McLane's email referred to a meet and confer. That was part of Dr. Nordella's advocacy. He wrote letters, he made phone calls, *and* he went to a meet and confer where two Blue Cross medical directors were present. That meet and confer is specifically referenced in Ben McLane's email, exhibit 71."

Again the exhibit popped up onto the big screen to reveal exactly that: "This provider was terminated from our network in 2003 . . . after a meet and confer took place in June of 2001."

"And let's go to Dr. Lehrfeld. If you recall, when I first asked him if he did any appeals for Dr. Nordella, he emphatically told me, 'No, I have not.' He didn't say, 'I don't remember.' And even when I showed him the letters, he claimed 'I don't recall them.'"

Some of the jury members actually nodded. Yes. They definitely remembered the letters. The same ones Junga had missed in those twenty boxes.

"Now, why is that important? Because when this case first started, Blue Cross' attorney told you that no one on the credentials committee knew Dr. Nordella, had ever heard of Dr. Nordella, and had any dealings with Dr. Nordella. That was *completely untrue.* I try not to use the word 'lie,' but that was *not true.*"

If only this were a baseball game. I would have gotten to my feet to cheer in the homerun that Theresa just slammed over the centerfield wall.

She was so good at this. I looked again toward the jury. A few of them cut a not-so-friendly look Junga and Ken's way. Theresa continued to fuel the fire.

She turned her attention to Blue Cross' claim of "no network need" and specifically exhibit 72, which Blue Cross said showed 137 providers in my area. The document that was only two pages long—with one page missing.

"I asked Mr. McLane, 'Was this a search you did for Dr. Nordella? Are you certain?' He said, 'No. I'm not absolutely certain.' Then I asked, 'Where is page 2?' And *really* interesting, Mr. McLane said, 'I don't know. I didn't print it out.' Then he turned around and said, 'I did print it out.'

When I asked him, 'Where is it?' he replied, 'I don't know.' He's gone back and forth."

"The other interesting thing is, why would page 2 be important to see? If Blue Cross had 137 providers and 7 appear on page 1, are there really 130 on page 2? It just doesn't make sense.

"And when I asked Blue Cross, 'What are the *names* of the 130 physicians?' they said, 'We cannot locate that information.' I cannot believe that Blue Cross could not go back and, either in its database or its physician directory, find the names of the other 130 doctors *if they really existed*."

Again eyes went toward the Blue Cross attorneys who now began scribbling madly on their legal pads as if they were far too busy to listen. I felt a warm glow building inside my chest. Theresa was saying out loud what I had been carrying inside me for all these years. She was making it known. She was exposing their lies. She was telling the truth. I was almost giddy with a sense of relief and vindication.

"You have to decide whether Blue Cross engaged in malice, oppression, or fraud."

*Yes,* I thought. This is the punitive portion that Theresa wanted to nail them on. She was just winding up for the big one-two punch.

"This is an interesting part," Theresa said, "because it has to do with intent. And how do we show intent in a lawsuit? Because it never happens in a real trial like it does on TV. No witnesses show up on the stand and say, 'I admit it. I did it. I meant to do it.' It just never happens.

"You only see intent by circumstantial evidence, which is like going to a pond and not seeing a duck. You see feathers. You hear the duck quack. You see duck prints everywhere. And even if you don't see the duck, you can infer from the circumstantial evidence there's a duck somewhere."

Here it was. She was pulling out the duck analogy she'd told me about at Starbucks. I turned to check the jurors' reaction. They were smiling. They liked this.

"No one has to say we did this. But the evidence infers that Blue Cross intentionally lied and concealed or covered up. It's simple. Lies and covering up happen, because somebody did something wrong.

"Let me use an example. I have two daughters, a teenage daughter who drives."

The jurors' heads swiveled to Lauren, Theresa's younger daughter who came to court nearly every day to watch her mom do her thing. Lauren and I had spent a lot of time together during the trial, getting Starbucks and talking about her school and friends while her mom stayed back conferring with the Blue Cross attorneys, the judge, or doing paperwork. The sad thing was this story was about Jordan, who was her older sister. But nobody knew that at the time.

"Probably three or four months ago, I went out to the car in the morning and found wet beach towels and sand everywhere. So I went in and asked her, 'What did you do last night? I thought you guys were going to a movie."

Some of the jurors smiled and nodded. They got this completely. I knew many of them were parents.

'Yeah. We saw the movie. 7 O'clock.'

'Okay. What did you do after that?'

'Well, I went over to Melissa's house.'

'Did you do anything else?'

'No.'

'Are you sure?'

'Yeah.'

'Really? Because I found wet beach towels and sand in the car.'

"What's the relevance? We have a rule. No going into the ocean at night. You can't go in the dark. Too dangerous.

'You must have gone to the beach,' I told her. 'You must have been down there.'

'No,' she said. 'Actually, we went before the movie.'

'How did you go before the movie? You left here at 6:30. How did you do that?'

"All of a sudden, the story starts to change. It's not corporate conspiracy. It's simple. She got caught doing something she wasn't supposed to do and had to cover it up. So she tells a lie. Doesn't tell the whole story. She got caught."

By that point, the jurors were snickering and staring at poor Lauren. It was a good story, but I couldn't help wondering where Theresa was going. She was talking about Code 35, network need, and now she's talking about Jordan going to the beach.

Theresa continued on, tying the story up in a perfect bow.

"Why is that important? That's what happened here in this courtroom. The evidence shows that. A lot of inconsistencies. A lot of things that don't fit."

Now she was really going for the jugular.

"When Code 35 said 'Refer to Vice President,' you heard the testimony about that. McLane said, 'We didn't have a vice president.' Dr. Lehrfeld said, 'I was the vice president,' and someone else said, 'I don't know who the vice president was.' All their stories were going in different directions.

"What about when McLane said he did an analysis of network need and the standard was one primary care physician to every 1200 enrollees. I said, 'Really?' Then he said, 'Wait. It was 1 to 1,500 enrollees.' And when I pushed one more time he said, 'The standard is actually two doctors within five miles.' Which is it? You have all these stories going on. What is it? We're not getting the truth. We're not getting what really happened. So I come back to malice, oppression, or fraud, intentional concealment or misrepresentation."

The point was clear: You could see the feathers, hear the duck, and see the duck prints. You can even almost see his tail disappearing as he dives under the water.

"So we have the lies, the cover-up, the fraud. Intentional conduct to hurt Dr. Nordella. And why would they want to hurt Dr. Nordella? They knew who he was. We know that. He was one of those doctors who fights back for patient care."

The jurors turned and looked at the Blue Cross attorneys. Their expression wasn't happy. Not at all.

I swallowed a lump of pride for Theresa. She nailed it. Home run. Grand slam.

Ken gathered his notes and strutted to the podium. But once there, his confidence seemed to evaporate. Whereas Theresa had really grabbed the jury, summing up how Blue Cross was nothing more than an oversized evil adolescent trying to cover its tracks with the entertaining anecdote about her daughter, Ken's eyes barely strayed from his notes.

He droned on and on for almost an hour.

"When you get back to the jury room," he'd mumbled, "look at exhibit 63 and remember the other part? That's exhibit 21, so look at that, too." It was as boring as it was confusing. The jury stared at him, their faces slack, unreadable.

But it was his final thoughts that woke them up.

He sauntered behind me, and I could feel myself bristle.

"Doctor Nordella and his attorney claim Blue Cross is all about the money. But it's Dr. Nordella who is asking you for money, isn't it? He calls himself a patient advocate, but don't believe that for a minute. Are you *really* going to pay him millions of dollars and he's never going to see another patient?

"Two themes have percolated during closing and in the case. Entitlement and guarantee. Dr. Nordella feels entitled to a contract from Blue Cross and he wants Blue Cross to guarantee his business. He wants to be paid millions of dollars whether he treats another patient tomorrow, a year from now, or five years from now. He wants to be guaranteed $200,000 even if he doesn't work another day in his life. "

It took a lot of control not to jump out of my chair. Of all the lies, all the ways Blue Cross had tried to discredit me, Ken's allegation might have been the worst. *You're never going to get it, are you?* I thought. *This was never about the money. This was about your client. The one who could just wave its hand and destroy my professional life with the flick of a wrist after I had spent fourteen years sacrificing everything I had to become a doctor. Then another fourteen years fighting for my life as I fought against your client's injustice. This was about exposing the lies of a company who talks about the power of Blue. This is about your client's greed. And you have the audacity to even insinuate this was about* my *greed?* It was an obscene claim.

As the judge thanked the jury, winding up the last day of the trial, I was left feeling numb. Theresa had presented a brilliant case. I had the truth on my side.

But I still couldn't help wondering...

Was it enough?

Either way, I'd find out soon.

# Chapter 21

## The Verdict

The trial ended on a Thursday.

Instead of obsessing over the verdict, I decided to just focus on Jamie's wedding.

I set my sights on the field. Jamie would have the wedding and reception there, and it was in desperate need of reseeding. I wanted the aisle I walked my little girl down to be lush, soft, and perfect. The wedding was twelve weeks out. If I didn't get started soon, it might be too late.

It was a beautiful distraction.

I still couldn't get used to the idea that it was over. Without realizing it, my battle against Blue Cross had seeped into my very DNA. In some ways it defined who I was and who I could be. As much pain as they had caused me, as much as they had taken away, the case had given me something to funnel my grief and anger over Carole into.

Now that was gone.

I still had my Porter Ranch practice. I still loved practicing medicine, but it would be an adjustment. No more interrogatories, motions, or depositions. No more legal strategizing over that favorite Starbucks.

Now that the lawsuit was over, even before the verdict, I experienced an unexpected feeling of closure. What I had really wanted all those years was to have a platform to air my grievances against Blue Cross. I realized it was sparring with thin air that had really ground my gears. But once I had that opportunity to tell the truth to a judge and twelve people who would actually listen, once Theresa tied up everything in her perfect legal bow in her closing, I felt content. I felt content because we had exposed Blue Cross. We had shone a center stage light on all their manipulations, lies, and deceit and they couldn't scurry out of the light and into the darkness where they normally operated.

Of course I cared tremendously about the outcome. I still wanted the vindication of a finding against Blue Cross. I wanted them to be punished for what they did to me, but underneath my nerves about the verdict, an uncharacteristic calm pervaded my psyche. Now that it was essentially over I found I didn't want to discuss the upcoming verdict with anyone, not even my children.

There was nothing to really discuss now anyway. I felt like, *Okay. We gave it the best shot we could. We told the truth. We told our story and they're either going to go with us or not.*

As I rototilled the ground with my tractor, I realized I was okay. No matter what the verdict was, I was going to be okay.

I had been heard and I was thankful.

I'd finally had my day in court.


Theresa: *When the court calls you and says they have a verdict, it is the worst feeling in the world. You've been waiting and waiting and waiting.... It's all going to happen now.*

*It's either good or it's not.*

*Here it is.*

*And it's going to happen as quickly as I can snap my fingers.*

*I'd been working the case for ten years and now it was in the hands of twelve people I've never even met. I've never even had a conversation with them. I didn't know what they were thinking.*

*It's just sickening.*

*I literally felt like I was going to throw up. And I was just tired.*

*The other side is going through the same thing. You're just jittery.*

*We finally got the call and I came into the courtroom. The jurors are out in the hallway and the lawyers are in the courtroom. We were so cramped in that courtroom. It's not a big room to begin with and with all the boxes everywhere also taking up space, I had to pull out my chair as the jurors brushed right by me into the jury box.*

*I didn't want to look at them, but they've already decided...*

*It is what it is.*

*Someone came in and I got a little smile, but then another juror looked down, avoiding my eyes. I'm really good at reading people, but I just couldn't read them. I'm just like, Dear Lord, please...*

*I can't even explain the feeling other than to say it's like being suspended in midair. You just know that in one second it's just going to go really well, or really shitty.*

*This case was even more important for me than any other case I've ever had because it had taken so long and because I knew what Jeff had been through. Most of my other cases, they're important, and I still get that same sick feeling right before they give the verdict, but they didn't have the same kind of emotion as this.*

*We were together, Jeff and I, for ten years. It felt like we were quite literally never going to get to trial.*

*And then it was Jeff's mother, and then my breast cancer, and then Jeff's wife... my God, the hell we'd lived through.*

*This one was just so emotional because I knew it was so important for Jeff to feel vindicated.*

*It could make Jeff feel like there was somebody else who recognized how bad this insurance company was. It would tell him that the fight was worth it. Not just this fight, but really fighting against anything you know is wrong.*

*This day in court was going to be so important. It was more than just a case.*

*So the moment to read the verdict finally arrived...*

*Usually the judge silently reads the verdict and hands it to the bailiff to read to the court. But this time, the judge did something totally different.*

*She read through the verdict silently and then looked up. "I typically don't do this, but I'm going to have counsel come to sidebar for a moment."*

What the heck...?

*I filed over and stood alongside Junga and Ken at the bench. It was very awkward. I kept wondering why I was even standing there.*

*"I'm going to have each one of you review the verdict before we have it read," the judge said. It may have been her way of giving us fast relief because otherwise when the bailiff reads all the counts it's so slow.*

*I took a deep breath and start reading...*

*Question number one: Did Blue Cross violate fair procedure?*
*Yes! They violated fair procedure! We won that point!*

*Number two: Did it cause Dr. Nordella damage? Yes!*

*There's a percentage and a yes box and then a number. I skip down to look at the dollar amount: $4,490,000.00!*

What?! Oh my gosh! We did it!

*I looked at Ken and Junga. I'm waiting for them to turn the page to the punitives.*

*They're both just standing there, stock-still.*

*Frozen.*

*Catatonic.*

*They lost. And they lost big.*

*This never happens. A sole practitioner winning against a major insurance company? It is unheard of. And they were in complete disbelief.*

*I hear the blood just thundering in my ears, my heart racing. I glanced over to the jury and they were all smiles.*

*Their faces were like,* Are you happy?

*I smiled back.*

*Yes. Very. Thank you.*

*I turned back to Ken and Junga. They haven't moved a muscle. They literally couldn't turn to the next page to see the punitive portion. They're still just standing there in shock.*

*They really never even imagined they'd lose. Apparently it had never crossed their minds.*

*"Are you ready?" I said and slowly turned my page. Breaking out of their trance, they followed my lead.*

*I turned the page...*

*Under punitive damages I see, "Yes."*

*My heart stopped.*

*The actual dollar amount would be decided over the next few days, but I knew, based on the 4.5 million dollar judgment, that it was going to be multiples of that judgment.*

*It was going to be a lot of money.* A lot!

*Throughout the trial Ken had made a big point, over and over, that Jeff really didn't lose any money because of Blue Cross. They wanted to convince the jury that this wasn't a big case. This wasn't a big deal at all.*

*But it was. And the jury wanted to send the message that they knew it was a big deal.*

*Even making those allegations, minimizing what Jeff had suffered had really backfired on them.*

*I couldn't have been happier.*

*The judge looked at the Blue Cross attorneys, "Are you good?"*

*They didn't even respond.*

*They just sat down.*

As I walked back to my seat, I could see that the back of the court was jammed with reporters. When I got out into the hall, I was swarmed. "Where's your client?" they wanted to know.

"I don't know. I haven't talked to him yet. I have to call him..."

The dog was running around and I was standing on the porch with the cell phone to my ear. I started to pace, really quickly, up and down the edge of the pool, waiting for Theresa to come back on the line.

I knew where she was going—she was stepping into the hallway outside the courtroom so she wouldn't have to whisper.

Finally, I heard her fumble with the phone. "Jeff! You won! And you won *big*!"

The moment stopped. Everything stopped. It was over. It was really over.

"Hallelujah!" I breathed into the phone. I didn't have words...

"Four-point-five million dollars."

"What?" I couldn't quite take it in. Everything was a blur. I had no idea what that really meant.

"Am I going to get the contract to get back into Blue Cross?" I asked.

"No, you can't get the contract, but they're going to pay for all your losses until you're 72 years old."

It wasn't what I'd hoped for. I could continue to be a doctor, but just not for Blue Cross.

The point was I'd won, they had been exposed and someone was listening.

And now, Blue Cross was accountable in the only way they understood: money.

"They also found them guilty on our request for punitive damages, Jeff."

"What does that mean?"

"The jury found that Blue Cross intended to harm you."

This was big.

I later learned that it was the first time a solo practitioner doctor had sued an insurance company and won in thirty years.

My thoughts swirled like a tornado: *Who do I call? Where do I go? What do I do?* In that moment, I felt a hitch in my gut. *Carole should be here.* How I would have given anything to rush in and tell her. Take her in my arms and tell her we'd won. I realized any victory from then on would be bittersweet.

But it was a victory nevertheless.

Once again, just as throughout my life, hard work had finally paid off.

Kristen: *Dad came into the house, filthy from having been on the tractor.*

*"Well, I got the call," he said.*

*I just held my breath—are we going to be sad, or are we going to be happy? Please... Please God...*

*"We did it! We won! We won!" he shouted.*

*It was an instant celebration. We cheered, we clapped our hands, we screamed. Our three Labs, Buck, Kinzie, and Powell, jumped around going crazy, celebrating with us.*

*He won. He'd finally won. And in a way, so had we all...*

Jamie: *Right after my mom died, my dad was going to put this place up for sale. He asked, "Are you sad?" I was. It just felt like it was the end of an era. And it made me sad because I felt like there was going to be so much good stuff that was going to happen with this place before he sold it.*

*As it turned out, we couldn't sell the house and Dad decided not to move after all.*

*But I was right when I said good stuff was going to happen in that house. The same grass my mom had been medevacked out of was the same grass where my husband proposed and where we had our engagement party. It was the same field where we had our wedding and the same field where my dad found out he'd won the lawsuit. When I was pregnant and trying to walk a lot I walked laps on that field, the same place where my mom and I and each of us kids would walk laps, running the dogs, praying, going over Bible verses, and talking about what was going on that week. When I was in the hospital in labor—the worst pain of my life—every time I would close my eyes I had flashbacks of that field. It was just so peaceful.*

*I can't describe it. That grass, that house was my happy place in the midst of the worst pain I ever had. That's where my mind went to when I just needed to hang in there, it's what my dad built, what my parents built.*

*There are just so many memories. It's come full circle and then some. So the fact that my dad found out about the lawsuit out there is just pretty ironic. It's extremes—just like my dad's personality. That's why he could take on this lawsuit. And win.*

*So when he called me, I was just so relieved and happy. So happy for him.*

*He did it. He stuck it to the Man.*

*Ever since my mom died, Dad had wanted justice. He just wanted to bring some kind of justice into the world somehow.*

*My feeling was that he got his justice. He did it. He needed that. And I needed that for him. It was the end of an era.*

# Chapter 22

## The Pony

Theresa: *My partner always jokes with me and says, "No matter how bad things are going you'll always find the pony.*

*Here's the story: The joke concerns twin boys of five or six. Worried that the boys had developed extreme personalities—one was a total pessimist, the other a total optimist—their parents took them to a psychiatrist.*

*First the psychiatrist treated the pessimist. Trying to brighten his outlook, the psychiatrist took him to a room piled to the ceiling with brand-new toys. But instead of yelping with delight, the little boy burst into tears.*

*"What's the matter?" the psychiatrist asked, baffled. "Don't you want to play with any of the toys?"*

*"Yes," the little boy bawled, "but if I did I'd only break them."*

*Next the psychiatrist treated the optimist. Trying to dampen his outlook, the psychiatrist took him to a room piled to the ceiling with horse manure.*

*But instead of wrinkling his nose in disgust, the optimist emitted just the yelp of delight the psychiatrist had been hoping to hear from his brother, the pessimist. Then he clambered to the top of the pile, dropped to his knees, and began gleefully digging out scoop after scoop with his bare hands.*

*"What do you think you're doing?" the psychiatrist asked, just as baffled by the optimist as he had been by the pessimist.*

*"With all this manure," the little boy replied, beaming, "there must be a pony in here somewhere!"*

*In this case, if we had tried the wrongful termination case, we never would have gotten to where we are now because that was arbitration, not a jury trial. When the doctor is in the network, he has a contract and that contract requires him to arbitrate before a retired judge. So you have a retired judge deciding your case and it's very corporate*

America. It's not conducive to plaintiffs. Rarely do you get punitives. Rarely are the awards very big because those judges know those cases are going to keep coming back to them.

And the jury trial was the most important part for Jeff. He was so upset for the longest time that we couldn't get our day in court. I believe things always happen for a reason. If you think about it—and here's the pony—because Jeff wasn't in the network, and because they wouldn't let him in the network, there was no contract, so he could take them to court. He could be heard by a jury. He could have his day in court, which is exactly what he did.

Winning was just the cherry on top of the sundae.

## Chapter 23

## Forgiveness, and Then...

Since the victory against Blue Cross I've had time to reflect. Not from a vacation resort overlooking the beautiful beaches of the Caribbean but from my medical office in Porter Ranch.

Life's journey has showed me some incredible highs as well as some tortuous lows. The emotional wounds from the tragedies had been well healed. I've changed, evolved, for better or for worse, and have learned much through the process of trauma and tragedy. I now share this information with patients hoping it will aid them through their own personal darkness. It makes me a better physician.

I've continued my practice of medicine and still enjoy seeing patients as much as I did the day I started doctoring. I have to admit life is different though, the family is different, and the profession is different.

It's ironic, as a single parent I did everything I knew to teach my kids right from wrong, to protect them and to help build their character. In the end, it was my own children who ended up teaching me a lesson I will be eternally grateful for. After Carole's death, I was still struggling with all my questions about God, about evil, and about the world. I became obsessed, I needed answers, and no one had them. Not the members of the church, nor the pastors, or even the Bible. I remember thinking there has to be an answer somewhere. I was like a dog chasing its tail, never to catch it, but I never ran out of energy.

My kids came to me one day.

"I don't know if you realize this, Dad, but you're very intimidating. No one really wants to talk to you." It wasn't an accusation. On the contrary, they were words from their hearts. I believe they felt sorry for me. It made me stop in my tracks and look up from the floor having that epiphany moment. It made me realize I was just so angry at everything. That anger fueled the way I constantly challenged my friends' beliefs. I couldn't comprehend how our close friends who loved Carole so much, could just go on with life. How they could sit in church, sing the worship songs, and listen to the pastors pontificate about how God loves us, how we should trust in him and that he is in charge.

Sorry, it just made no sense to me.

My questioning people's personal beliefs certainly alienated me and further exacerbated the fact that I was on my own.

When my children had turned the mirror on me so I could see myself through the eyes of others, I realized they too were in pain, confused, and frightened by Carole's death. They had their own questions and were unsuccessful in attempting to make sense from insanity.

They needed their church, their fellowship, and their beliefs. Without it the world and afterlife would make no sense to them and life would become an empty journey.

Because I was blinded by my own anger and unable to extend grace to them in their weakness, I realized I needed their forgiveness more than I needed to forgive.

My kids helped me gain an entirely new perspective on life.

And so it stopped. I gave it all up, the searching, the questioning, and most importantly, the intimidation.

I had to live in the "here and now" because as they say, tomorrow is not guaranteed. I certainly learned that the hard way. It was at this point I think the healing process really started to take hold.

As the years have worn on, I've seen more and more that each of my children contained a different piece of Carole. Her wisdom, fairness, humor, and love for life was embodied in different ways within each one of them. So in a very real way, Carole is still with me. Her spirit remains.

My children are doing well and have grown into independent young adults, just as it should be. One is married, one has started her own business, and one is well on his way to dental school. I couldn't really blame him for not wanting to go to medical school. All have moved out of the nest, and yes, it's empty, both physically and emotionally. I have witnessed their growth over time and I couldn't be more proud of them. I now celebrate being a grandpa. All is good.

And the cycle of life continues.

# Epilogue

## Finding Purpose

It was a pretty ordinary day at the office in Porter Ranch. The waiting room was packed as usual. I was flipping through my paperwork waiting for patients to be roomed when I was approached from the receptionist.

"This message just came in for you."

"Ok, what is it regarding?"

"Something about a death in the family and it being questionably related to the Porter Ranch gas leak. They knew about your Blue Cross case and thought you stood up for patients. He stated they were referred from a law firm."

"Wait, what?"

She handed me the message receipt.

Porter Ranch was exposed to the biggest gas leak in the nation's history. After all, I was the medical director of the urgent care clinic sitting right in the middle of the mess and the supplier of the noxious chemicals, Southern California Gas Company.

I returned the call from my private office.

I introduced myself and spoke with the son of the patient who had passed away.

He stated he had power of attorney and confirmed the fact that he was referred to me by a large legal firm that was using Erin Brockovich of *Erin Brokovich* fame. He gave me a quick synopsis of the unfortunate events leading to his mother's death. I have to admit, medically, it was very unusual.

"I'm afraid it's related to the gas leak; we don't know. She lived in Porter Ranch," the receptionist said.

"What were you told that was the cause of her death?"

"Well, that's the problem. There are different diagnoses from different doctors, so we really don't know. They're taking her to UCLA to do the postmortem."

I smelled something and it wasn't the sulfur from the gas leak.

"I'm concerned about our family's health. My child, wife, neighbors, and myself are having unusual symptoms. Our HMO is doing nothing to help. We get the feeling that we are being prejudged, like we're looking for financial gain. Or they just don't want to spend the money. I know how the HMO system works. We can't get any answers."

I could feel his frustration.

"I apologize for the loss of your mother and I'm sorry that you're going through so much difficulty."

He anxiously interrupted.

"Can you help us...please?"

# About The Author

One of six children, Jeffrey B. Nordella, M.D. grew up in very humble circumstances in the East San Fernando Valley, California. Dr. Nordella watched his ailing father's health deteriorate before his sudden death, which inspired him to become a physician.

Dr. Nordella received a Bachelor of Science degree in Human Biology from the University of California at San Diego. He received his Medical Doctor degree from the University of California at Los Angeles. He completed his internship and residency at the UCLA Hospital and Clinics in the Departments of Family Medicine and Emergency Medicine. After working for seven years in a Los Angeles Level 2 trauma center, he decided to open a unique medical clinic with the philosophy of offering Urgent Care, Family Medicine and Occupational Medicine at a single site for patient convenience. For 14 years and as an independent physician, he was the owner and Medical Director of Santa Clarita Valley Quality Care in Santa Clarita, California. Presently, he is the Medical Director at Porter Ranch Quality Care in Porter Ranch, California.

Dr. Nordella has served patients in the Santa Clarita and the San Fernando Valley for over 25 years. Dr. Nordella has a long history of confronting the Anthem Blue Cross' business practices that focus on profit instead of facilitating access to quality healthcare and treatment for patients. After a 10-year litigation history with Anthem Blue Cross, Dr. Nordella was successful in receiving a favorable judgment that the LA Times stated had not been done in over 25 years by a solo practitioner.

"Healthcare should not be about profit over patients."

*If you would like to have Dr. Nordella speak to your organization or to learn more, visit his website at* http://deniedjeffreynordellamd.com

Made in the USA
San Bernardino, CA
05 October 2017